Survival Guide for Traders

Founded in 1807, John Wiley & Sons is the oldest independent publishing company in the United States. With offices in North America, Europe, Australia, and Asia, Wiley is globally committed to developing and marketing print and electronic products and services for our customers' professional and personal knowledge and understanding.

The Wiley Trading series features books by traders who have survived the market's ever changing temperament and have prospered—some by reinventing systems, others by getting back to basics. Whether a novice trader, professional, or somewhere in-between, these books will provide the advice and strategies needed to prosper today and well into the future.

For a list of available titles, please visit our Web site at www.WileyFinance.com.

Survival Guide for Traders

How to Set Up
and Organize Your
Trading Business

BENNETT A. MCDOWELL

WILEY

John Wiley & Sons, Inc.

Published by John Wiley & Sons, Inc., Hoboken, New Jersey.
Published simultaneously in Canada.

For general information on our other products and services or for technical support, please contact our Customer Care Department within the United States at (800) 762-2974, outside the United States at (317) 572-3993 or fax (317) 572-4002.

Wiley also publishes its books in a variety of electronic formats. Some content that appears in print may not be available in electronic books. For more information about Wiley products, visit our web site at www.wiley.com.

Library of Congress Cataloging-in-Publication Data:
McDowell, Bennett, 1957-
    Survival guide for traders : how to set up and organize your trading business / Bennett A. McDowell. — 1st ed.
        p. cm. — (Wiley trading)
    Includes index.
    ISBN 978-0-470-43642-4 (hardback); ISBN 978-1-118-15941-5 (ebk);
    ISBN 978-1-118-15940-8 (ebk); ISBN 978-1-118-15939-2 (ebk)
        1. Electronic trading of securities.   2. Online stockbrokers.   3. Investments.
    4. Finance, Personal.   5. Small business—Management.   6. Home-based businesses—Management.   I. Title.
    HG4515.95.M395 2011
    332.640285'4678—dc23

                                                                            2011025466

Printed in the United States of America
10 9 8 7 6 5 4 3 2 1

To each and every trader who has
the perseverance and courage to live their dreams
and turn those dreams into reality.
Godspeed to you all on this
miraculous and rewarding journey.

Contents

Foreword

"**B**utter!" we'd yell, our eyes glued to flashing level II screens on our monitors. "Bu-utter!"

It was the mid-1990s. About two dozen of us jeans-clad traders sat at long tables littered with keyboards and banks of monitors. We pounded out trades as we yelled. "Butter" was our code word for a rapidly melting level of ask prices on our level II screens. It meant gluttonous bulls were slicing through—buying—each price level of stock offered for sale—and fast. Our stocks' prices were soaring. Life was good!

Outside the squat stone office building that housed our trading room, the cold, concrete city spread below. Smokestacks, streets, parking garages, and skyscrapers all reflected the steel-colored New York skies.

In our neon-lit room, however, shades of gray dissolved. Black or white ruled. Why? Because the stock market took no prisoners. Each day, we won . . . or we lost. Our hearts, minds, and trading accounts flew high on the white wings of each victorious trade. Or they descended into black holes of despair on the agony of trades gone sour.

What did we trade? "Any four-letter stock that moves," we declared staunchly. Of course, we were referring to the four-letter symbols of the high-flying stocks listed on the NASDAQ exchange. Most were Internet bubble stocks—but we didn't know about bubbles back then.

We did know that they exploded 20, 30, or more points a day (higher or lower), fueled by the high-octane energy twins, volume and volatility.

Ask any of us if we knew to which sector or industry group our stocks belonged, and you'd usually get a shrug. Who cares? If it moved, we traded it.

Miraculously, my trading account and I survived those go-go days. Of course, I learned a lot of lessons, some more enjoyable than others. I do know that had I and my trading buddies been given access to the commonsense content now put forth in *Survival Guide for Traders*, our losses would have been leaner and our wallets fatter.

In *Survival Guide for Traders*, author and trading expert Bennett McDowell offers you the framework of decision-making tools you need to establish and execute a successful trading business. And make no mistake. Trading is a business.

After all, who would we nominate for "Most Likely to Succeed"? The trader who has set up and organized his or her trading business with the kind of well-thought-out planning Bennett details in this book? Or would we nominate the "I'm-gonna-get-rich-by-Friday" trader, who jumps into trades without forethought of account size, share size, protective stops, and other risk management tactics that Bennett reveals in these pages?

Survival Guide for Traders tells you how to set up and organize your trading business in the best possible way. In each chapter, you will find a virtual cornucopia of helpful graphs, tables, and information you can personalize and apply to your trading business.

Survival Guide for Traders is divided into two parts: (1) Survival Basics and (2) The Financial Pie. Five appendixes at the book's conclusion provide the reader with additional resources, from online brokers to books and movies that feature trading and Wall Street themes to discussions of Bennett's ART trading platform.

In Chapters 1 and 2, Bennett warns traders that "It's a Jungle Out There," and advises readers of the importance of formulating a business plan.

Too many times, novice traders jump into the market with a fistful of cash and a burning desire to "beat the Street." Either they aren't aware that successful trading demands a business plan or they don't think that kind of planning is necessary. The mind-set that accompanies that approach lacks discipline. Result? The stock market drools, smacks her lips, and eats those unlucky traders before the closing bell chimes.

Chapters 3 and 4 help you create your net worth statement. Such a statement is a vital action for all of us to complete. For traders, knowledge of your exact net worth is essential for creating your financial profile. Moreover, Bennett kindly provides several Sample Financial Profile templates for you to choose from. You can also study the Sample Net Worth Curve table; it can assist you in anticipating and guiding the direction of your discretionary capital.

In Chapter 5, the discussion centers on the entrepreneurial lifestyle. Six points detail actions you can take to ensure that your trading business moves forward in the best way.

Bennett also talks about simple, yet often ignored concepts that are so important to success. For example, "reduce expenses and increase revenue" is a given for any business owner. Yet as traders, it's easy for us to get so immersed in market action that we forget to keep an eye on everyday business expenses that drain our funds. Confession: I am guilty of subscribing to too many expensive financial newspapers, some of which I haven't time to read each morning. I just canceled those extra subscriptions. Thank you, Bennett, for the valuable reminder to use money management in every area of our trading business.

In Chapters 6, 7, and 8, Bennett spotlights the order flow process, types of orders, margin and leverage, the bid-ask spread, data feeds, and more—essential information traders need to begin executing trades. He goes on to talk about the four types of market cycles and shows readers how to recognize them. Again, here is more vital information that will help you excel.

The content in Chapter 9 provides readers with a comprehensive business plan. Bennett also includes a Vision Statement form, and ones for Money Management Strategy, Order Execution, and Profit and Loss History, among others. This is another chapter in *Survival Guide for Traders* that I wish I'd had access to a dozen years ago. Taking the time to fill out these planning tools embeds the seriousness of our trading business into our psyches.

Chapter 10 delves into trading and investing rules. If you apply these to your trading plan and use them with discipline and forethought, your trading results can improve nicely.

In Chapters 11 and 12, Bennett discusses scanning tools for both technical and fundamental analysis. While many traders do not incorporate fundamental analysis into their daily trades, I'm delighted to see that Bennett's view aligns with mine—that applying at least the most basic fundamental knowledge to trades can give you an edge. Bennett also moves into one of the most neglected—but most important—aspects of trading, risk management. He offers a comprehensive list of all types of protective stops, which every trader should have at his or her elbow. As Bennett says, using risk management in the form of planning and placing stops "allows you to be wrong and not go bust." Well said and so true!

Chapter 13 is devoted to the trader's mind-set. Bennett furnishes readers with several checklists to consider, and they all pertain to establishing the proper mind-set with which to approach the markets. To me, this chapter alone is worth the price of the book. We've all seen traders who have rows of monitors and the best trading platforms money can buy. Know that all the equipment—and even gobs of financial knowledge—works only when those traders approach the markets with an appropriate frame of mind.

Survival Guide for Traders shows traders efficient and effective ways to build a strong and lasting foundation for their trading careers. Read it, then reread it and take full advantage of the fountain of information in these pages. This book belongs in every trader's library as a timely and compelling guide to success.

Toni Turner
Author, *A Beginner's Guide to Day Trading Online,*
A Beginner's Guide to Short-Term Trading,
Short-Term Trading in the New Stock Market;
President, TrendStar Trading Group, Inc.
www.ToniTurner.com

Preface

Survival is at the heart of this book, more than getting rich quick or making a fast killing. Maybe on the surface that idea appears to lack ambition, but many of you who have been caught off guard even once by the power and speed of the financial markets know and understand the need for caution when entering even a routine investment or trade. Surgeons will say that there is no such thing as "routine" surgery. The same applies in the financial markets—there is no such thing as a routine transaction. Even deceptively safe vehicles can surprise the individual who is not alert and respectful of the markets' overall supremacy.

What this means is that you cannot control the markets; instead you have to learn to listen to the markets and follow their lead, whether they be in a bullish cycle or a bearish one. The markets have the ultimate power to do as they desire despite any of us who may hope and wish for them to behave as *we* want them to. Much like Mother Nature, the markets can wield their strength swiftly and unexpectedly. For this reason it is best to study the markets, to be educated and prepared, and to never let your guard down.

Having outlined the goal—to survive (and as a result prosper)—the next step is to look at managing your hard-earned money as a business. It is not a hobby or an afterthought—or a nonexistent thought; your money is most absolutely serious business, and this book, *Survival Guide for Traders*, is going to teach you how to survive and prosper by treating it that way.

You'll learn how to run a profitable trading business by keeping your eye on the ball and keeping expenses down and revenue up. Most important, we'll show you why the old fashioned buy and hold strategies are not as effective as they used to be and why we all need to take more control over our finances—and even if we have qualified advisers, why we need to be in the driver's seat. With the ammunition in these pages, you'll have tools that can guide you through any market moving up, down, or sideways, and safeguard your trading and investment portfolio against unnecessary risks.

Ultimately, this book is intended to teach you how to personally build a profitable business using all your assets—financial, physical, and intellectual—that will succeed and last a lifetime.

Bennett A. McDowell
San Diego, California
September 2011

Acknowledgments

The very first edition of the *Survival Guide for Traders* was self-published back in the year 2000. The goal of the first survival guide was to outline the formula for success in the business of trading, and that first paperback edition covered the basics in less than 100 pages.

Fast-forward to the year 2011, as we're just sending off the manuscript to the publisher for this new John Wiley & Sons edition of the *Survival Guide for Traders*, and my editor tells me this edition will be more than 300 pages. The growth of this book is symbolic of the fact that we've come a long way in the past decade. And that is in no small part thanks to the many fantastic clients, business partners, and family members who have been supportive all along the way. You have all helped shape the content of this book, and I thank you.

The journey started in 1998 when I first obtained the domain name for my website at www.TradersCoach.com back when the Internet was just taking off. At the time my brokerage business kept me busy with clients who liked active trading, and my methodology, now known as the ART® software, was what I used to trade their accounts for them. If you can believe it, back then I drew all my charts by hand to determine entries and exits.

We later transformed my manual approach into the ART software so that my clients could follow along at home, and that was released in 2003. Since then we have seen the popularity of the ART software grow to where it is today used by clients in over 50 countries around the world. The journey continues to 2008, when my first two John Wiley & Sons books were released. Their titles are *The ART of Trading* and *A Trader's Money Management System*.

This brings us to 2011 and the release of this new book. My thanks go out to the entire staff at John Wiley & Sons, the greatest publisher on the planet. Laura Walsh, my editor, thank you for being so nice, patient, and professional—you are a gem! Judy Howarth, you are terrific at keeping everything right on track and Claire Wesley you are my production super hero! And of course thank you to David Pugh for your cherished friendship and for discovering us in New York City back in 2007.

Thanks also go out to a number of industry partners who were generous with their time in giving me input on a number of the chapters in the book, especially Chapter 6. John Gromala and Ryan Sindelar at NinjaTrader, Julie Craig at eSignal, Mark Grieco and Michelle Moore at TradeStation, Glen Larson and Pete Kilman at Trade Navigator, and Matt Verdouw at Market Analyst, thank you all for your generous feedback—it is greatly appreciated.

Then of course there are a number of wonderful educators in this industry that I am fortunate to have worked with over the years and to whom I am sincerely grateful. These exceptional people include Larry McMillan, Steve Nison, Stan Dash, Larry Pesavento, Bill Williams, and Leslie Jouflas, to name a few. Thank you all.

Thank you also to Ed Schramm and Jayanthi Gopalakrishnan from *Technical Analysis of Stocks & Commodities* magazine and Larry Jacobs from *Traders World* magazine. You are my favorite media moguls.

And of course, thank you so much to Toni Turner. It is an honor for her to write the Foreword to this book—in this business of trading geeks, she is one of the few traders who is a fabulous writer as well. (And I love having her as a neighbor here in southern California!)

Last but not least, thanks to my terrific partner and wife, Jeannie. Many of you have met her at the trade shows or talked to her on the phone. I will let you know that without her this book might not have been finished, since she did all the tables and organizing of the manuscript. Thank you, sweetheart; you are the best!

Just as with running a successful trading business, writing a book takes more than just one player to pull it off. Teamwork from my wife, industry partners, and my fantastic clients has all contributed immensely to this work. Thank you all for making the *Survival Guide for Traders* a reality!

Bennett A. McDowell
San Diego, California
September 2011

Disclaimer

The information in this book, *Survival Guide for Traders*, is intended for educational purposes only. Traders and investors are strongly advised to do their own research and testing to determine the validity of any trading idea or system.

Trading in the financial markets involves substantial risk, and Traders Coach.com, Bennett A. McDowell, or affiliates assume no responsibility for your success or failure in trading or investing in the markets. For this reason you should use only money you can afford to risk. Furthermore, past performance does not guarantee future results. Thus, even if you were successful with your trading and investing in the past, you may not be successful in the future. TradersCoach.com and Bennett A. McDowell make no performance representation or guarantee of any kind or nature. Traders Coach.com encourages you to conduct your own research and engage in numerous practice trades prior to risking any actual money.

Hypothetical or simulated performance results have certain inherent limitations. Unlike an actual performance record, simulated results do not represent actual trading. Also, since trades have not actually been executed, results may have undercompensated or overcompensated for the impact, if any, of certain market factors, such as lack of liquidity. Simulated trading programs and ideas in general are also subject to the fact that they are designed with the benefit of hindsight. No representation is being made that any account will or is likely to achieve profits or losses similar to those discussed.

Survival of the Fittest

By striving to be the fittest, you may not be the biggest, but you can develop your unique strengths to outperform the average financial market participant. Sometimes the smaller fish is more nimble and can adapt to changing environments more efficiently. The smaller trader or investor may realize he or she has a smaller margin for error and may in turn be smarter than the larger fish that may carelessly lose money in the markets, simply because they can afford to.

Regardless of your portfolio size, be smart. Work smarter, not harder. Your survival and prosperity depend on it. This will be your edge in the market.

YOUR FINANCIAL PIE

Many of my students have heard me talk over the years about the "financial pie" concept when it comes to successful trading and investing. The illusion that so many novices in the market believe is that all they need is one magic system, or adviser, or software package, or market tip. The reality is that it takes a lot more than that to be consistently successful in the markets.

Take a look at Figure I.1, and you'll see the four essential slices of the "financial pie" you will need to master in order to be successful in the markets. They are your: (1) *trading and investing rules*, (2) *scanning for opportunities*, (3) *money management*, and (4) *financial psychology*. We cover all of these four important slices of the pie in detail in the coming chapters, but let me plant the seed of an idea in your mind: that you must approach the market with a broad view and an open mind.

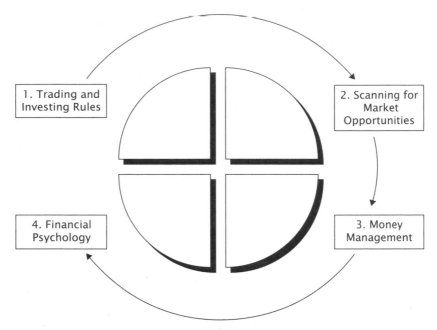

FIGURE I.1   Financial Pie
You will need to master all four pieces of the "financial pie" to become consistently successful in the markets.

You will see how to improve your portfolio's performance by acquainting yourself with a variety of techniques and tools, all of which are important to the process. It is the weakest link that will hinder your development, so try to identify where you need the most improvement and dive into that area until all the links have uniform strength.

LAYOUT OF THIS BOOK

This book is laid out into two parts plus five Appendix sections in a way that takes you step-by-step through the most important aspects of preserving your capital and growing your capital. The format is meant to help you get at the survival basics quickly before you have a chance to get into trouble.

For that reason, the book is written in simple, clear language and does not go into enormous depth on any one topic. There are other books that you can turn to once you have fully absorbed the topics covered here. The main focus is to highlight the most essential areas for study so that you develop a vocabulary that you can expand on at your own pace.

In addition to the hard copy of this book, you will have access to a website link that will be constantly updated with the latest and most current information. This link will provide you with free videos, printable PDF files, and other related survival guide information. You will also have access to free trials to a number of TradersCoach.com software products. You can access all of this current *Survival Guide Central* information and free software trials by going to the following link:

www.traderscoach.com/survivalguide.php

Part I: Survival Basics

This part introduces you to the most important aspects of survival in the markets. Here you will learn how important it is to treat your trading as a serious business and you will determine how to implement a process to monitor and evaluate your progress. This includes setting up accountability procedures, determining what your net worth is, and learning how to best utilize all of your natural resources.

You'll learn the importance of always keeping an eye on revenue and expenses, the core of any business. These two line items can sneak up on you if you're not paying attention, and it is crucial to keep costs down and revenue up at all times.

Then we help you understand financial markets from order flow to data feeds to getting the most value from your broker. You will find out about the nature of a variety of market cycles and how they can dramatically affect your profitability. And last, you will see how to design an effective business plan that will get results.

Part II: The Financial Pie

Successful trading or investing is not dependent on just one single skill, approach, or idea. Instead, it is achieved by mastering a number of areas that are all equally important. My way of explaining this concept is to break it down into four equal parts of a pie, which is what I call the "financial pie." (See Figure I.1.) Part II of this book covers all four of these important "financial pie" areas and shows you how to master them.

1. **The first slice of the pie is designing a set of trading and investing rules that are consistently profitable.** Designing your trading and investing rules requires that you match your own unique personality and experience level with an appropriate approach that you can

effectively implement. This means you have to know yourself, and identify your strengths and risk tolerance, to find the right combination of tools and strategies in order to become consistently profitable. In Chapter 10 you will learn about a variety of approaches to use to achieve this goal.

2. **The second slice of the pie is scanning for market opportunities.** The key to any successful financial approach is finding high-probability opportunities in the market. Traders must learn that the markets offer us infinite opportunity—it is just a matter of developing the skills to uncover the highest-probability trades at any given moment. Chapter 11 shows you fundamental and technical ways to find opportunities. You will learn about ways to use technology to do the heavy lifting of scanning for the best trades every day.

3. **The third slice of the pie is money management.** This area of the markets is so often ignored and yet is one of the areas where you will generally see the quickest progress when properly implemented. In Chapter 12 we talk about all areas of money management from record keeping to managing risk. You will learn to use some simple formulas that will help keep you out of harm's way and maximize your profit potential.

4. **The fourth slice of the pie is financial psychology.** Psychology is by far the most difficult and abstract piece of the financial pie to master and in Chapter 13 we address this very important topic. Very often we can be our own worst enemy in financial endeavors, and understanding this will enable us to secure our own survival. What is it that motivates us to succeed? How do fear and greed factor into our decision making? How dedicated and persistent are we at attaining our goals? These questions are the tip of the iceberg, and opening up the discussion will surely start you on the road to a better understanding of yourself.

All four of these pieces of the pie are important to master. The trading success chain is only as strong as its weakest link, so you need to self-evaluate to determine which of these four areas needs the most attention. You will find information in Part II that can assist you in fine-tuning all four of these areas.

WWW.TRADERSCOACH.COM/SURVIVALGUIDE.PHP

This website, www.traderscoach.com/survivalguide.php, combined with your purchase of this book is your free access ticket to *Survival Guide Central,* SGC. This feature will enable you to keep your copy of the

Survival Guide for Traders current for years to come. Plus, you will have access to a printable version of the business plan found in Chapter 9. Just visit this website and you will find these features, along with access to the free software trials that the purchase of this book entitles you to. Be sure to have a copy of your *Survival Guide* handy when visiting this link, as you will be asked a security question to ensure that you are a current owner of this book before gaining free access to *Survival Guide Central*. If you have any questions or need assistance in registering for this special online feature, you can call us at 858-695-0592 or e-mail us via Info@TradersCoach.com.

YOU CAN SURVIVE AND PROSPER IN TODAY'S FINANCIAL MARKETS

It is all up to you, and there is no doubt in my mind that if you apply yourself and are persistent you will be able to use these ideas and will look at your trading and investing in a new way. This will open up infinite possibilities for your financial future. You can reach me at any time with questions and comments by sending an e-mail to Team@TradersCoach.com.

PART I

Survival Basics

CHAPTER 1

It's a Jungle Out There!

I t doesn't matter what country you live in, or what business or company you work in, or what financial market you invest in—it's a jungle out there! And by that I mean to survive financially you will need to identify and focus on your top priorities with precision and be wary of possible adversaries, competitors, and obstacles that exist in each respective environment.

Around the world in each country, there are political developments that to one degree or another affect your livelihood for better or worse. In every business or company there are individuals who may exploit your weaknesses to further their own survival or prosperity. And of course in every financial market there are "sharks," as I like to refer to them, who will gladly eat you alive if they can so that you are on the losing side of a trade or investment and they are on the winning side.

The only law of the jungle is survival, and that is the focus of this book. With your trading and investing you will of course be following the rules of law in your country and whatever your personal ethics are. But within that framework you need to be diligent and be absolutely determined to survive and prosper. In this day and age, you need to be more involved and aware than ever to advance your personal financial prosperity, and there are many effective ways to do so. We cover these techniques in the coming chapters.

BRAWN, BRAINS, AND TECHNOLOGY

Historically when talking about survival of the fittest, it comes down to the strongest, biggest, and most intelligent creatures that are at the top of the food chain and that outlive the others. For example, in the jungle the lion is the king of the beasts because of his strength and size. But, in contrast, man is king of the planet because he has used his brain to ultimately outsmart all other living creatures.

The intellectual superiority of the human race is really what adds technology and strategy to the mix. It's not their physical brawn, but instead it is their brains that have elevated the human race to this current position of power. Consider the invention of fire on demand, the wheel, weaponry, transportation, and computers. Once a given invention is introduced, again it reverts back to the prevailing creature that is most able to put the technology to effective use with either brawn or brains. And it comes down to which individuals have *access* to new technology as well. In underdeveloped regions computers are not readily available, where as the more developed regions have greater access to technology and as a result have a greater opportunity to survive and dominate. As Bill Gates, Microsoft's creator and the world's richest man, has so accurately said, technology and computers will determine which modern cultures will survive and excel.

So really strength and intelligence and access to technological opportunity are equally important in the game of modern day survival, and individual circumstances determine which is needed most at any given time or place. (See Table 1.1.)

The paradox around brawn versus brains makes me think about a program that appeared on the History Channel. It was about the Vikings in Europe during a global climate change. The strength and physical size of the legendary Viking warriors, which were exceptional compared to the attributes of some other cultures during the same time period, were not enough to ensure their survival. What sadly happened was that the Viking

TABLE 1.1 Survival in the Financial Arena Depends on Using All of Your Available Assets and Resources, Including Brawn, Brains, and Technology

Brawn	Brains	Technology
Confidence	Experience	Computers
Emotional strength	High IQ	Software
Persistence and focus	Education	News feeds
Financial strength	Street smarts	Fast order execution
Stamina and endurance	Strategic skills	Live market data

culture became extinct because they did not adapt to the changing climate, which was becoming much colder in their region. Strategically they did not move their villages south and were unable to develop enough technology to obtain food in the new colder climate that offered declining crops and less wildlife to feed them.

There were other cultures in that region during the end of the Viking era that were less impressive in physical size and strength, but they fared better than the Vikings due to their ability to adapt to the changing environment around them. They used their reasoning and intelligence to develop primitive but effective techniques for obtaining food and shelter and to move to different locations to escape the challenges that they had faced in the changing climate of their former homes. They were able to identify a changing environment and adapt in order to survive.

This example shows that it is not imperative that you be the biggest and strongest to survive and prosper. It is imperative, though, that you use every asset at your disposal to continually improve and protect your financial ground. You may in fact be more nimble as a smaller investor or trader than some of the bigger financial giants and Vikings that have fallen in recent times.

This is due to the fact that you have less red tape and political quagmires to navigate through than the huge institutions. You can take immediate action at a moment's notice and you need no sign-off or approval from a committee of bureaucrats. The bottom line is you need to be quick on your feet and to identify changing circumstances and effectively adapt to them.

TECHNOLOGICAL AND INNOVATION TIME LINE

Technology and innovation throughout the ages have changed the course of history. Table 1.2 illustrates a time line of developments that have impacted the way humans live their lives. These innovations and discoveries have also enabled humans to survive and prosper in a constantly evolving world.

Necessity is the mother of invention, as well as the mother of technology and innovation. That is how all good ideas are born; they are in answer to a need. And technology is often developed in answer to a need for military and transportation products first, and then, once developed, these products are applied to other everyday endeavors.

You can see how some of the more modern innovations such as the computer, Internet access, and search engines have changed the way that traders conduct business. Now information and data are more accessible than ever before to the average individual. Technological innovations have

TABLE 1.2	This Time Line of Technological Developments throughout History Illustrates the Impact That Technology and Innovation Have Had on Our Survival and Prosperity

Year	Technological Innovation or Discovery
500,000 B.C.	Fire tamed by Homo erectus
20,000	Invention of the bow and arrow
3500	First wheeled carts used in Mesopotamia and Central Europe
3000	Abacus invented by the Chinese
700	First purpose-made sundials appear
650	Standardized coins used by the Greeks
400	Greeks invent the catapult, the first artillery weapon
1180 A.D.	Windmills introduced in Europe
1440	Printing press invented by Johannes Gutenberg
1492	Columbus discovers the New World and proves the world is not flat
1800	Electric battery invented by Alessandro Volta
1821	Difference engine, first primitive computer, invented by Charles Babbage
1876	Telephone invented by Alexander Graham Bell
1880	Lightbulb invented by Thomas Edison
1888	Kodak camera invented by George Eastman
1889	Automobile invented by Karl Benz
1895	Wireless telegraph (radio) invented by Guglielmo Marconi
1903	Airplane invented by the Wright brothers
1913	Mass production developed by Henry Ford
1925	Television invented by John Logie Baird
1927	Charles Lindbergh makes nonstop solo trans-Atlantic flight from New York to Paris
1936	Multiplane animation camera invented by Disney studios used to produce animated cartoons
1940	First McDonald's fast-food restaurant opened by Ray Kroc
1958	U.S. Defense Advanced Research Projects Agency (DARPA) created (agency that began the Internet)
1962	First Wal-Mart discount department store opened by Sam Walton
1966	Handheld calculator invented by Jack Kilby
1969	U.S. NASA Apollo 11 mission lands the first two men on the moon
1970	First Intel i1103 computer chip released
1975	Charles Schwab starts offering discount brokerage services
1984	Microsoft Windows operating system released by Bill Gates
1984	First Macintosh computer and first mouse introduced by Apple Computer, Inc., which was founded by Steve Jobs and Steve Wozniak
1991	World Wide Web invented by Tim Berners-Lee
1998	Google Internet search engine founded by Sergey Brin and Larry Page
2004	Facebook social networking site launched by Mark Zuckerberg

leveled the playing field. We as traders must apply the latest available technology in our day-to-day operations. We must also be aware of the constantly changing and evolving technological advances, since our survival depends on it. You want to be on the cutting edge whenever possible regarding technology.

DON'T BRING A KNIFE TO A GUNFIGHT

As we saw in Table 1.2, technology has been developing and changing the world since the beginning of time. Anyone with a computer today knows that the minute you open the box of your brand-new super-spectacular computer, it is already outdated. It seems every time I open the box of the latest and greatest new multiple-core computer of mine, an e-mail arrives in my inbox moments later for another with twice the speed and functionality; and such is life.

With this understanding, remember that when entering the financial markets it is important to obtain the best technology you can afford at the time, as this will improve your odds for success. If your competitors in the market are using technical analysis and live streaming data from the markets, you will want to be similarly equipped. And, if they have access to up-to-the-minute news and fundamental information, you will want that information as well if your approach requires it.

Don't bring a knife to a gunfight, and don't bring antique technology and information to the markets when you are trading and investing. Get as up-to-date as you can so that it's a fair fight.

RIGHT IN MY OWN BACKYARD

Night after night I'm reminded of the reality of nature and the struggle of all living things to survive. We live on a hilltop overlooking a canyon here in southern California, and there are acres and acres of wide-open spaces all around us. When we first moved here in 1997 from New York City, which is the ultimate concrete jungle, the sounds of the night in my own backyard here in San Diego were new and fascinating to me.

The variety of wildlife you can see right out there beyond the fence range from deer, coyotes, bobcats, and raccoons to quail, owls, bats, and rattlesnakes—hardly the type of wildlife I'd been used to in the big city. The most you would see in New York City might be some pigeons, squirrels, or ducks in Central Park. Here on the canyon, it's like getting a front-row seat for the National Geographic channel and all the inner workings of our eco-system. And the brains and brawn issue comes up when you can see that each species has certain skills, strengths, and weaknesses.

All these animals coexist and live in balance as they have done for hundreds of years. And for those of us, like me, who have lived in mostly residential areas, it is rare that we see up close the brutal realities of nature and what maintains the balance. There's a food chain; some of my backyard animals are herbivores, some carnivores, and others omnivores. Just the other day there was a blue jay on my fence that was chomping on a beautiful monarch butterfly. And then there is this giant flying egret that visits our pond every so often to feast on our goldfish, much to my children's dismay.

In one sense it seems harsh, but in another way it's just nature—very much like when the coyotes use their cunning and shrewd strategies to trap a much larger deer down there in that canyon. You can hear the "yip-yip" howls of the coyotes as they work themselves into a frenzy, until there is total silence and you know they are feasting on their latest kill.

The markets are no different; in fact, they are exactly the same. It is the cycle of life—there are winners and losers, and that is the reality. Maybe it is not exactly life and death in the markets in a physical sense, but it can be your financial life and death. To help protect you in the jungle of the financial markets, we are going to educate you step-by-step about the brawn, brains, and technology you need in order to compete with the kings of the financial jungle and to help you come out ahead.

CHAPTER 2

Managing Your Money Is Serious Business

Often we, as a society, are so focused on the day-to-day job of earning a living that we forget the fact that managing our overall finances is important business. It is just as important as our day job. We can get in a rut and without even realizing it become like hamsters on a treadmill.

In grade school when we're kids, there are really no required courses that highlight the importance of personal finance. Rather, as children growing up, we are left to figure it out on our own. We're required to take general courses in math, science, English, and such, but there are no required courses that teach us how to manage the big picture from a purely financial standpoint. Instead, we are prepared to identify a vocation and a job and to make a living at that job. But what about how to manage the money we earn at our day job and how to manage our home finances? Your home in essence is like a mini corporation. You could even call your household "Home Incorporated."

It seems that every kid in high school should be required to take a course in personal finance to show them how serious this business is from the very start. And in doing that they'd need to learn basics like how to balance a checkbook, identify (and increase) revenue, identify (and reduce) expenses, develop a budget, and plan for the expected (and unexpected) future. This course would teach kids the value of making difficult choices in order to stay on track and achieve their own planned goals.

Sounds a lot like a business plan, doesn't it? Well, yes, in my mind the world would be a better place, financially at least, if every household prepared a business plan and followed it. If you treat your money like a hobby or an afterthought, you are not giving it the attention it deserves.

Now is the time to take control and treat your personal finances and your trading and investing as the serious business that it is.

TRUST AND FINANCIAL ADVISERS

Before Charles Schwab came onto the scene and enabled the average investor or trader to place their own trades, things were different than they are today. The only way for the layman to enter and exit the market was for them to work through an adviser or broker, and pay this person commission fees that were astronomical compared to what they are today.

During those times, most folks hired a broker to manage their money and to make entries and exits into the market. They trusted the broker to do what was best for their financial stability.

In reality, most brokers are basically salespeople, and if you go into a firm and ask, "Who is the best broker here?" you'll most certainly be directed to someone in a private office who has the largest portfolio of assets under management. The problem is that the broker may not be delivering a high annual yield on clients' accounts; instead that broker is just talented and the best at acquiring lots of new and big clients.

In a bull market, most financial advisers like this all look pretty smart. It is during a bear market that you can really pick out the truly talented advisers from the mere salespeople. The truly talented advisers see the bear coming, convert a large portion of your account to cash, and preserve your capital. They've got your asset allocation in line with your goals, take into account your age and tolerance for risk, and have your best interests at heart. They've got a contingency plan, and they've probably given you a "business plan," or "investment management plan," to review and comment on. This plan outlines the goals and objectives for your portfolio over the next five, 10, and 20 years.

In contrast, the pure salespeople do not have your best interests in mind, will attempt to churn your account, and will sell you whatever the head of their firm is pushing that week regardless of whether it is the right move for you. And they probably have not taken the time to map out your plan for you on paper, because that frankly will take time away from the cold-calling for new prospects that their boss insists they do every day.

How do I know this? Simply because I've been there, been a registered securities broker for the big wire houses, and been in the position of doing what's right for my clients regardless of what the firm wanted. There's a conflict going on in the big brokerage houses that the average client doesn't ever see. The conflict is that the brokerage firm's primary goal is to increase *its* revenue, which sometimes is in direct conflict with increasing *the client's* revenue.

Now, this is not to say that there are not amazing and talented financial advisers available to you. It is to say, however, that they are few and far between and you'd best do your homework before handing over your portfolio to a broker at a big firm. If you do take on an adviser, continue to closely monitor the activity in your portfolio on a quarterly basis. As the saying goes, past performance does not guarantee future results.

TIPS ON SELECTING A QUALIFIED FINANCIAL ADVISER

Selecting a qualified financial adviser is a task that deserves your undivided attention. If you have a sizable net worth, you owe it to yourself to bring a specialist onto your team who has experience in portfolio management and can guide you. There are costs involved in hiring a specialist, but a competent adviser is well worth the investment. Remember, you are the boss. Make it clear to your adviser that you have goals and expectations and the portfolio's performance will be monitored.

Here are some tips that will serve you well in finding the right person for the job:

- Interview two or three advisers in person at their offices prior to making your final choice.
- Have a list of questions to ask such as: What is your investment strategy? What are your credentials? Are you a Certified Financial Planner (CFP)? How many years have you been a financial adviser? What fees would be charged? Do you use risk control? How do you diversify a portfolio? What kinds of annual returns do you get on your clients' portfolios?
- Ask for references of other clients you can talk to, and if references are available, call them and ask questions such as: How long have you been using this adviser? Are you happy with the adviser? Can you name one strength and one weakness of the adviser? What kind of annual return have you received on your portfolio while using the adviser? What kind of monthly statements or reporting are you receiving?
- Outline a list of priorities that you want the adviser to address and ask how the adviser would handle them.

- Check to see if there are any complaints registered on the adviser made with the National Association of Securities Dealers (NASD) or the Securities and Exchange Commission (SEC).
- Do an online Google search on the adviser and see what comes up.
- Check the adviser's firm with the Better Business Bureau (BBB) by going to www.bbb.org/us/Find-Business-Reviews/.
- Make sure the adviser will prepare a written financial plan for you, and find out what the fee for that would be, if any.

As Steve Cox, BBB spokesperson, said, "The fact that Bernie Madoff was well-known and respected despite operating an elaborate Ponzi scheme for years—that cost his clients upwards of $50 billion—shows that finding someone to trust with your money isn't as simple as choosing the firm that yields the highest returns. Consumers need to apply the same care and concern in selecting a financial planner that they would use in selecting a doctor, lawyer, or other professionals."

Your relationship with any adviser is built on trust and confidence in the person's ability, so take the time to do your homework and fully research the planner you choose to handle your portfolio. Continue to evaluate performance every quarter to keep a close eye on the markets, your adviser, and the status of your financial health.

SO, WHO ARE YOU GOING TO TRUST?

So, in the end without a doubt the best person for you to trust is yourself. That is because you know your needs and goals better than anyone else, you will always have your best interests at heart, and you have the most at stake.

If you agree with me on this, then it makes sense for you to educate yourself so that you know enough to choose a truly talented financial adviser and to supervise and police that adviser. Or you may decide to create your own business plan and in effect hire yourself as a financial adviser so that you can fulfill your own financial goals. You can even use various asset allocation models that are available on the Internet or through the American Association of Individual Investors (AAII) to determine how you should structure your portfolio.

Generally, if you have a large portfolio, it is best to hire a talented and fully vetted adviser and put that professional to work for you. Have the adviser do a complete analysis on how far you've come, where you are now, and where you want to go. Adding a talented adviser to your team can pay you dividends in the end. The key to increasing those dividends is to participate in the process completely. Don't just blindly hand over your cash and expect miracles; the more you know, the more you will prosper.

The book you are reading now will help you to manage your adviser and participate to maximize your annual yield.

If you've got a smaller portfolio, you should manage everything yourself so that you are not spending fees on advisers. Use your own skills to grow that portfolio and grow your net worth. The knowledge you gain in the building phase will serve you well when it comes time to bring in an adviser as part of your team.

Keep it lean and mean; watch expenses and find out what works for you and your circumstances and what does not. The trial-and-error phase of your development will help you refine your personal business model.

CREATING YOUR OWN BUSINESS PLAN WILL STRENGTHEN YOUR ABILITY TO PROSPER

With the understanding that you are the most qualified person to trust when managing your finances, you will want to begin thinking about developing a personal business plan. Whether you develop this plan independently or bring in an adviser to assist you, the ultimate goal is to map out on paper where you've been, where you are now, and where you are going.

In Chapter 9 of this book we provide you with a thorough outline so that you can get your plan on paper. In the meantime, paint in the broad strokes of your plan. We can fill in the details later.

To start thinking about your business plan, identify the following data to get a sense of what your current profile is:

- Net worth: _____.
- Age: _____.
- Tolerance for risk (circle one): High Medium Low.

If you do not have the information readily available to fill in your net worth or you are uncertain about your risk tolerance, that is okay. We will work on these areas in greater detail in the coming chapters. The reason for introducing these three items now is to have you begin to see the value of knowing where you are now, so that you can more effectively get to where you want to be later.

After thinking about your current profile, you will then begin to look at a variety of areas that will affect your personal business plan. Some of the areas to consider for now are:

- Current annual gross revenue.
- Average annual gross revenue over past three years.
- Projected future gross revenue.

- Current gross overhead—personal and/or business expenses.
- Projected future gross overhead—personal and/or business expenses.
- Investment portfolio dollar amount.
- Annual yield on investments.
- Active trading account dollar amount.
- Annual yield on active trading account.
- Areas to cut expenses.
- Areas to increase revenue.

Again, if you do not have the information readily available to address these areas, that is fine. We will be working on this material in the coming chapters and you will be able to finalize this information when you prepare your business plan.

TRADE, INVEST, AND LIVE WITHIN YOUR MEANS

As any competent accountant will tell you, a business (and a household) must have enough revenue coming in to cover the expenses going out. Of course at times businesses and individuals take on debt, but what is the cost of that debt? *Does the end justify the means?*

For example, if you buy a house you take on a mortgage and owe the bank money for the house that you live in. For that service the bank collects interest, and there is a monthly cost to you that goes toward paying the interest on that secured loan. The interest you pay enables you to have a roof over your head, so in most cases this end justifies the means. If for some reason you stop paying the bank, it has the right to take back the house since a mortgage is a secured loan. Taking on debt can offer you great value, as long as the end justifies the means and as long as the probability is high that you can sustain the debt for the duration of the loan.

For your business plan you will need to look at your own circumstances to ensure that the revenue coming in will cover the expenses going out. Remember, past performance does not guarantee future results. So, if things change and what was once a balanced budget becomes unbalanced, the quickest remedy is to cut expenses and increase revenue. From a survival standpoint, that is rule number one.

Another issue to address is that most start up businesses don't get into the black and don't become profitable right away. Keep this in mind when budgeting, so that you can plan for a period of adjustment and reduced revenue.

Keep your budget balanced and you will stay the course for the long term.

CHAPTER 3

Accountability, Setting Stops, and the Rogue Factor

One of the biggest challenges for most independent traders is to create a system of accountability. Generally traders work alone and have no mandatory checks-and-balances hierarchy to work within such as a day job or corporation would require. They have no one to answer to.

This is quite different from corporate life. In a corporation every employee from the janitor to the CEO answers to someone on a daily, weekly, or at least quarterly basis. Even the big kahuna has to report to the board of directors or the company shareholders, and the boss's job security is vulnerable if the company's performance fails.

The accountability that employees in corporations are subject to results in them having formal annual reviews. Many of them are awarded bonuses for quantifiable performance results and receive raises to their annual salaries based on the previous year's achievements.

In the corporate world when individuals are *not* performing their job adequately, they receive a series of verbal warnings and written warnings before they are officially fired. There are even times when employees get fired for not doing their job adequately and can still get unemployment paychecks every week or better yet, some top executives will get a golden parachute that many of us only dream of.

This is not so for the independent professional trader. Unless the individual trader sets up a system for accountability, the trader's financial stability can erode ever so quickly, without any warning or notice. Traders can find themselves making less than minimum wage and often can find themselves losing money as opposed to making any money at all.

They might even get their pink slip (meaning their trading account balance has gone to zero) without so much as a whisper of a reprimand or warning from their boss, who of course is none other than themselves. There are no federal and state laws to protect them from making less than minimum wage or from a harsh and painful termination.

They are on their own.

TRADERS ARE THE ULTIMATE ENTREPRENEURS AND MUST BE HELD ACCOUNTABLE

I've always said that trading is the perfect business.

That is because all traders are in fact entrepreneurs, whether they realize it or not. In essence, a trader has no boss; they call all the shots, and they benefit from all the winnings. The price they pay for that freedom is that they take on all of the risk and the headaches when things go wrong. Yes, they are on their own.

And that is a good thing.

The way to make that a good thing is to run your business with a profitable balance sheet and as few headaches as possible. With any business, accountability and honesty are key components in achieving this. So how do you hold yourself accountable and keep yourself honest?

By maintaining daily records you'll always be accountable and will always be forced to be honest with yourself. When you have daily numbers, there is no guessing as to what you are doing in terms of revenue.

You need to be just like the manager of a local restaurant or clothing store. The manager will know exactly to the penny how much money came in every day since opening the doors for business. It is likely that the manager compares these numbers and looks for trends in revenue from month to month, quarter to quarter, and year to year.

Depending on whether the revenue trend is up or down, the manager will need to make adjustments to the business model. This might involve unpleasant choices such as laying off employees when the revenue trend is down or exciting choices such as expanding the square footage of the retail space to accommodate the hordes of customers during a revenue trend that is up.

Trading is similar, and the choices are the same, but the vocabulary is different. So when the revenue trend is down, a trader may reduce the risk percentage; and when the revenue trend is up, the trader might increase the risk percentage. These are the same concepts with a different vocabulary. Your survival will depend on whether you can make difficult choices and whether you can do so in time for them to make a difference.

If you look at some infamous corporate debacles such as the Barings Bank and the Enron collapse, you can see that dishonest accounting just delays the inevitable. Facing bad news and solving problems rather than covering them up is the best way to succeed.

Your survival will depend on your ability to be honest with yourself in this process and to problem solve. We can sometimes try to avoid painful truths, but to be successful that is not an option. The honesty factor is key to your success.

SETTING STOP-LOSS EXITS IS ESSENTIAL

Setting stop-loss exits and adhering to them is usually difficult for new traders. There is often a strong psychological resistance to this concept. The resistance is linked to a variety of emotions, including fear and greed: fear of being wrong about the trade and greed of not wanting to get out and take a loss even if it is a small loss.

The other aspect linked to stops is ego. Many traders almost feel they can make the market do what they want it to do. When the market defies them and does not cooperate it can then create anger.

The key to setting stops is to develop skill in setting effective stops that are in alignment with current market dynamics. In other words, don't use arbitrary stops that are not directly related to support and resistance levels. You will want to give your trade enough room to breathe so that you don't get whipsawed and get stopped out repeatedly. Once you have confidence in your stop-setting skills, you will be more likely to adhere to your stops.

Also, the time to set your stop is *before* you enter a trade, not after. You will not be able to make rational decisions on your exit if you wait until you are already in a trade. The heat of the moment can overcome you and cloud your judgment.

For more information on money management and setting stops, refer to Chapter 12.

THE INFAMOUS ROGUE TRADER NAMED NICK LEESON

Oftentimes fact is stranger than fiction and can teach us lessons that steer us away from danger in the future. Surely if we cannot learn from our own mistakes and the mistakes of history, then we are doomed to repeat them.

And so it is with the true story of Nick Leeson, who is infamous for causing the collapse of the Barings Bank in February 1995. Barings was the oldest bank in the world, operating for 233 years before the collapse. It had in fact financed the Napoleonic Wars and counted the Queen of England among its clients. The story that follows illustrates that no entity is too big to fail, despite popular belief.

Leeson, a young trader for the bank, allowed small losses to spiral into $1.3 billion (£600 million) in losses in just three years. His own fear, greed, denial, and nonexistent risk control drove him to cover up his losses (in the now famous 88888 account) while he desperately attempted to trade his way back into profitable territory.

He stopped at nothing to fund his department's trading activity. In his own words Leeson says, "I saw the cuttings and shreds of paper and glue which I'd used to forge Ron Baker's and Richard Hogan's signatures. I couldn't believe what I'd done. . . . With my scissors, stick of glue and paper and fax machine, I had created £50 million."[1]

What's even more astounding than Leeson's lies and deceit is that Barings' upper management was oblivious to his deception and did not implement simple checks and balances to prevent just such a disaster. Their own greed and incompetence blinded them to glaring discrepancies that could have been detected and addressed.

If we are to learn anything from the original rogue trader, Nick Leeson, it is that accountability along with checks and balances go a long way to ensure our survival as traders. If we are to be independent entrepreneurs, we then need to institute some type of overseeing authority. This might be in the form of a trading buddy, a spouse, a trading partner, an accountant, or a coach. Basically, we need someone to whom we can be accountable so that we stay on track and follow the rules we have established for ourselves. You will read about more ideas on this topic in Chapter 8.

Ultimately, it is crucial to identify an individual to be your sounding board and eliminate the isolation that can lead to rogue behavior. When healthy accountability and benchmarks are not present in your day-to-day operations, you will be subject to the temptation to ignore important signs that you as a business owner need to face head-on. Working in an isolated vacuum over the long term will hinder your performance.

WATCH THE *ROGUE TRADER* MOVIE

If you haven't already done so, you really owe it to yourself to watch the movie about the true story of Nick Leeson. *Rogue Trader* was released by

---

[1]Nick Leeson, *Rogue Trader: How I Brought Down Barings Bank and Shook the Financial World* (Little, Brown, 1996), 189.

Miramax in 2000; Ewan McGregor starred and James Dearden directed. The book that Leeson wrote in 1996 is also enlightening.

The movie and book are much like a late-night thriller to any trader who has felt the emotions of a trade gone bad, very bad. One reviewer on Amazon.com stated that he trades for a living and watches the movie once a year to be reminded to use risk control. You probably don't need to go that far (once is no doubt enough), but it does drive the point home.

INSURMOUNTABLE, LARGE LOSSES USUALLY START AS SMALL LOSSES

Remember, most large, insurmountable losses start out as small losses. It is that snowball effect that you've got to watch out for, since the momentum is difficult to harness and control.

Don't become a rogue trader.

CHAPTER 4

What's Your Net Worth?

To be successful, it is critical to know where you stand at any given moment, and in the case of your finances, that means knowing what the dollar amount of your net worth is. This fluid number may increase or decrease as years go by, and checking in on what your current net worth status is should be at minimum an annual exercise. The number in itself will unlock the answers to a number of questions, including "How big should my active trading account be?"

NET WORTH STATEMENT

For starters, you will need to develop a current net worth statement, which is an accounting of all your assets and your liabilities. Take a look at Table 4.1, which is a sample that shows you a very basic accounting of a hypothetical household. Yours of course will vary, and you may add items or delete them to suit your individual situation. The concept of this statement, though, is the same for everyone. The concept is to add up all your assets and your liabilities into one easy-to-read statement.

The next step in figuring out your net worth is to subtract the liability amount from the asset amount, and that gives you your current net worth. It looks something like this equation:

$$\text{Total Assets} - \text{Total Liabilities} = \text{Net Worth}$$

TABLE 4.1   Sample of a Net Worth Statement

Assets		Liabilities	
Description	**Amount**	**Description**	**Amount**
Real estate—home	$805,000	Mortgage—home	$425,000
Automobiles	$ 55,000	Automobile loans	$ 17,000
Jewelry	$ 29,000	Credit cards	$ 23,000
Checking accounts	$ 13,000	Current bills	$ 19,000
Savings accounts	$ 48,000	Business loan	$ 45,000
Trading accounts	$ 45,000	Other	$ 8,000
Total assets	**$995,000**	**Total liabilities**	**$537,000**

Total assets $995,000 – Total liabilities $537,000 = Current net worth of $458,000

And if we use the numbers from our sample net worth statement in Table 4.1, the numbers look like this:

$$\$995,000 - \$537,000 = \$458,000 = \text{Current Net Worth}$$

Once you have this information, you will be able to more effectively create your financial profile, which is the first step in starting your trading business.

CREATING YOUR FINANCIAL PROFILE

Knowing yourself and where you stand financially is important in any business endeavor. The following exercise will enable you to visualize where you are now, and how you will structure your trading business.

Fill out your own custom profile by using the blank triangle chart in Figure 4.1. You can see that your profile consists of four important pieces of information: (1) your net worth, (2) your tolerance for risk, (3) your age, and (4) your trading account size. This profile will be the cornerstone to your business plan, which you will be developing when you read Chapter 9 of this book.

Next, look at Table 4.2 and Figures 4.2 through 4.7, which show six different profiles that are for example only. These six sample illustrations can be used for reference to get a sense of what the spectrum of possibility is. Remember, where you start today is just the beginning. The plan is to grow your net worth and trading business by setting up a solid foundation in the beginning.

Typically, you will allocate about 10 percent of your net worth for your trading account. This percentage is not one that needs to be carved in stone, but it is a general rule of thumb that I like to go by.

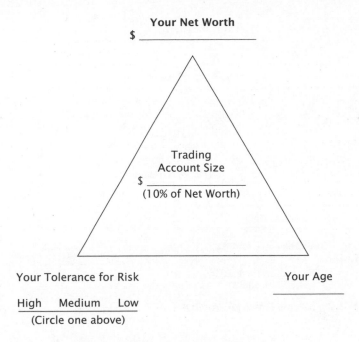

Your Net Worth

$ _____

Trading
Account Size

$ _____
(10% of Net Worth)

Your Tolerance for Risk   Your Age

High   Medium   Low   _____
(Circle one above)

FIGURE 4.1   Blank Financial Profile for You to Fill Out

At times, younger traders with a longer time horizon until retirement can afford to put more than 10 percent into this account. To do this means that the trader must be fully aware of the nature of the business and the risk involved and must be comfortable with that risk.

At other times, an individual will structure this as a business venture. The trader will have to fund and capitalize this start-up business with risk capital that may or may not be independent from personal net worth. As with any new business venture, there is an inherent high risk of failure.

TABLE 4.2   Financial Profile Samples

	Figure #	Net Worth	Age	Risk Tolerance	Trading Account Size
Profile A	4.2	$1,000,000	60	Low	$100,000
Profile B	4.3	$ 500,000	50	Medium	$ 50,000
Profile C	4.4	$ 100,000	40	High	$ 10,000
Profile D	4.5	$ 50,000	30	Low	$ 5,000
Profile E	4.6	$ 10,000	30	High	$ 1,000
Profile F	4.7	$ (50,000)	30	Medium	$ 250

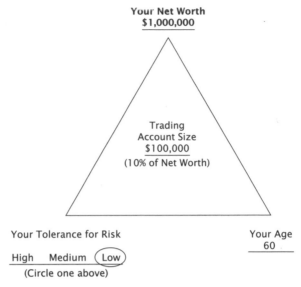

FIGURE 4.2   Sample Financial Profile A

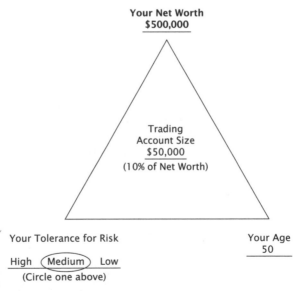

FIGURE 4.3   Sample Financial Profile B

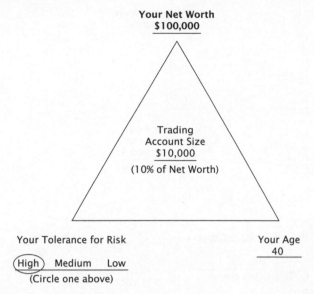

FIGURE 4.4 Sample Financial Profile C

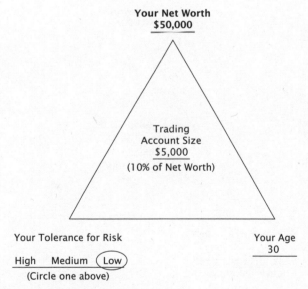

FIGURE 4.5 Sample Financial Profile D

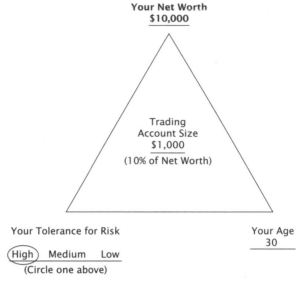

FIGURE 4.6   Sample Financial Profile E

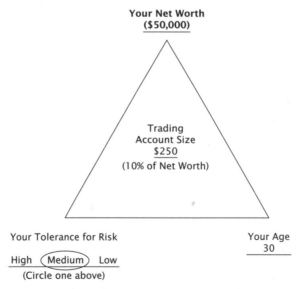

FIGURE 4.7   Sample Financial Profile F

This must be taken into consideration when developing the plan. You will find out more about these topics in Chapter 5 and Chapter 9.

Here is a quick take on each of the sample profiles so that you can get an idea of how each of these traders could structure their plan:

- **Profile A** in Figure 4.2 is for a trader with a $1,000,000 net worth at age 60 with a low risk tolerance and a trading account size of $100,000. This person is close to retirement, so it is crucial not to jeopardize net worth. The trader will have a diminishing opportunity to recoup any large losses. For that reason, even though he can afford to have a $100,000 trading account, it may be useful to be especially conservative when it comes to risk control. For example, if the payoff ratio and win ratio warrant a 2 percent trade risk amount, this individual may elect to reduce that to 1.5 percent. Refer to Chapter 12 for more information on how to calculate the percentage of money to risk on each trade based on your trading performance results.
- **Profile B** in Figure 4.3 is for a trader with a $500,000 net worth at age 50 with a medium risk tolerance and a trading account size of $50,000. This person is not as close to retirement as the trader in Profile A, so she is able to comfortably design a business plan that can absorb drawdowns and have enough time to recoup prior to retirement. This person's trading account is half the size of the one in Profile A, and will potentially generate one-half the annual revenue of the account in Profile A.
- **Profile C** in Figure 4.4 is for a trader with a $100,000 net worth at age 40 with a high risk tolerance and a trading account size of $10,000. The individual has funds to allocate toward trading and is not close to retirement age. This trader has two options when setting up a trading business. If he works with a $10,000 trading account, he will need to maintain another source of income, such as a day job, during the start-up phase of the business to cover living expenses and overhead. Or he could take a more aggressive, high-risk approach and put more than 10 percent of net worth toward the trading business. These decisions should be carefully worked out in the planning phase that is outlined in Chapter 9.
- **Profile D** in Figure 4.5 is for a trader with a $50,000 net worth at age 30 with a low risk tolerance and a trading account size of $5,000. This person has a similar scenario to the one in Profile C in that they both are young and have funds that are available to put toward a business. However, they differ as to risk tolerance. It is a matter of considering all factors and preparing a plan prior to launching any approach.
- **Profile E** in Figure 4.6 is for a trader with a $10,000 net worth at age 30 with a high risk tolerance and a trading account size of $1,000. This person's limited resources will make it challenging, but not impossible,

to launch a trading business. The likely path that this individual will take is to work a full-time day job and focus all energies on nights and weekends to developing a profitable paper trading approach. This person will have greater stress than those in the previous profiles, but sometimes when resources are limited people are more motivated and effective with their approach. Sometimes the hungrier traders and investors are, the more dedicated they are and the more they care about the outcome.

- **Profile F** in Figure 4.7 is for a trader with a negative net worth of minus $50,000 at age 30 with a medium risk tolerance and a mini trading account of $250. Much like Profile E, this person has minimal resources. If his net worth is negative $50,000, he is carrying that debt by paying interest. This increases one's monthly overhead. Depending on what kind of day job the person has, allocating resources to a trading business will be difficult. The first goal for this individual is to reduce the debt by cutting back any expenses that are not absolutely essential. Just go with the bare-bones essentials and every day chip away at the debt. Then, with the trading business, it is important to be lean and mean and get any and all education and services for free. You would be surprised at how many brokers are looking for your business and will offer you services for little or no money down. Focus on paper trading and developing a winning strategy while reducing debt.

These six profiles are by no means the only ones that exist, and yours will be unique and will fall somewhere between them. Try to play out in your mind how you see your financial profile and how you will structure your plan. Then, go to Chapter 9 when you're ready to set up your formal business plan.

ARE YOU MOVING FORWARD, FALLING BACKWARD, OR STANDING IN PLACE?

If you plotted a graph from when you were age 15 to the present and you drew in what your net worth was on that chart over the years, what would it look like? Most likely, it would reflect whether you were moving forward, falling backward, or standing in place.

Much like the financial markets, our net worth is a chart and a graph, and it has meaning for us. Our net worth has bull runs, bear runs, and bracketed or sideways runs, just like the financial markets. It's a reflection of what is happening in our life.

Here is an example of one net worth scenario: Your parents may give you money before you begin college, and your net worth goes up. While

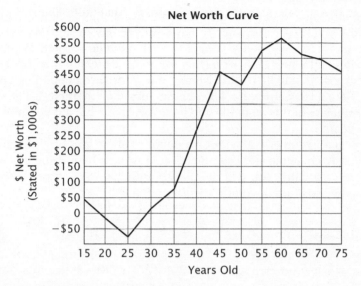

FIGURE 4.8 Sample Net Worth Curve

attending college you may spend the funds you were given and then need additional funds; your net worth will fall backward. When you get out of college and get your first job you are paying off student loans, your net worth will be negative, but it will slowly begin to go forward. Then when you get your first big break at work and your salary does more than cover the essential food, shelter, and clothing expenses, your net worth will go

TABLE 4.3	Hypothetical Net Worth Progression from Age 15 to Age 75
Age	**Net Worth**
15	+$ 45,000
20	−$ 15,000
25	−$ 75,000
30	+$ 15,000
35	+$ 78,000
40	+$268,000
45	+$458,000
50	+$416,000
55	+$528,000
60	+$568,000
65	+$515,000
70	+$498,000
75	+$458,000

forward more quickly. Sometimes you will have an illness or lose a job, and the family will dip into savings to pay for everyday expenses to compensate. Other factors will nudge your net worth up or down such as inheriting money, landing a super job, or paying for your own children's college.

Your goal should be to consistently move forward in building your net worth. Take a look at Figure 4.8. You can also look at Table 4.3 to see the actual numbers in this example and how they move up and down throughout the years.

This is a hypothetical net worth curve to show you how this number is constantly changing and is a reflection of what is happening in your life. With some planning, you will be able to anticipate and, more effectively control, the direction of your net worth curve.

CHAPTER 5

The Life of an Entrepreneur

You—the entrepreneur, that is—can decide at a moment's notice to take off on Tuesday or just take off all next week, because you are the boss. You have the freedom to call the shots and make your own hours, and come in late every day if you want to. No one tells you what to do. It's just a life of leisure and luxury, right?

Well, not really. It's not *all* glamour and glitz. Yes, there is someone to answer to, and that would be your bank account. That is because if you are not making a profit, the party is over and the business shuts down. And, let's face it— there's nothing glamorous about that.

The truth about being an entrepreneur and running your own trading business is that it is a lot of hard work, a lot of taking on risk, and a lot of not giving up when the going gets tough. These are things that most people don't know until they dive in and start their own business. From the outside looking in, most people think that having your own business is all fun and fancy free. But when the business throws you its first curveball, what are you going to do? That's what separates the men from the boys and the women from the girls.

NEW START-UP BUSINESSES HAVE HIGH FAILURE RATES

The Small Business Administration (SBA) keeps the statistics on business failures and claims that more than half of new businesses will disappear in the first five years. The debate about this figure is that not all the businesses that disappear do so because of failure. Some disappear because they get bought out by another company, or are reborn under another name, or move to another state.

Even so, it is pretty agreed upon that the failure rate is high, despite the ongoing debate about the exact number and cause. The next staggering statistic is that in the first year, nearly one-quarter of the new businesses will disappear. Again, the debate regarding what causes the *disappearance* continues, but any rational person will know that a large number of these disappearing businesses do in fact fail.

The good news is that if you can make it beyond the first year and then if you can make it to five years, your odds at staying in business for the long run are not bad. So, you ask: How do I ensure that my new trading business will make it to the five-year mark?

WHAT DOES IT TAKE FOR A NEW BUSINESS TO SUCCEED?

Longevity in the start-up business world is dependent on a number of very important factors. All of these factors are basic common sense, so how hard could it be to make this new business a slam-dunk winner, right?

Yet, I'll bet that a good share of the modest folks reading this book will admit to a time or two when they brazenly were overly enthusiastic about a project and got in a little too deep and a little too fast. Even I at times have energetically and enthusiastically dived into a project without using common sense. What can we say? We are human and the word *human* is *not* synonymous with *perfect*.

The upside to this is that the energy and enthusiasm and innovation that get us in over our head at times reflect a passion and creativity that are essential to making a business successful. So, in that important sense, we have the right stuff. Now it is a matter of harnessing these qualities and channeling them into the right direction with a certain amount of structure.

Here are six things you need to do to have a shot at being successful in your new business:

1. **Understand it will be a *lot* of work.** No one can prepare you for how much work it will be, but you can be assured you will work harder as a business owner than you ever worked when you were working for someone else. At least this will be true in the beginning. Until you are out of the red and into the black, you will need to be tireless at putting the time in to meet the anticipated and unanticipated challenges

that will arise. Prepare yourself so you are not surprised and discouraged by this fact. It doesn't hurt for you to be in good health and have above-average stamina when you launch your business venture. These two assets are more essential than most realize.

2. **Get adequate financing.** Business owners often underestimate how much money is needed. The estimate may be off due to a lack of planning or research in the development phase. Or it may be off due to an unexpected event that depletes the capital reserve. The trick with financing is that you always need to be ahead of the curve. What I mean is: You don't want to find out about a shortfall two days before it hits. Your cash flow is your lifeline; without it your business will die, or cease to exist. Plan for financing before you need it. This will take some of the pressure off and enable you to negotiate better terms on your loans. Two things happen when your back is up against the wall due to a financing shortfall: (1) You can't think clearly and can't trade well. (2) You will be faced with getting a loan where your interest is astronomical. High interest rates on financing only reduce your chances for success. Negotiate wisely and from a position of strength.

3. **Plan, plan, and plan some more.** When caught up in the romance and enthusiasm of an innovative new business venture, it is very easy to forget to plan. You get swept off your feet, and before you know it you've invested time and money into the venture before you've done a feasibility test and business plan. It's like falling in love; your adrenaline is raging and you get blinded by the excitement of new possibilities and opportunities. It's totally normal and very common. The problem is that if you don't catch yourself in time, you can get too far in and set yourself up for failure without even realizing it. There are things you may do that are irreversible, and that may jeopardize the entire operation. Caution: Plan early, plan well, and plan now. You can refer to the business plan in Chapter 9. That will get you on the right track. And, yes, it goes back to item number one in this list—doing a business plan is a *lot* of work. Trust me; the time you spend on your plan now will save you money and time later.

4. **Start your business for the right reasons.** If you are starting a trading business because you want to get rich quick and not work very hard, you are doing so for the wrong reasons. First of all, trading is like any important occupation or business; it takes a lot of effort to get to the master level. And let's define *master level* as being able to earn a living that supports your lifestyle. Becoming a doctor or lawyer takes years of education and intense dedication. Trading is no different. Are doctors and lawyers and traders rich? Let's define *rich* as living comfortably

and having a nice lifestyle for their families. Then yes, doctors and lawyers and traders can be rich. But there's no free ride; they all have to work at it. The right reasons to start your trading business are that you love the work and have a passion for it, you have an aptitude for the business, and you believe you can be successful.

5. **Be resilient and persevere.** All great visionaries, entrepreneurs, and innovators have qualities of resilience and perseverance. You may start up your business and there will be smooth sailing and then out of the blue you may get blindsided by some unforeseen disaster. Those who know how to survive have a cool head, know how to turn a bad situation into an opportunity, and if nothing else learn from the experience. The nonsurvivors will panic, become paralyzed, get excessively angry, and miss opportunities to counteract the disaster. Nonsurvivors tend to feel victimized by events and people and usually have an excuse for everything instead of taking responsibility and working on the problem. With any problem, it is not a question of "Is there a solution?" but a question of "Which is the best solution?" Remember that. Another thing to remember is: No matter how well your business is going, do not get overconfident or cocky. That is the kiss of death and will cause you to miss warning signals and vulnerabilities to your model and to changing environments.

6. **Create a model that can be profitable.** Here's where you need hands-on experience to prove that you have a profitable model. You can do this in the form of paper trading, and trading as a parallel test (see Chapter 10) while you retain other employment that pays the bills.

SMALL BUSINESSES ARE THE BACKBONE OF THE ECONOMY

Remember how important small businesses are to the economy. The Small Business Administration website states that small businesses in the United States:

- Represent 99.7 of all employer firms.
- Employ just over half of all private-sector employees.
- Pay 44 percent of total U.S. payroll.
- Have generated 64 percent of net new jobs over the past 15 years.
- Represent 40 percent of high tech workers (such as scientists, engineers, and computer programmers).
- Are 52 percent home-based.

The real innovation and creativity always come from the entrepreneurial sector. That's where the new ideas are. Just like Bill Gates starting Microsoft in his garage, or Mark Zuckerberg starting Facebook in his dorm room or Larry Page and Sergey Brin starting Google while they were at Stanford, you are part of an elite and creative group of individuals.

Entrepreneurs are often misunderstood and don't always fit in. They think outside the box, try things that other people think are crazy, and generally take on more risk than the average person would ever consider. But they love what they do and wouldn't trade it for anything else; that's what makes them special.

Because, if they beat the odds and succeed at doing what they love, there is no better job in the world. To be able to create something, a profitable company, out of nothing is quite simply a miracle. Yes, miracles do happen, but you have to make them happen. They don't just fall into your lap.

Granted, the life of an entrepreneur is not for everyone, and the true test is in the launching and maintaining of a business. You will never know if you can succeed until you try.

REDUCE YOUR EXPENSES AND INCREASE YOUR REVENUE

Any successful small business owner will tell you that the secret to success is to always be looking for new ways to reduce expenses and increase revenue. It is a constant, ongoing process that never ends. It requires a creative mind-set, since there are always new ways to create efficiencies that save money and time, especially with new and emerging technology on an almost daily basis.

In addition to efficiency, there are also ways to just do without. If it comes down to the possibility of closing down your shop or instead cutting some nonessential items, what are you going to do? You betcha—get rid of the fat and cut anything you don't absolutely need.

Make the hard choices earlier rather than later. The earlier you make them, the more positive effect they will have in the long run. Doing too little too late is a sad state of affairs, since there are times when a business could have been saved if more had been done sooner. Don't fall prey to that mistake.

And don't forget, in the end, it is *all* about the revenue.

You've got to keep your eye on the revenue and keep your eye on the ball. Donald Trump is quoted as saying that when one of his enterprises went bankrupt in the 1990s, it was because he took his eye off the ball. That is a luxury a businessperson cannot afford. Diligence is the key.

HOW TO REDUCE EXPENSES

There are a variety of ways to cut expenses, some of them painful, to be sure, and then some more creative ways that just require a bit of ingenuity. Best that you do a little of both and strive to be lean and mean, even in times of prosperity.

For example, take a page from the book of Sam Walton, who founded Wal-Mart in 1962; he walked the walk and talked the talk of a lean, mean discount machine. His top executives had to stay in budget motels when on business travel, because his mind-set was all about stripping down costs to the bare minimum.

We can take another useful example of cost cutting and reducing expenses from the story of American Airlines back in 2003 when it was attempting to avoid bankruptcy. The airline took the usual obvious measures, such as laying off personnel and implementing lower salaries for pilots.

What interests me more about American Airlines is its uniquely innovative groundbreaking ideas, such as getting rid of magazines on all flights, dumping all the heavy stainless steel machines for brewing coffee, getting guard dogs instead of paying night watchmen, and not carrying more fuel than the planes needed—which, interestingly, would be dumped in flight prior to landing to avoid the danger of combustion.

As you can imagine, every time gas prices increase at the pump, the airlines struggle to stay alive. Extra weight on an airplane uses more fuel and costs more money. American Airlines systematically went through every single line item in their budget and lightened up the load to save money on fuel. And it worked. The airline avoided bankruptcy and weathered that storm and lived to see another day.

Here it seems that necessity is the mother of invention! The first commercial flights took place in the 1930s, and it took around 70 years for the airlines to finally look at fuel efficiency the way American did. Of course the measures that American took have now been adopted by every major airline around the world. But what took them so long to think of these ideas in the first place? The answer lies in the fact that American had to look at everything possible when faced with bankruptcy.

When running your business, you do not need to be faced with bankruptcy to get creative and think of new and innovative ways to cut costs. You just need to have the mind-set to think that way in the first place. I urge you to do so.

Here is a list of ways to cut costs:

- **Delay expenses.** If you are not going to use an item right away, delay the expense. If you have expenses like insurance, rather than paying in one big lump sum once a year, make monthly payments and spread the expense out over time.

- **Lay off personnel.** Do whatever you can do yourself. Lay off the cleaning service, gardener, receptionist, bookkeeper, and so on.
- **Restructure debt to get lower interest rates.** This includes business debt, your mortgage, and credit cards. You can negotiate with anyone; just get on the phone and start the conversation and come from a position of strength since you can take your business elsewhere.
- **Lower rates with your vendors.** Call every service provider you have and ask if your monthly payment can be lowered. The answer may be no, but they understand you can go elsewhere for services, so they may try to work with you, and any discount is a good discount.
- **Use it or lose it.** If you are *not* using a product or service, get rid of it. Cancel magazines and newsletters that don't make you money; shut off subscriptions to news feeds or data feeds you don't actually use. Do you really need three land line phones plus a cell phone?
- **Cut down services that are needed to half.** For example, if you have a cleaning service come every week, try having them come every other week or once a month. You will be surprised that sometimes you don't need as much service as you are getting currently and you may not experience a significant change in overall benefit.
- **Cut down your use of electricity.** Try energy-saver lightbulbs and other green measures if you work at home. Residential users of electricity generally are subject to a penalty for using more kilowatts than their neighbors who are not home all day; it's called going over your baseline. If you go over your baseline, you can get hit with four times the price per kilowatt than your neighbor pays. Call your energy company to find out more.
- **Use a professional tax accountant.** An accountant can guide you on ways to save on your taxes; it may save you money to spend money on a professional tax advisor that knows how to structure your business and personal taxes to maximize savings.
- **Bundle or renegotiate your phone, cable, and Internet access.** These companies are getting increasingly aggressive about competing in the marketplace, and even if you have a relatively new plan (a year or two old) it is worth looking into current prices and terms. Bundling landlines, cell phones, Internet, and cable can make a big difference.
- **Shop around for lower health insurance rates.** Maybe a higher deductible can save you a bundle per month, since health insurance is one of those skyrocketing budget items; it is crucial to keep tabs on what the increase is every year and reevaluate current needs versus expense.
- **Think before you buy!** How often do you go to Staples office supply and load up the cart with everything you *might* need, only to find that a lot of it sits in your supply closet untouched a year later? Make a shopping list *before* you go shopping and stick to the list.

- **Return items you haven't used.** If you do go to your supply closet, only to find that you have 10 boxes of staples when you use maybe one box a year, or ink cartridges from a printer you don't even own anymore, return them! You will be pleasantly surprised at how much all that stuff adds up to on a gift card the nice sales clerk will give back to you. Don't worry about not having a receipt; many stores will take back items and give you a store credit as long as the items are still in their system.
- **Reduce inventory.** Excess inventory costs money, big money, in outlay of funds at the time of purchase and space to house the inventory. When you go to your local Costco or Sam's Club, do you really need to buy 24 pads of paper that may take you two years to use? Purchase what you need right now, and only what you need right now.
- **Negotiate on everything.** If you don't ask, you don't get. So, pose the question: "Can you sell this to me for less?" It costs nothing to ask.
- **Comparison shop.** Check with three vendors that have similar products and services and find out which gives you the best value for your dollar.
- **Empty your storage unit.** If you have a storage unit and pay $200 per month just to store items you don't really need and haven't looked at in years, get rid of it.

This is a list to get started with and it is mostly commonsense ideas. The list helps to cover all the bases and get your mind thinking in the right direction. You can probably come up with a few ideas that would work for your personal situation.

The best mind-set for every entrepreneur to be in is to spend every dollar as if it were your last. It is surprising what you can live without when you set your mind to cutting costs. For example, imagine yourself stranded on a deserted island; how would you survive if you had only the bare minimum? The bare minimum would be food, shelter, and clothing. It is a useful exercise, because that is how you can get innovative in cutting costs without feeling any change in lifestyle or business style.

A PENNY SAVED IS REALLY ONE AND A HALF PENNIES EARNED

Good old Benjamin Franklin—he was a smart man. His saying that a penny saved is a penny earned cuts right to the heart of cutting costs.

When you think about it, though, in this day and age it is more like saving a penny is more like saving one and a half pennies. Franklin didn't take into account state, local, and federal tax on every penny we earn. Then of course there is sales tax. It can add up, and if you earn a penny you might get to keep only half of that penny.

So, choose wisely how you spend your pennies.

IT'S ALL ABOUT THE REVENUE

Generally, the more skilled you become in the trading business, the more able you are to go from one winning trade to another. And yet, when there are changing market cycles and market dynamics that catch even the most seasoned trader off guard, it can be challenging to get back on track.

For this reason, the famous line that past performance does not guarantee future results rings true, and you must be sure to have safeguards in place so that you can see a change in revenue activity early. Then make adjustments, and just like in cutting expenses, use your creative ingenuity to capture unique and ever-abundant opportunities in the marketplace to maximize revenue.

You are the captain of your ship; you have the ability to navigate and steer your business away from dangerous rocky waters. You call the shots and can set the sails to capture the winds of prosperity. But you must use all the tools and resources at your disposal and never rest from searching for new ways to increase revenue.

CHAPTER 6

Understanding Financial Markets

U nderstanding financial markets and how they work will be a constant education for you, because they are constantly changing. With every new technological advance and with every new geopolitical structure introduced into the marketplace, the markets will adapt and change. Prepare yourself to be on the lookout for the latest developments in the markets at all times, since what is written on these pages will no doubt change as the months and years go by.

Compared with the simplicity of the caveman days, in today's world we have a variety of new developments that did not exist until recently, such as:

- Electronic markets have replaced many open-outcry pits.
- Introduction of the euro currency in 1999 replaced the existing currency of 15 European countries at the time.
- Decimalization in the U.S. markets replaced fractions in 2000.
- Around-the-clock 24-hour trading for *all* markets is on the horizon.

So now in today's world we have all these new and exciting developments, which needless to say weren't around in the year of the Great Crash, 1929. Who knows what we will have in another 80 years? There may be a completely different financial landscape with a completely different vocabulary to match.

If we go way back to the beginning, finance consisted primarily of a barter system. There was a time when a farmer might give a number of bushels of grain to a rancher up the road in exchange for a cow. They each got something they needed and it was a fair trade. In essence, they were trading commodities, which we still do today. The only difference is that today it's not as literal as it was back then. Now the trade generally takes place on paper or through a fiber-optic cable, as opposed to physically handing over a living, breathing, mooing cow in exchange for some bushels of grain.

Barter was essentially the beginning of the financial markets. There were trades being made, and liquidity (or lack thereof) existed just as it does in modern-day markets. The sophistication of today's technology and computers and the many channels an order goes through do not change the essence of it all.

BUYER AND SELLER AGREE ON PRICE, BUT THEY DISAGREE ON VALUE

It is still the same, where on one side of a trade there is a *buyer* and on the other side of the trade is the *seller*. And this is important; both the buyer and seller agree on price, but disagree on value. The farmer and the rancher exchanged commodities; they were buying and selling. They agreed on how much to make the exchange for, but they disagreed on the value of the item they were exchanging. They each had a surplus of one commodity and were willing to give it up for something else.

When you sit behind your computer screen and you place a buy order or a sell order, it goes through many more channels and systems than the farmer and the rancher shaking hands on a deal, but it is basically the same.

Many of my students have struggled with the idea of two parties in a transaction that *disagree* on value. How can that be if they both agree to a fair trade, don't they believe the *value* to be equal, therefore agreeing on value?

Let me try to explain this with an example. Suppose there was a man who owned an automobile that he drives to work every day. This car has value to him until all of a sudden he loses his eyesight and now has to take a taxi cab to work. The man decides to sell his car to a young woman and they both agree on a price of $15,000.

They agree on the price, but they disagree on the value of what they are trading. In this example, the man does not value the car, because he no longer can use it. And the woman does not value the currency, because she needs the car more than she needs the cash. It is a fair trade where they agree on the price and disagree on the value of what they are trading.

BUYERS AND SELLERS AND THE FINANCIAL ORDER FLOW PROCESS

In the world of buy and sell orders there are many players that contribute to the process. The journey that an order takes from the time it is initiated by the trader or investor until the time it is confirmed by the clearing firm may take just seconds, and yet in slow motion it is quite an amazing series of events.

Take a look at Figure 6.1, which is a diagram of a simplified order flow process, to get an idea of how your buy and sell orders are handled. Keep in mind that the process will vary among a variety of markets, whether they are options, futures, foreign exchange (forex), or stocks. But the basic idea is the same. The job of all the players is to be a matchmaker for a buyer and a seller, and to be sure that the transaction is handled properly so that both the buyer and the seller are treated fairly.

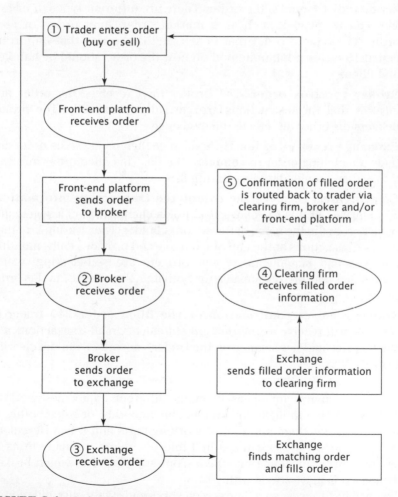

FIGURE 6.1 Order Flow Diagram
This diagram shows the path that a trade takes from the time it is placed to the time it is filled and then cleared.

Important Note: In some cases, one firm functions as a front-end platform, broker, and clearing firm all in one. TradeStation is an example of a firm like this because it is a self-clearing broker that has a front-end platform as well. There are many other firms that have this same scenario, and they are usually larger firms.

The series of five events for a typical order transaction goes something like this:

1. **Trader enters order.** The investor or trader enters a buy or sell order through the front-end platform or in some cases calls the broker directly to initiate the order. There are different types of orders that can be placed, such as a market order, limit order, or stop order. The type of order that is selected is the way that important instructions are communicated on how the order should be handled and filled.

2. **Broker receives order.** The broker then receives the order and ensures that the instructions are carried out correctly. The broker delivers the order directly to the exchange.

3. **Exchange receives order.** The exchange then receives the order and finds a matching order to complete the fill. This filled order information is then provided to the clearing firm.

4. **Clearing firm receives the completed transaction information.** The clearing firm is the player that holds client funds in a segregated bank account in the name of the account holder. The clearing firm then clears transactions at the end of each day and provides daily, monthly, and year-end statements. (Some brokers are self-clearing, which means that they are responsible for both item 2 and item 4 in this order process.)

5. **Trader receives confirmation of the filled order.** The trader or investor will receive a confirmation statement on all transactions and the fill price and net balance on the trader's account from the clearing firm.

There are many employees in many different companies working together worldwide to make the system run smoothly, or as smoothly as possible. Basically, there are a lot of working parts and it is a Herculean effort, to be sure. As you can see in Table 6.1, there are many firms to choose from when deciding on which front-end platform, which broker, and which exchange to trade with.

You will have access to online screen shots and statements and reports of all of your trading activity with your front-end platform and your broker.

TABLE 6.1 Examples of Players in Today's Order Flow Process

Front-End Platforms	Brokers	Exchanges	Clearing Firms
NinjaTrader	TradeStation	NYSE	R.J. O'Brien
eSignal	Mirus Futures	CBOT	Dorman Trading
Trade Navigator	AMP Futures & Forex	CME	GAIN Capital
Market Analyst	Interactive Brokers	NYMEX	RCG*
QuoteTracker	PFGBEST.com	NASDAQ	Penson Financial
TradeStation	Global Futures	ICE	Wedbush

There are many players that participate in the order flow process. This table shows just a few examples of some of the current players and their functions in the process. There are many more players in the marketplace for you to choose from when designing your business plan. You can find more thorough lists of the players in Appendix C (Resources) and in Appendix E (Market Exchanges) at the back of this book. Those sections include complete contact information so that you can do your own research on current products and services.
*RCG is an acronym for Rosenthal Collins Group LLC.

See Figures 6.2 through 6.9 to get an idea of the information you will be provided with in order to monitor your positions and your account balances.

There are fields on these screens for account balance figures, orders placed, orders filled and canceled, symbols, interval and time frame of chart, position short or long, type of order, quantity filled, quantity left, time of order placed and filled, average price, and so on.

You will notice that the look of the statements will vary depending on which platform you are using. For example, in Figure 6.6 you can see the order status on the TradeStation platform for a number of trades that have been filled and canceled. Then in Figure 6.9 on the NinjaTrader platform with Mirus Futures as the broker and Zen-Fire as the connection, you can also see a number of orders that are filled and canceled. However, the two platforms are quite different in appearance, meaning depending on which platform(s) you decide to use, it is important to know where to find all the relevant information to stay on top of your trades.

There will be a learning curve with any new front-end platform and/or broker, and it is important to get acquainted with any new provider. Place small test trades to get your feet wet before you begin your actual trading. Order-entry mechanics will also vary from platform to platform. If you are going to encounter any operator errors or surprises, it is best to experience them on small sample trades first.

Once you are up and running, the next important concern for your survival is to reconcile all of your account statements daily. If a glitch in the order flow system occurs, you need to address it immediately. With the volume of transactions and the volume of personnel processing these transactions, there is always a margin for error.

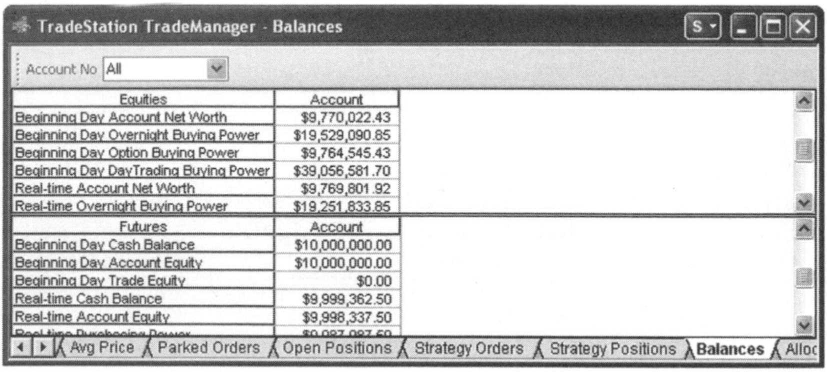

FIGURE 6.2   Screen shot of TradeStation TradeManager—Balances
Source: Created with TradeStation. © TradeStation Technologies, Inc. All rights reserved.

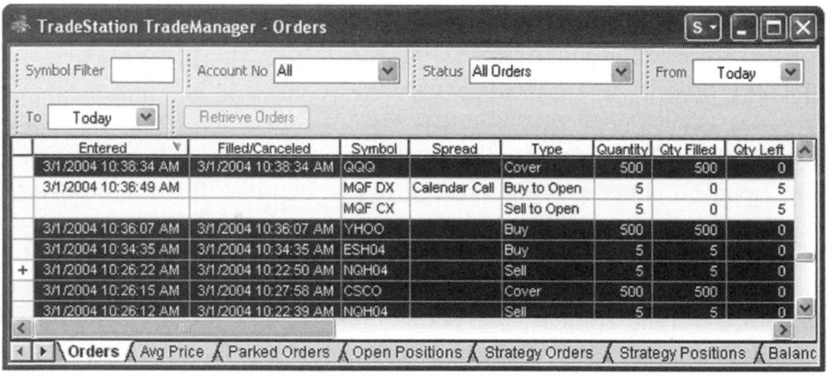

FIGURE 6.3   Screen shot of TradeStation TradeManager—Orders
Source: Created with TradeStation. © TradeStation Technologies, Inc. All rights reserved.

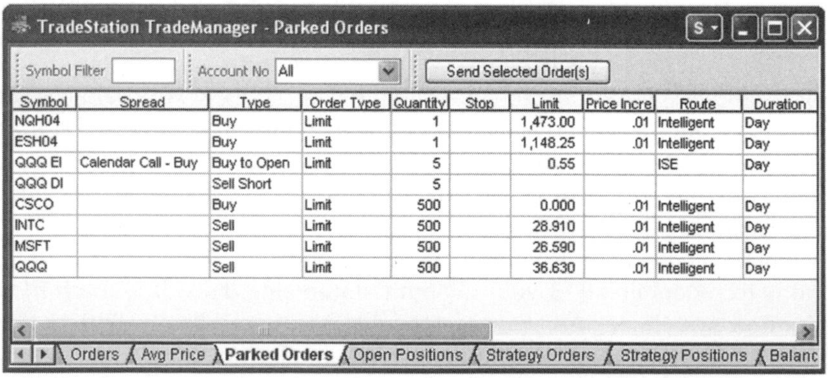

FIGURE 6.4   Screen shot of TradeStation TradeManager—Parked Orders
Source: Created with TradeStation. © TradeStation Technologies, Inc. All rights reserved.

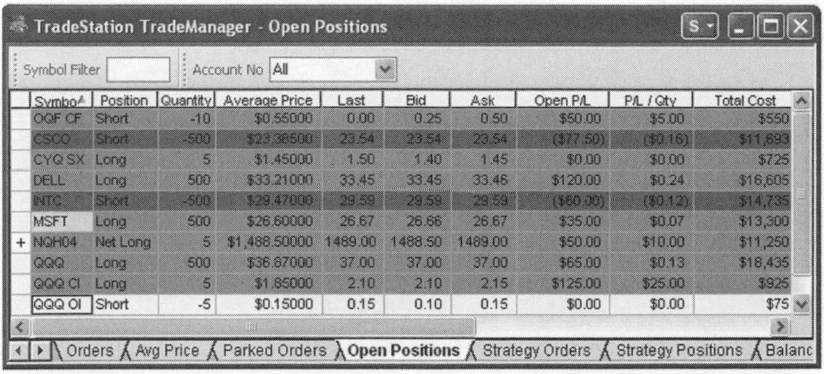

TradeStation TradeManager - Open Positions

Symbol Filter [ ]   Account No [All ▾]

Symbol▲	Position	Quantity	Average Price	Last	Bid	Ask	Open P/L	P/L / Qty	Total Cost
OQF CF	Short	-10	$0.55000	0.00	0.25	0.50	$50.00	$5.00	$550
CSCO	Short	-500	$23.38500	23.54	23.54	23.54	($77.50)	($0.16)	$11,693
CYQ SX	Long	5	$1.45000	1.50	1.40	1.45	$0.00	$0.00	$725
DELL	Long	500	$33.21000	33.45	33.45	33.46	$120.00	$0.24	$16,605
INTC	Short	-500	$29.47000	29.59	29.59	29.59	($60.00)	($0.12)	$14,735
MSFT	Long	500	$26.60000	26.67	26.66	26.67	$35.00	$0.07	$13,300
+ NQH04	Net Long	5	$1,488.50000	1489.00	1488.50	1489.00	$50.00	$10.00	$11,250
QQQ	Long	500	$36.87000	37.00	37.00	37.00	$65.00	$0.13	$18,435
QQQ CI	Long	5	$1.85000	2.10	2.10	2.15	$125.00	$25.00	$925
QQQ OI	Short	-5	$0.15000	0.15	0.10	0.15	$0.00	$0.00	$75

◄ ► \ Orders ∧ Avg Price ∧ Parked Orders ∧ **Open Positions** ∧ Strategy Orders ∧ Strategy Positions ∧ Balanc

FIGURE 6.5   Screen shot of TradeStation TradeManager—Open Positions

Source: Created with TradeStation. © TradeStation Technologies, Inc. All rights reserved.

TradeStation TradeManager - Strategy Orders

Symbol Filter [ ]   Strategy Order Type [All Orders ▾]

Generated ▼	Symbol	Interval	Quantity	Qty Filled	Qty Left	Strategy Status	Order Status	Type
3/1/2004 3:19:34 PM	NQH04	1 min.	5	0	0	Canceled	Unsent	Sell
3/1/2004 3:19:34 PM	ESH04	1 min.	5	5	0	Filled	Filled	Buy
3/1/2004 3:19:34 PM	ESH04	1 min.	5	0	0	Canceled	Unsent	Cover
3/1/2004 3:16:34 PM	ESH04	1 min.	5	0	0	Canceled	Unsent	Buy
3/1/2004 3:16:34 PM	ESH04	1 min.	5	0	0	Canceled	Unsent	Cover
3/1/2004 3:13:34 PM	NQH04	1 min.	5	5	0	Filled	Filled	Buy
3/1/2004 3:13:34 PM	NQH04	1 min.	5	0	0	Canceled	Unsent	Cover
3/1/2004 3:13:34 PM	INTC	5 min.	500	500	0	Filled	Filled	Sell Short
3/1/2004 3:13:34 PM	INTC	5 min.	500	500	0	Canceled	Filled	Sell
3/1/2004 3:13:34 PM	ESH04	1 min.	5	0	0	Canceled	Unsent	Buy

◄ ► \ Orders ∧ Avg Price ∧ Parked Orders ∧ Open Positions ∧ **Strategy Orders** ∧ Strategy Positions ∧ Balanc

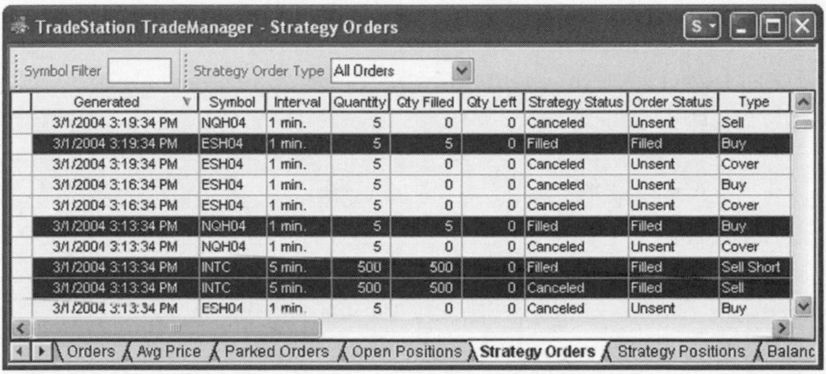

FIGURE 6.6   Screen shot of TradeStation TradeManager—Strategy Orders

Source: Created with TradeStation. © TradeStation Technologies, Inc. All rights reserved.

TradeStation TradeManager - Messages

Time	Action	Message
3/1/2004 3:31:10 PM	<Received>	Buy to Close 5 Calendar Call - Buy QQQ Apr 36 Call/Apr 36 Call @ 0.5500 Limit
3/1/2004 3:31:09 PM	<Sent>	Buy to Close 5 Calendar Call - Buy QQQ Apr 36 Call/Apr 36 Call @ 0.5500 Limit
3/1/2004 3:31:09 PM	<Sending>	Buy to Close 5 Calendar Call - Buy QQQ Apr 36 Call/Apr 36 Call @ 0.5500 Limit
3/1/2004 3:28:35 PM	<Filled>	Bought 500 INTC @ Market - Filled @ 29.6400
3/1/2004 3:28:35 PM	<Received>	Buy 500 INTC @ Market
3/1/2004 3:28:35 PM	<Sent>	Buy 500 INTC @ Market
3/1/2004 3:28:34 PM	<Cancel Rejected>	Cover 500 INTC @ Market - Reason: No shares left to cancel
3/1/2004 3:28:34 PM	<Sending>	Buy 500 INTC @ Market
3/1/2004 3:28:34 PM	<Filled>	Covered 500 INTC @ Market - Filled @ 29.6400
3/1/2004 3:28:34 PM	<Cancel Sending>	Cover 500 INTC @ Market

◄ ► ∧ Open Positions ∧ Strategy Orders ∧ Strategy Positions ∧ Balances ∧ Allocations ∧ **Messages** /

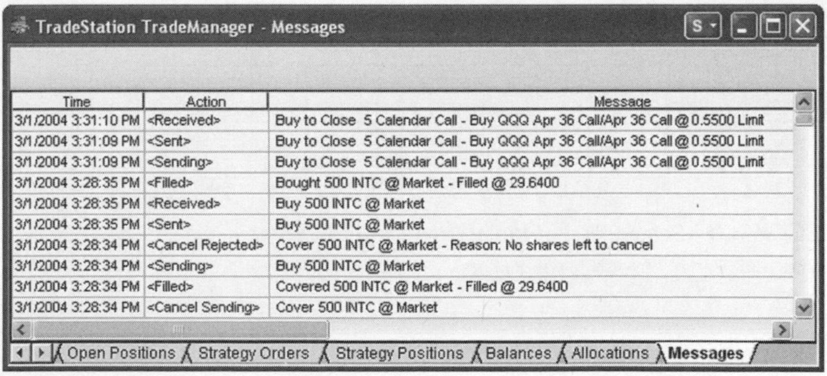

FIGURE 6.7   Screen shot of TradeStation TradeManager—Messages

Source: Created with TradeStation. © TradeStation Technologies, Inc. All rights reserved.

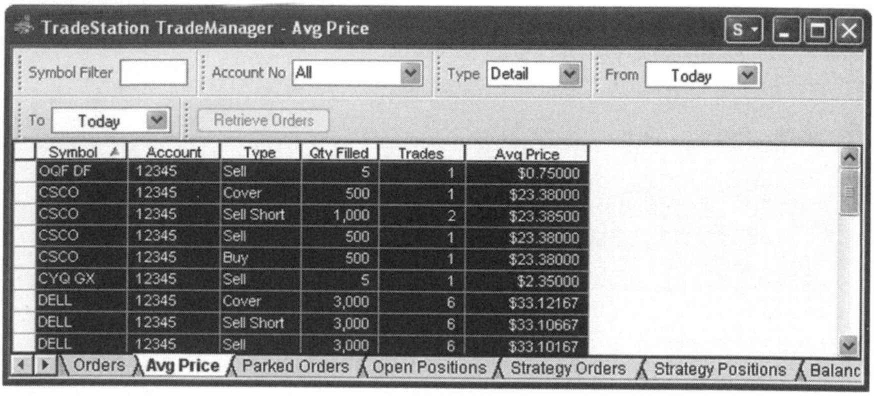
TradeStation TradeManager - Avg Price
Symbol Filter
Account No All
Type Detail
From Today
To Today
Retrieve Orders
Symbol Account Type Qty Filled Trades Avg Price
OQF DF 12345 Sell 5 1 $0.75000
CSCO 12345 Cover 500 1 $23.38000
CSCO 12345 Sell Short 1,000 2 $23.38500
CSCO 12345 Sell 500 1 $23.38000
CSCO 12345 Buy 500 1 $23.38000
CYQ GX 12345 Sell 5 1 $2.35000
DELL 12345 Cover 3,000 6 $33.12167
DELL 12345 Sell Short 3,000 6 $33.10667
DELL 12345 Sell 3,000 6 $33.10167
Orders
Avg Price
Parked Orders
Open Positions
Strategy Orders
Strategy Positions
Balanc

FIGURE 6.8 Screen shot of TradeStation TradeManager—Average Price

Source: Created with TradeStation. © TradeStation Technologies, Inc. All rights reserved.

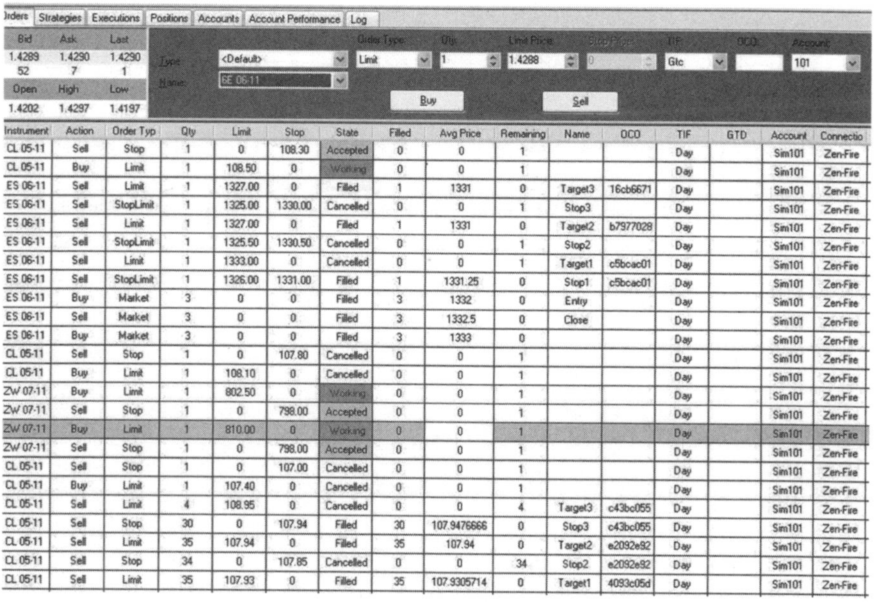
Orders Strategies Executions Positions Accounts Account Performance Log
Bid Ask Last
1.4289 1.4290 1.4290
52 7 1
Open High Low
1.4202 1.4297 1.4197
Type <Default>
Name 6E 06-11
Limit
1
1.4288
Gtc
101
Buy
Sell
Instrument Action Order Typ Qty Limit Stop State Filled Avg Price Remaining Name OCO TIF GTD Account Connectio
CL 05-11 Sell Stop 1 0 108.30 Accepted 0 0 1 Day Sim101 Zen-Fire
CL 05-11 Buy Limit 1 108.50 0 Working 0 0 1 Day Sim101 Zen-Fire
ES 06-11 Sell Limit 1 1327.00 0 Filled 1 1331 0 Target3 16cb6671 Day Sim101 Zen-Fire
ES 06-11 Sell StopLimit 1 1325.00 1330.00 Cancelled 0 0 1 Stop3 Day Sim101 Zen-Fire
ES 06-11 Sell Limit 1 1327.00 0 Filled 1 1331 0 Target2 b7977028 Day Sim101 Zen-Fire
ES 06-11 Sell StopLimit 1 1325.50 1330.50 Cancelled 0 0 1 Stop2 Day Sim101 Zen-Fire
ES 06-11 Sell Limit 1 1333.00 0 Cancelled 0 0 1 Target1 c5bcac01 Day Sim101 Zen-Fire
ES 06-11 Sell StopLimit 1 1326.00 1331.00 Filled 1 1331.25 0 Stop1 c5bcac01 Day Sim101 Zen-Fire
ES 06-11 Buy Market 3 0 0 Filled 3 1332 0 Entry Day Sim101 Zen-Fire
ES 06-11 Sell Market 3 0 0 Filled 3 1332.5 0 Close Day Sim101 Zen-Fire
ES 06-11 Buy Market 3 0 0 Filled 3 1333 0 Day Sim101 Zen-Fire
CL 05-11 Sell Stop 1 0 107.80 Cancelled 0 0 1 Day Sim101 Zen-Fire
CL 05-11 Buy Limit 1 108.10 0 Cancelled 0 0 1 Day Sim101 Zen-Fire
ZW 07-11 Buy Limit 1 802.50 0 Working 0 0 1 Day Sim101 Zen-Fire
ZW 07-11 Sell Stop 1 0 798.00 Accepted 0 0 1 Day Sim101 Zen-Fire
ZW 07-11 Buy Limit 1 810.00 0 Working 0 0 1 Day Sim101 Zen-Fire
ZW 07-11 Sell Stop 1 0 798.00 Accepted 0 0 1 Day Sim101 Zen-Fire
CL 05-11 Sell Stop 1 0 107.00 Cancelled 0 0 1 Day Sim101 Zen-Fire
CL 05-11 Buy Limit 1 107.40 0 Cancelled 0 0 1 Day Sim101 Zen-Fire
CL 05-11 Sell Limit 4 108.95 0 Cancelled 0 0 4 Target3 c43bc055 Day Sim101 Zen-Fire
CL 05-11 Sell Stop 30 0 107.94 Filled 30 107.9476666 0 Stop3 c43bc055 Day Sim101 Zen-Fire
CL 05-11 Sell Limit 35 107.94 0 Filled 35 107.94 0 Target2 e2092e92 Day Sim101 Zen-Fire
CL 05-11 Sell Stop 34 0 107.85 Cancelled 0 0 34 Stop2 e2092e92 Day Sim101 Zen-Fire
CL 05-11 Sell Limit 35 107.93 0 Filled 35 107.9305714 0 Target1 4093c05d Day Sim101 Zen-Fire

FIGURE 6.9 Screen shot of NinjaTrader Control Center

Source: NinjaTrader. (www.NinjaTrader.com).

It's like balancing your bank statement and credit card statements every month. You want to catch a problem immediately so that you have grounds to contest it. If you snooze, you lose—you will have less power to prove your point, rectify the situation, and seek reimbursement.

TYPES OF ORDERS

The type of order you place is part of your trading and investing rules and can affect your bottom line. There are many different kinds of order types that you can use, and not all brokers offer all order types. So check with your broker to find out what it offers.

The purpose of selecting an order type when you place your order is to achieve a number of objectives, including but not limited to the following:

- Limit risk.
- Control the speed of the fill (as soon as possible or not).
- Control the price of the fill (specific price or not).
- Control when you will be filled (day or time).
- A combination of all of the above.

Depending on market dynamics and liquidity, any attempts to achieve these stated objectives may or may not be possible. This means you may not get filled at the speed and price you desire, or you may not get filled at all. You are at the mercy of the market, and your selection of order types is merely a way to *attempt* to control the outcome of any trade.

The most common order types are:

- **Market order.** This is the simplest and most common of the order types. It does not allow any control over the price received and is a buy or sell order to be executed immediately with no limits. As long as there are willing sellers and buyers, market orders are filled. Market orders are used when certainty of execution is a priority over price of execution at current market prices.
- **Limit order.** A *buy limit order* is an order to buy a security at not more than a specific price. A *sell limit order* is an order to sell a security at not less than specific price. This gives the trader control over the price at which the trade is executed; however, the order may never be filled. Limit orders are used when the trader wishes to control price rather than certainty of execution.
- **Cancel order.** This is an order that cancels an existing order already placed.

Conditional orders that have one or more conditions to be met prior to being filled include:

- **Stop order.** A *buy stop order* is an order to buy a security once the price of the security has climbed above a specified stop price. It is used to limit a loss (or to protect an existing profit) on a short sale. A *sell stop order* is used to sell a security once the price of the security has dropped below a specified stop price. On both of these stop orders, when the specified stop price is reached, the stop order is entered as a market order (no limit). This means the trade will definitely be executed, but not necessarily at or near the stop price, particularly when the order is placed into a fast-moving market, or if there is insufficient liquidity available relative to the size of the order.
- **Stop limit order.** A stop limit order becomes a limit order once the specified stop price is attained or penetrated.
- **Trailing stop order.** A trailing stop for a *sell trailing stop order* sets the stop price at a fixed amount below the market price. If the market price rises, the stop loss price rises by the increased amount, but if the stock price falls, the stop loss price remains the same. The reverse is true for a *buy trailing stop order*.
- **Bracket order.** This order is designed to help limit your loss and help lock in a profit by bracketing an order with two opposite-side orders using the same quantity as the original order.
- **All or none (AON) order.** This order will remain at the exchange until the entire quantity is available to be filled.
- **Market if touched (MIT) order.** This is an order to buy (or sell) an asset below (or above) the market. It is held in the system until the trigger price is touched, and is then submitted as a market order.
- **Market to limit order.** This order is sent in as a market order to be executed at the current best price. If the entire order does not immediately execute at the market price, the remainder of the order is resubmitted as a limit order with the limit price set to the price at which the original order was executed.
- **Limit if touched (LIT) order.** Is an order to buy an asset below the market *or* sell an asset above the market, at the defined limit price or better. This order is held in the system until the trigger price is touched, and is then submitted as a limit order.
- **One cancels all (OCA) order.** This kind of order is used when the trader wishes to capitalize on only one of two or more trading possibilities. For instance, the trader may wish to trade stock ABC at $10 *or* stock XYZ at $20. In this case, the trader would send in an OCA order composed of two parts: A limit order for ABC at $10 and a limit order for XYZ at $20. If ABC reaches $10 first, ABC's limit order would be executed, and the XYZ limit order would be canceled.

- **Basket order.** This is a group of individual orders that are saved in a single file and submitted as a package.
- **Block order.** This is a large-volume limit order with a minimum of 50 contracts.
- **Volatility order.** This is a Trade West Systems (TWS)-specific order where the limit price of the option or combination is calculated as a function of the implied volatility.
- **Spreads order.** This is a combination of individual orders (legs) that work together to create a single trading strategy. You can combine stock, options, and futures legs into a single spread.

Order time limits that affect the time it takes to fill the order include:

- **Day order.** This order is in force from the time the order is submitted to the end of the day's trading session. For equity markets, the closing time is defined by the exchange. For the foreign exchange market, this is until 5:00 P.M. EST/EDT for all currencies except NZD.
- **Good till canceled (GTC) order.** This order requires a specific cancel order to close it out. It can persist indefinitely, although brokers may set time limits, for example, 90 days.
- **Good till date (GTD) order.** This order will remain working with the broker system and in the marketplace until it fills or until the close of the market on the date specified.
- **Immediate or cancel (IOC) order.** This order will be immediately filled or it will be canceled by the exchange. Unlike a fill or kill (FOK) order, immediate or cancel orders allow for partial fills.
- **Fill or kill (FOK) order.** This type of order is usually a limit order that must be filled or canceled immediately. Unlike immediate or cancel (IOC) orders, fill or kill orders require the full quantity to be filled.
- **Market on close (MOC) order.** This is a market order that is submitted to fill as close to the closing price as possible.
- **Market on open (MOO) order.** This is a market order that is filled at the market's open at the market price.
- **Limit on close (LOC) order.** This limit order is filled at the closing price if the closing price is equal to or better than the limit price, according to the rules of the specific exchange. There is often some deadline; for example, orders must be in 20 minutes before the auction.
- **Limit on open (LOO) order.** This limit order is executed at the market's open if the opening price is equal to or better than the limit price. There is often some deadline; for example, orders must be in 20 minutes before the auction.
- **Pegged to market order.** This is an order that is pegged to buy on the best offer and sell on the best bid.

TABLE 6.2 Order Types Listed by Category

Limit of Risk	Speed of Fill	Control of Price	Time to Fill	Advanced
Stop	Market	Limit	Day order	All or none
Trailing stop	Market if touched	Limit if touched	Fill or kill	One cancels all
Stop limit	Market on open	Limit on open	Good till canceled	Basket
Market to limit	Market on close	Limit on close	Good till date	Spreads
Block	Pegged to market	Block	Immediate or cancel	Volatility

Determining your order type will help you achieve an ultimate goal, whether it is limiting risk, speed of execution, or improvement of price. This table is an overview of some types of orders and what they can achieve for you. Keep in mind that when you place your order, the fill you receive depends on market dynamics and liquidity. There is no guarantee on the outcome of any order you place. An order may not fill at your optimum desired price or time.

Privacy order types that keep your strategies hidden from the market include:

- **Hidden order.** This is generally a large-volume order that shows no evidence of its existence in the market data.
- **Iceberg order.** This is an order that allows you to submit an order, generally a large-volume order, while publicly disclosing only a portion of the submitted order.

As you can see when looking at Table 6.2, the use of order types is crucial in achieving your objectives. By selecting the correct order type when placing a trade, you can attempt to control your risk, speed, and price of any resulting fill and much more. It is important to realize though, that none of these objectives are guaranteed. Whether your placed order gets filled at the price and time you want is dependant entirely on current market dynamics.

USING MARGIN AND LEVERAGE

The definition of margin is borrowed money that is used to purchase market instruments. This practice is referred to as *buying on margin.*

Using margin can dramatically increase risk because both gains and losses are amplified. That is, while the potential for greater profit does exist, it comes with a heavy price—the potential for loss is great. Margin also subjects the trader to additional risks, such as interest payments for using the borrowed money. There is also the possibility of experiencing a *margin call*. This is when traders would need to supply additional funds immediately if the market goes against them.

Adding margin to your plan is similar to trading on a day trading time frame versus trading on an investor time frame: *It speeds up the action.* Information will come at you more quickly, the size of your losses and gains will come at you more quickly, and your reaction time has to be at lightning speed. You will need to determine what the impact of margin has on your stress level and trading psychology. In other words, are you a more profitable trader using margin or not?

Another way to look at margin is purely as a debt, and in the corporate world debt ratios can determine the health of an entity. Too much debt means a generally unhealthy company. However, debt can also be a positive tool.

For example, debt can fund a new start-up company that can change a generation—just as when 20-year-old Mark Zuckerberg got his first investment of $1,000, and a few months later obtained $16,000 to launch Facebook in 2004. In the beginning Zuckerberg took on proportionally high risk and high debt. This assessment is based on the fact that at the start Facebook generated *zero* revenue. Now, of course, in the year 2011, just seven years after the launch, Facebook has a corporate value of around $15 billion. In 2008, Zuckerberg became the youngest self-made billionaire in the world at the time (at age 24). So, you can see how that turned out.

Ultimately, how you handle margin, leverage, and debt needs to be a calculated business decision on your part. You must carefully weigh the pros and cons of using margin and determine how much margin to use and when to use it. The bottom line is: Beware of the dreaded margin call. It's all about risk and managing that risk.

My suggestion is that only experienced traders and investors use margin. When a novice trader begins to apply this tool, they should do so slowly and carefully. It is crucial that trade size be carefully calculated to prevent yourself from overextending risk. Refer to Chapter 12 on money management. There are formulas to help you determine how to size your positions effectively when using margin.

THE IMPORTANCE OF LIQUIDITY AND VOLUME

Liquidity is the degree to which an asset or security can be bought or sold in the market without affecting the asset's price. In order for the asset's price to be unaffected, there must be a balance of *buyers* and *sellers* on both sides of the trade, which offers liquidity to both the buyers and the sellers at the same time.

Volume is the total number of shares or contracts being traded in a given period. Typically when there is high volume, there is high liquidity. Volume adds additional pressure to the market system, in that when there is a sudden unprecedented increase in volume the existing systems become over loaded.

When there is an imbalance of buyers and sellers, such as when Enron stock was falling in 2001 and there were all sellers and no buyers, the stock price will gap down out of control. This type of event will cause low liquidity for sellers because there are no buyers in the market. Liquidity is extremely important, and most traders don't fully understand the importance of it until they are faced with an open trade in a market that has *poor* liquidity such as in the Enron example.

Awareness of the importance of liquidity is crucial to avoiding devastation to your account. Some risk management techniques are useful in softening the effect of a low-liquidity event.

Here are three risk management techniques you can use to minimize the effect of low liquidity:

1. Diversify your trading portfolio among a variety of sectors.
2. Trade with only 10 percent of your net worth, which limits your overall risk.
3. Seek markets and trading hours that are known for high liquidity due to their high volume.

Generally, liquidity is reflected in the *volume* of trades being made on any given day or hour or minute. The number of active traders in the market at any time and place will affect the amount of liquidity. For example, in the Standard & Poor's E-mini S&P 500 futures market, there is high liquidity during open market hours and low liquidity at night. After regular market hours there are fewer active traders in the market; hence there is less liquidity.

In the forex market, which trades around the clock, there is high liquidity throughout the entire day and into the night. There are a lot of night owl forex traders who are busy trading when everyone else is sleeping, and that provides ongoing liquidity. In addition, the forex market is a global market with currencies around the world being traded. When one country ends its day another country is just beginning, which also contributes to the round the clock trading activity in this market. It is the market that never sleeps.

TABLE 6.3	Examples of Assets and Market Conditions That Have Varying Levels of Liquidity	
	Level of Liquidity	**Notes**
Cash	High	Typically cash is the most liquid asset, and most day traders convert their accounts to cash every evening.
Blue-chip stocks	High	Have higher liquidity by nature of the sheer volume and size of shares traded.
E-mini S&P 500 futures	High	Popular day trading market, has high liquidity during regular trading hours.
E-mini NASDAQ futures	High	Popular day trading market, has high liquidity during regular trading hours.
Forex currencies	High	The 24-hour forex market has high liquidity due to global active trading.
Penny stocks	Low	Penny stocks have low liquidity due to the low trading volume.
Unlisted stocks (Pink Sheets)	Low	Pink Sheets have low liquidity due to the low trading volume.
Financial market closure	Zero	Markets can be closed to trading due to significant drops in market value (see Tables 6.4 and 6.5).
Market risk event	Low to Zero	Acts of God (earthquakes, hurricanes, etc.) and acts of war can cause markets to be closed to trading.

This table is intended to be a frame of reference for educational purposes only. It is designed to acquaint the reader with a variety of liquidity conditions. Keep in mind that all of these assets and market conditions are subject to change, and there may be times when a blue-chip stock, for example, may have low liquidity depending on the current market dynamics. Typically a blue-chip stock has statistically higher liquidity than a penny stock, but that is not a guarantee. Cash or currencies can devalue, so again this chart is for reference only. Past performance of any market, asset, or market condition does not guarantee future results.

Take a look at Table 6.3 to see a variety of instruments and market conditions and details on their liquidity components. They are each categorized as having either high, low, or zero liquidity. You will find information relating to market dynamics in the Notes column in this table.

Table 6.3 is geared toward giving you a head start in understanding the spectrum of possibility with regard to liquidity. But by no means is this list meant to be a guaranteed liquidity guide. Because the markets ebb and flow and will change with time, this table is meant to help you to understand what the possibilities are and as a result begin to think about how to prepare for these possibilities in your business plan and model.

One more note about liquidity: Speculators, traders, and market makers all create liquidity in the markets. These individuals are seeking to profit from anticipated increases or decreases in market prices. By doing this, they provide the capital needed to facilitate the liquidity. They generate revenue for themselves when they are on the winning side of a trade. In essence, their profits are the price that the world pays in order to maintain adequate liquidity in the financial markets.

ZERO LIQUIDITY

There are rare occasions when you will be faced with *zero liquidity*, meaning there is no volume at all because no one is able to trade. A variety of events can occur to affect an exchange's ability to function, including snowstorms, hurricanes, acts of war, excessive volume that over loads the system, labor strikes, computer failures, and circuit breaker halts. When an exchange is closed or halted, no one can enter or exit, no matter how much they may want to.

Take a look at Table 6.4, which illustrates an action schedule for a circuit breaker system that was instituted by the New York Stock Exchange (NYSE) in an attempt to slow down future market crashes. And then look at Table 6.5 to see a sampling of days and times when the NYSE was actually closed or halted from the year 1914 to 2001 and the reasons for the closing; it's very interesting to see.

| TABLE 6.4 | The First Circuit Breaker System (Rule 80B) That Halts the NYSE Trading Activity When Market Drops Occur, was instituted on October 19th 1988 by the NYSE |

Percent Drop in Market	Time of Drop	Trading Closed
10%	Before 2:00 P.M.	One-hour halt
10%	2:00 P.M. to 2:30 P.M.	Half-hour halt
10%	After 2:30 P.M.	Market stays open
20%	Before 1:00 P.M.	Two-hour halt
20%	1:00 P.M. to 2:00 P.M.	One-hour halt
20%	After 2:00 P.M.	Close for the day
30%	Anytime during day	Close for the day

Source: Chris Farrell, "Where Are the Circuit Breakers?" October 16, 2008, www.publicradio.org/columns/marketplace/gettingpersonal/2008/10/where_are_the_stock_market_cir.html. Another good source of information on this topic is found at http://usequities.nyx.com/markets/nyse-equities/circuit-breakers and also at www.ehow.com/list_5807156_rules-stopping-stock-market.html.

TABLE 6.5 Examples of NYSE Special Closings

Date(s)	Period of Closing	Reason for Closing
July 31, 1914, to November 27, 1914	Market completely closed for over four months	Closed pending outbreak of World War I. All restrictions were removed April 1, 1915.
September 16, 1920	Closed @ 12:00 noon	Wall Street explosion.
May 21–28, 1928	Closed @ 2:00 P.M. every day for one week	Shortened hours to allow offices to catch up on work due to heavy volume.
August 4, 1933	Closed @ 12:30 P.M.	Gas fumes on trading floor.
February 20, 1934	Opened @ 11:00 A.M.	Delayed opening due to severe snowstorm.
November 22, 1963	Closed @ 2:07 P.M.	Assassination of President John F. Kennedy.
January 6–14, 1966	Closed @ 2:00 P.M.	Shortened hours due to transit strike.
July 7, 1969, to September 26, 1969	Closed @ 2:30 P.M. every day for over two months	Paperwork crisis.
August 9, 1976	Closed @ 3:00 P.M.	Hurricane watch.
July 14, 1977	Closed all day	Blackout in New York City; no electricity.
March 30, 1981	Closed @ 3:17 P.M.	Assassination attempt on President Reagan.
October 23–30, 1987	Closed @ 2:00 P.M. every day for one week	Shortened hours following market fall of October 19, 1987 and record-breaking volume.
November 9–11, 1987	Closed @ 3:30 P.M.	Shortened hours due to trading floor and clerical staff strike.
December 18, 1995	Opened @ 10:30 A.M.	Delayed opening due to computer systems trouble.
October 27, 1997	Closed @ 2:35 P.M. for 30 minutes	Circuit breakers triggered for first time, after DJIA dropped 350 points.
September 11–14, 2001	Market completely closed for four days	Terrorist attack on the World Trade Center in New York City.

The information on this table is excerpted from a link that has a list of every closing of the NYSE from 1885 to January 2011: www.nyse.com/pdfs/closings.pdf.

In addition to being just plain interesting, both Tables 6.4 and 6.5 illustrate a very real possibility: a *market risk* possibility where you can get trapped in a trade for a longer period of time than you planned on. In this situation, even your most carefully selected stop-loss exit cannot protect you from the price activity and volatility that may result when trading resumes.

Some traders fare better in these events than others. For example, "trader Paul Tudor Jones predicted and profited from the [1987] crash, attributing it to portfolio insurance derivatives which were 'an accident waiting to happen' and that the 'crash was something that was imminently forecastable.'"[1]

In the end, whether you have a profit or a loss after a zero liquidity event, it is crucial that you play the "What if?" game beforehand. Work this into your business plan.

VOLATILITY AND MARKET GAPS

The term *volatility* refers to dramatic, short-term fluctuations of price in a market or individual financial instrument. Quick drops or increases in price in a market or financial instrument can create *gaps*. On a chart a gap looks like a hyperbolic move to the upside or downside. Volatility and market gaps can be caused by a number of factors, including overall market crashes, breaking news, scheduled Federal Reserve announcements, and such.

Typically, traders love volatility because when the market is volatile, there is movement, and traders make money when they are correct about which way the market is moving. When there is no movement or volatility in the market, traders are not able to capitalize on their ability to pinpoint what direction the market is moving, and they are not given opportunities to profit from their skills.

If we look at the history of the markets up until this point in time, we can study Tables 6.6, 6.7, and 6.8 to find patterns of volatility in the Dow Jones Industrial Average (DJIA). Table 6.6 shows a top 10 list of the largest daily changes to the *downside* in the DJIA. Here you can find statistics on some of the most significant drops in the U.S. market, such as the crashes of 1929, 1987, and 2008. During these drops the volatility was high.

When you look at Table 6.7, which shows the top 10 list of largest daily changes to the *upside* in the DJIA, you can see that typically when there is a crash to the downside, as in 1929, shortly afterward there is usually high volatility to the upside during the period where the market is in a correction.

In Table 6.6, items ranked 2, 3, and 4 show three days when the DJIA market dropped 12 percent, 11 percent, and 9 percent, respectively, during the period between October 28 and November 6, 1929. Interestingly, though,

---

[1]*Wikipedia*, "Black Monday (1987), Causes."

TABLE 6.6	Top 10 List of Largest Daily Percentage Changes to the Downside in the Dow Jones Industrial Average (DJIA)			
Rank	**Date**	**Close**	**Net Change in Points**	**% Change Downward**
1	10-19-1987/Mon.	1,738.74	−508.00	−22.61%
2	10-28-1929/Mon.	260.64	−38.33	−12.82%
3	10-29-1929/Tues.	230.07	−30.57	−11.73%
4	11-06-1929/Wed.	232.13	−25.55	−9.92%
5	12-18-1899/Mon.	58.27	−5.57	−8.72%
6	08-12-1932/Fri.	63.11	−5.79	−8.40%
7	03-14-1907/Thurs.	76.23	−6.89	−8.29%
8	10-26-1987/Mon.	1,793.93	−156.83	−8.04%
9	10-15-2008/Wed.	8,577.91	−733.08	−7.87%
10	07-21-1933/Fri.	88.71	−7.55	−7.84%

Information on this table is excerpted from the following link: http://en.wikipedia.org/wiki/List_of_largest_daily_changes_in_the_Dow_Jones_Industrial_Average.

TABLE 6.7	Top 10 List of Largest Daily Percentage Changes to the Upside in the Dow Jones Industrial Average (DJIA)			
Rank	**Date**	**Close**	**Net Change in Points**	**% Change Upward**
1	03-15-1933/Wed.	62.10	+8.26	+15.34%
2	10-06-1931/Tues.	99.34	+12.86	+14.87%
3	10-30-1929/Wed.	258.47	+28.40	+12.34%
4	09-21-1932/Wed.	75.16	+7.67	+11.36%
5	10-13-2008/Mon.	9,387.61	+936.42	+11.08%
6	10-28-2008/Tues.	9,065.12	+889.35	+10.88%
7	10-21-1987/Wed.	2,027.85	+186.84	+10.15%
8	08-03-1932/Wed.	58.22	+5.06	+9.52%
9	02-11-1932/Thurs.	78.60	+6.80	+9.47%
10	11-14-1929/Thurs.	217.28	+18.59	+9.36%

Information on this table is excerpted from the following link: http://en.wikipedia.org/wiki/List_of_largest_daily_changes_in_the_Dow_Jones_Industrial_Average.

when you look at Table 6.7 you will see items ranked 3 and 10, when the DJIA actually rose by 12 percent and 9 percent, respectively, around the same time period as the crash.

The market was extremely volatile during the 1929 crash, and it had huge swings to the downside blended in with huge swings to the upside. As always, the market never moves in a perfectly straight line. It has corrections along the way until it finds its direction. If you were trading in 1929 and could read the market correctly, you would have been able to make an enormous amount of money because of the volatility. Huge swings in price activity to the downside and then to the upside and then to the downside again offer talented traders a unique opportunity to profit.

Unlike buy-and-hold investors, traders benefit from volatility in the market. Buy-and-hold investors, in contrast, have a tendency to buy during the euphoria phase at the top of the market and sell during the panic phase at the bottom of a market cycle. This is precisely the wrong thing to do. When you enter and exit the market based on group psychology, there is a high probability that you will be entering the market when it is at the top and exiting the market when it is at the bottom.

Table 6.8 shows the top 10 list of largest intraday point swings in the DJIA. You can see that nine of the top 10 ranking intraday swings took

TABLE 6.8 Top 10 List of Largest Intraday Point Swings in the Dow Jones Industrial Average (DJIA)

Rank	Date	Close	Day High	Day Low	Point Swing	Net Change in Points
1	10-10-2008/ Fri.	8,451.19	8,901.28	7,882.51	1,018.77	−128.00
2	05-06-2010/ Thurs.	10,520.32	10,879.76	9,869.62	1,010.14	−347.80
3	10-13-2008/ Mon.	9,387.61	9,427.99	8,462.18	965.81	+936.42
4	11-13-2008/ Thurs.	8,835.25	8,876.59	7,965.42	911.17	+552.59
5	10-28-2008/ Tues.	9,065.12	9,082.08	8,174.73	907.35	+889.35
6	10-09-2008/ Thurs.	8,579.19	9,448.14	8,579.19	868.95	−678.91
7	10-16-2008/ Thurs.	8,979.26	9,013.27	8,197.67	815.60	+401.35
8	10-06-2008/ Mon.	9,955.50	10,322.76	9,525.32	797.44	−369.88
9	10-15-2008/ Wed.	8,577.91	9,308.76	8,530.12	778.64	−733.08
10	09-29-2008/ Mon.	10,365.45	11,139.94	10,365.45	774.49	−777.68

Information on this table is excerpted from the following link: http://en.wikipedia.org/wiki/List_of_largest_daily_changes_in_the_Dow_Jones_Industrial_Average.

place in 2008. So, if you knew how to read the markets correctly, this highly volatile period would be an ideal opportunity to trade and generate profit. This 2008 period is similar in volatility to the 1929–1933 and also the 1987 period.

Important Note: There will be times when a gap up or a gap down will blast right through your carefully set stop-loss exit. This type of event will be out of your control and you will lose more than your planned risk amount. This is something to be cognizant of so that you can be quick on your feet and not have your trading psychology thrown off. Keep a cool head in the event of a gap that goes against you.

And, in the reverse situation, when you have a gap that goes in your favor, my favorite approach is to scale out a portion of my position when there is a hyperbolic move in the direction of my trade. That locks in profit and reduces anxiety while in the trade.

HOW CAN THE BID AND ASK, SPREADS, FILLS, AND SLIPPAGE AFFECT YOUR PROFITS?

The terms *bid*, *ask*, *spreads*, *fills*, and *slippage* are interconnected in that they can affect your profitability at the end of the day. In reading blogs on trading websites, you will no doubt see lots of conversation about all of these terms. Accusations can abound toward brokers for providing bad fills and that the spreads are too wide. And others will tell you that slippage can kill your profits.

What everyone is really talking about is the bid-ask spread, and how it translates into your profitability (or lack thereof) at the end of the day, or week, or month or year.

Here are some basic definitions to begin our discussion:

- **Bid and ask.** The bid price is the highest price that a *buyer*, or bidder, is willing to pay for a good. In bid and ask, the bid price stands in contrast to the ask price. The ask price is the price a *seller* of a good is willing to accept for that particular good.
- **Spread.** The difference between the bid and ask price is called the bid-ask spread. The size of the spread will differ from one asset to another mainly because of the difference in liquidity of each asset. For example, currency is considered the most liquid asset in the world, and the bid-ask spread in the currency market is one of the smallest (0.01 percent of the asset's value). Less liquid assets such as a small-cap

stock may have spreads that are equivalent to 1 or 2 percent of the asset's value.

- **Fill.** There are three possible reasons for a trade to be perceived as receiving a bad fill. The *first* is that in fast-moving markets, the broker may do everything exactly right, but the market momentum was so fast that between the time you entered your order and the time your order was filled, the market got away from your ideal entry price. The *second* thing that can happen is that the broker may be slow in getting your order to the exchange and therefore your fill ends up being bad. A variety of factors can lead to one broker being slower than another, including the quality of their order execution technology. The *third* possibility is that you have slow or imperfect data on your front-end platform. The reason that would impact your perception of the quality of the fill is that what you were seeing as market reality when you entered the trade was not completely accurate or was delayed information. So the fill may have been fast and a good fill, but your perception of that is altered by the quality of the data you were looking at when you placed the order.
- **Slippage.** This is the difference between the expected price of a trade and the price the trade actually executes at. Slippage often occurs during periods of high volatility when market orders are used, and also when large orders are executed when there may not be enough interest at the desired price level to maintain the expected price of a trade. Slippage is a term often used in both forex and stock trading, and, although the definition is the same for both, slippage occurs in different situations for each of these types of trading.

Typically, bad fills and slippage are much less of an issue for investors and position traders than for day traders. It is never a good thing when you get a bad fill, but position traders feel less of an impact.

YOU CAN PARALLEL TEST YOUR BROKER AND DATA FEEDS

At times, though, even day traders are just splitting hairs when they are lamenting at the end of the day about bad fills and slippage. Generally, beating up the broker or data provider about bad fills or bad data isn't going to make you a more profitable trader. The blame game seldom achieves anything beneficial. Instead it creates negative energy. If you genuinely feel that your service providers are not the best you can get, then you should switch.

The best way to decide if you need to switch is to do a *parallel test*. Randomly moving from one provider to another like a nomad can be expensive in time and money. So, before you divorce or fire your current provider, do a trial with another vendor simultaneously to see how they compare in a side-by-side and apples-to-apples comparison. You might be surprised that your current provider is not as bad as you thought. Or you might find that the new provider is better.

Either way, conduct a parallel test before you switch. Relying on hearsay from other traders or trading blogs will not give you definitive or reliable data. The only way to know for sure what the impact of slippage, fills, speed of data, and speed of order execution will be on your profit-and-loss statement is by doing a test for yourself.

When you do your test, you must be sure to place exactly the same trade, with the same order type and the same number of shares or contracts at exactly the same time, and on the same day. Make it truly apples to apples, not apples to oranges. It will be a valid test only if all the variables are the same. If you do find a significant difference in the outcome, then run the numbers to determine hypothetical revenue impact on your monthly and annual profit-and-loss statement. Depending on the true impact, you then will need to consider doing additional tests to verify your findings. Consider having a large enough sample size to ensure that your results are accurate.

Important Note: *Fast-moving markets* will affect the outcome of your findings more than slow-moving markets. Generally, slow-moving markets with little volume and volatility will not affect the speed of execution and data flow. It is the fast-moving markets that more severely slow down the flow of information since there is more data flowing through the bandwidth of your vendor's system, which can create a *bottleneck* event. The best parallel test will be one that is done in a fast-moving market.

At the end of the day, one cost of doing business is having a glitch in the system every once in a while. The truly great traders handle those glitches with ease and move on to the next winning trade. They don't waste their time focusing on negative energy. So you need to attempt to take the occasional glitch in stride. For the endlessly reoccurring glitches or for poor performance scenarios, a parallel test is worth the time and effort if it enables you to systematically identify a valid way to increase your revenue.

"I FEEL THE NEED FOR SPEED"

As Tom Cruise in the movie *Top Gun* would say, "I feel the need for speed." Speed of data, speed of order execution, and the speed of your computer are all important factors that affect your success as a trader. Typically, speed is not as much of a factor for investors to be successful. But for day traders who use faster time frame charts like the one-minute, five-minute, and 10-minute charts, speed is essential.

Technology is changing by the minute in our world, and of course the more cutting-edge your technology is, the faster it will be. Can you remember the days of dial-up and rotary telephones? Maybe I am dating myself, but that can illustrate how much and how fast things can change in a short time period. It was only 10 years ago that there were still people using dial-up technology to connect to the Internet.

You must always be up to date on what new innovations are available at this moment in time. No doubt in a year or two after this book is released there will be new technologies on the horizon that can enable you to better profit from your business model. It is your task to continually be on the lookout for the next generation of speed and technology. And then your task is to determine if the end benefit of that technology justifies the expense to attain it.

SO MANY MARKETS TO CHOOSE FROM

Worldwide there is an overwhelming number of markets to choose from, and deciding what market or markets you will trade is an important decision in preparing your business plan. Table 6.9 is a sample of a number of markets and exchanges available to you. You can see a more extensive list of markets and exchanges in Appendix E at the back of this book.

TABLE 6.9   Financial Markets

Market	Increment of Movement	Market Exchanges
Stocks	Decimals	NYSE, NASDAQ
Options	Decimals	CFE, PSE, BATS
Futures	Ticks	CME, NYFE, NYMEX, CBOT, CBOE, ICE
Forex	Pips	CME, ISE
ETFs*	Decimals	NYSE, NASDAQ, CBSX
Indexes	Decimals	PHLX, CBOE, Russell
Bonds	Decimals	MuniCenter, Tradeweb
Mutual funds	NAV*	Janus, Dreyfus

This table has a brief list of financial markets and the exchanges that carry them. For a more complete list, refer to Appendix E (Market Exchanges) at the back of this book.
*ETF is an acronym for exchange-traded fund. NAV is an acronym for net asset value.

When choosing the best market for you to trade, there are a number of factors to consider, such as:

- Market cycle.
- Volatility.
- Liquidity.
- Trading or investment account value.
- Market price.
- Time frame you want to trade.
- Your skill level.
- How much time you have available to monitor the markets.

You may decide to move from one market to another, depending on market cycles and also depending on your developing skill level. Each market has its own unique personality and characteristics. For this reason you may enjoy one market more than another and ultimately be more profitable in one market over another.

Do not spread yourself too thin trying to learn about all the markets at one time. Pick one or two and develop confidence and skill in those before experimenting with new markets. When you become a master of one market, you will flow with it and will be more consistently profitable.

TICKER SYMBOLS AT A GLANCE

A stock symbol or *ticker symbol* is a short abbreviation used to uniquely identify publicly traded shares of a particular stock on a particular stock market. A stock symbol may consist of letters, numbers, or a combination of both.

The phrase *ticker symbol* refers to the symbols that were printed on the tape of a ticker tape machine back in 1870 through 1970. The word *ticker* refers to the ticking sound that the machine made as it printed the tape with the updated price and volume numbers. This machine became obsolete in the 1960s as it was replaced with television sets and computers to transmit this financial information.

The symbols themselves live on, though, and are still used to identify financial instruments. Table 6.10 illustrates some of the most common U.S. stock symbols. Symbols occasionally evolve and change when publicly traded companies merge. For example, in 1999 when Exxon merged with Mobil Oil, Exxon changed its phonetic ticker symbol XON to XOM to reflect the new company merger. In this day and age of mergers and acquisitions, changing a ticker symbol is a normal occurrence.

TABLE 6.10   Stock Symbols

Company Name	Symbol
Agilent Technologies	A
Apple Inc.	AAPL
AT&T	T
Bank of America	BAC
Citigroup	C
Coca-Cola Company	KO
Exxon Mobil	XOM
Ford Motor Company	F
Google	GOOG
H.J. Heinz Company	HNZ
Harley-Davidson Inc.	HOG
Hewlett-Packard	HPQ
Hyatt	H
Intel	INTC
Kellogg	K
3M Company	MMM
Macy's, Inc.	M
Microsoft	MSFT
Target Corporation	TGT
Texas Instruments	TXN
United States Steel	X
Visa, Inc.	V
Wal-Mart	WMT
Walgreens	WAG

HOW TO CHOOSE THE BEST DATA FEED FOR YOUR NEEDS

Live streaming price and volume data is your lifeline to the markets and gives you minute-by-minute and tick-by-tick readings on what is happening in the market at every given moment. There are many ways you can get data delivered to you. The quality and speed of the data you receive will vary depending on the way it is delivered.

Very often (not always), when you get data from a broker it is filtered and delayed and it is not the same quality as you would get from a data vendor or trading engine that specializes in only data. So it is vital to weigh the importance of the quality of the data you receive versus the cost of getting the data. Depending on your budget, either quality or cost may be a greater priority, and only you can weigh the decision to determine the best solution to achieve the greatest net profit.

Paying Exchange Fees

Ultimately all price and volume data comes directly from the exchange that is being traded. Anyone who receives data from the exchange must pay an *exchange fee*, which covers the exchange's cost of doing business.

If you are receiving free data through your broker, your broker is paying the fees to the exchange for you. The commissions you pay to your broker indirectly cover the cost of those fees. There's no getting around it; like death and taxes, someone has to pay for the exchange fees. Look at Table 6.11 for examples of some U.S. exchanges and the fees associated with them.

These current per-month nonprofessional exchange fees are stated in U.S. dollars. If you desire to get multiple markets and exchanges, then you will need to pay multiple fees. As you can see, depending on which markets you select and how many markets you choose, costs can add up. Plus, for professional status (anyone who is a professional broker) the rates are sometimes *quadruple* what they are for nonprofessionals.

Keep in mind that these are the fees that are current as of the printing of this book; for up-to-date figures you can contact the exchanges directly or your data provider or broker. There is also a comprehensive listing of market exchanges in Appendix E at the back of this book.

TABLE 6.11 Monthly Nonprofessional Exchange Fees

Exchange	Monthly Fee
NASDAQ Level I and indexes	$ 5.00
NASDAQ Level II (you must subscribe to NASDAQ Level I first)	$12.00
NYSE Level I	$ 5.00
CME Level I (includes E-minis and Globex Level I)	$68.00
CME E-minis only	$32.00
CBOE futures (CFE)	$ 4.00
NYMEX	$68.00
CBOT Level I (includes CBOT Mini futures)	$68.00
CBOT Mini futures only	$18.00
Russell indexes	$ 2.00
ICE futures U.S.	$70.00
NYMEX	$68.00
COMEX (includes COMEX E-mini futures)	$68.00
COMEX E-mini futures only	$18.00

This table is for educational purposes only. The fees stated in this table are current at the time of printing. They are stated in U.S. dollars. For more current information, you can refer to Appendix C and/or Appendix E for contact information so that you can directly request the latest information from either your data provider or the exchange you are interested in.

How Fast Does Your Data Need to Be?

You will need to decide on what data speed you will need: real-time data, delayed data, or end-of-day data. Typically, the faster the data, the more expensive it will be. The way you determine the speed you will need is by deciding what the time frame of your trading will be. In other words, will you be trading on a higher time frame and day trading or will you be trading on a lower time frame and investing?

If you plan on investing or position trading, you can make do with end-of-day data. However, if you will be day trading, you must have real-time lightning-speed data. Determine what your budget allows for and what type of trading you will be most profitable with.

In deciding where to get your data, you will need to take into account the following factors by answering this Q&A:

1. **Q:** What is your budget? Can you afford to pay for data? Do you have a current data feed?

   A: _____

2. **Q:** Can you afford to open a brokerage account? What is the minimum dollar amount required to open and maintain an account?

   A: _____

3. **Q:** What time frame are you trading in—real-time day trading or end-of-day position trading?

   A: _____

4. **Q:** Will you be paper trading or live trading?

   A: _____

5. **Q:** What broker(s) do you currently use, or what broker(s) are you interested in using in the future?

   A: _____

6. **Q:** Which of these brokers provide data?

   A: _____

7. **Q:** Which brokers pay for or waive your exchange fees?

   A: _____

8. **Q:** Do any of these brokers provide their own front-end charting platform? What, if anything, is the cost for that?

   A: _____

9. **Q:** Do these brokers plug into other front-end charting platforms?

   A: _____

10. **Q:** What market(s) have you decided to trade?

    A: _____

11. **Q:** Which symbols will you be trading and through which exchange(s)? What brokers carry these items?

    A: _____

12. **Q:** What trading tools and software do you currently use, and what platform do they plug into?

    A: _____

Once you have completed the preceding question-and-answer section, then you are ready to begin your brainstorming and research to get the best possible solution for your needs at this place and time. For starters, there are lots of choices at your disposal, including a number of front-end charting platforms and data providers that can connect you to brokers so that you can literally place trades right off your chart. You can see in Table 6.12 a variety of data choices.

You can always call our office at 858-695-0592 in San Diego, California, if you ever need current feedback on the latest solutions. Or you can also e-mail us at Info@TradersCoach.com if you would like another set of eyes on your situation.

For an updated version of Table 6.12 you can also go to the following link, since we will keep it current with any new developments:

www.traderscoach.com/survivalguide.php

What is exciting is that now more than ever, due to the connectivity of the Internet and ever-advancing technology, you will have a greater ability to customize your approach for a lower cost.

TABLE 6.12 Select a Data Feed That Matches Your Needs

	eSignal	Kinetick	Genesis	TradeStation	Zen-Fire
Front-end charting platform	eSignal *or* NinjaTrader	NinjaTrader	Trade Navigator	TradeStation	eSignal *or* NinjaTrader
Stocks	Yes	Yes	Yes	Yes	No
Options	Yes	No	Yes	Yes	Yes
Futures	Yes	Yes	Yes	Yes	Yes
Forex	Yes	Yes	Yes	Yes	Yes
Bonds	Yes	No	Yes	Yes	No
Mutual funds	Yes	No	No	Yes	No
ETFs	Yes	No	Yes	Yes	No
Indexes	Yes	No	Yes	Yes	No

This table of data feeds is current at the time of printing. Check with each individual provider for updates on information. You will find contact information and a variety of providers in Appendix C (Resources) at the back of this book.

Due to the structure of many front-end platforms, you can pull real-time data from some brokers and channel it through the front-end platform, thus avoiding the cost of data and exchange fees. This revolution has enabled traders with fewer resources to learn faster and start more quickly on the road to profitable trading.

NinjaTrader in particular currently offers a free front-end platform and free end-of-day Kinetick data, in addition to the fact that many brokers also plug into NinjaTrader and you can pull data from your broker for no cost.

Begin your research by using Appendix C (Resources) at the back of this book to find the contact information for a variety of providers. Then go on the Internet and learn more about how to effectively get a combination of quality data and excellent charting tools at a very reasonable cost (sometimes you can get this for *no* cost). Shop around to determine the best combination of products and services, and then you will be ready to begin.

HOW TO CHOOSE THE BEST BROKER FOR YOUR NEEDS

There are probably thousands of brokers worldwide and choosing the best for your needs can be challenging. They each have different niche strengths and varying price models. Your decision will be based on your needs, and the costs associated with those needs.

Choosing the best broker comes down to a number of factors, such as these six:

1. **Service.** How many products and services does the broker provide, and is this offering a good match for the products and services you will require? Does the broker provide good customer support?

2. **Markets.** What markets will you trade, and what markets will the broker provide?

3. **Cost.** What are the costs associated with commissions, exchange fees, and the products and services you will require? Typically, the more you trade, the more you save. Ask about the broker's pricing model and determine if your trading volume entitles you to savings.

4. **Account size.** What is the minimum account size required for opening and maintaining an account?

5. **Connectivity and Compatibility.** What front-end platforms is the broker able to connect to, and does the broker provide a quality

front-end platform itself? If the broker has a quality front-end platform, do you have to pay fees for using it, and are there exchange fees that you will be subject to as well?

6. **Speed of execution.** What is the quality of the order execution system that the broker uses, and how fast can the broker fill your orders?

Many traders and investors maintain a few different brokerage accounts, each serving a different purpose. This is a way to get the best of all worlds. Others have a one-stop shopping approach and choose a broker that serves all their needs. Depending on your unique situation at this moment in time, you will need to identify priorities and find a suitable broker to match those priorities. For a quick start, refer to Table 6.13 for an overview of some popular brokers and what they have to offer. You can get a more thorough listing of brokers at the back of this book in Appendix C (Resources).

You can at any time change your priorities and possibly change your broker. So don't feel like you are chained to one provider for life. Both you and the markets are evolving and are a work in progress. Reassess your needs on an annual basis to achieve optimal portfolio performance.

TABLE 6.13 Select a Broker That Matches Your Needs

	TradeStation	Mirus Futures	Interactive Brokers
Front-end charting platform	TradeStation	NinjaTrader and eSignal	NinjaTrader, eSignal, and Interactive Brokers
Stocks	Yes	No	Yes
Options	Yes	Yes	Yes
Futures	Yes	Yes	Yes
Forex	Yes	Yes	Yes
Bonds	Yes	No	Yes
Mutual funds	Yes	No	Yes
ETFs	Yes	No	Yes
Indexes	Yes	No	Yes
Clearing firm	Self-clearing	Dorman/RCG	Self-clearing

This table is current at the time of printing. Check with each individual provider for updates on information. You will find contact information and a variety of providers in Appendix C (Resources) at the back of this book.

HOW TO CHOOSE THE BEST FRONT-END PLATFORM FOR YOUR NEEDS

Today's technology has dramatically changed the landscape of trading from only 10 years ago. The speed of execution and the availability of extensive trading tools and products for a very reasonable price have altered the industry as we know it. This has helped to level the playing field for the independent trader.

This topic ties in with the power of today's front-end platforms. They can do almost anything; they can seemingly even get you a cup of coffee in the morning. (When they can do that, sign me up since coffee is my primary essential vice!) From enabling traders to place trades with their broker right from their chart to automating trades and scanning for opportunities in the market, the possibilities of what front-end platforms can do for you are endless.

Each front-end platform has its individual strengths, just like brokers and data feeds, so you will need to again identify your needs and find the

TABLE 6.14   Select a Front-End Platform That Matches Your Needs

	NinjaTrader	eSignal	Trade Navigator	Market Analyst
Brokers that connect to the front-end platform	Mirus Futures, IB*, RCG*, MB Trading, GAIN, MF Global, GFT, PFGBEST, FXCM, Zaner, Daniels, and more	IB*, PFGBEST, GAIN, FXCM, Infinity, Dorman, optionsXpress, Zaner, and more	PFGBEST, MF Global, Infinity Futures, TransAct Futures	GFT and IB*
Stocks	Yes	Yes	Yes	Yes
Options	Yes	Yes	Yes	Yes
Futures	Yes	Yes	Yes	Yes
Forex	Yes	Yes	Yes	
Bonds	Yes	Yes	No	
Mutual funds	Yes	Yes	No	
ETFs	Yes	Yes	No	
Indexes	Yes	Yes	No	

Note: IB is an acronym for Interactive Brokers; RCG is an acronym for Rosenthal Collins Group LLC. This table shows some of the choices you have to choose from. For a more complete list of resources in addition to contact information, refer to Appendix C at the back of this book.

This table is current at the time of printing. Check with each individual provider for updates on information. You will find contact information and a variety of providers in Appendix C (Resources) at the back of this book.

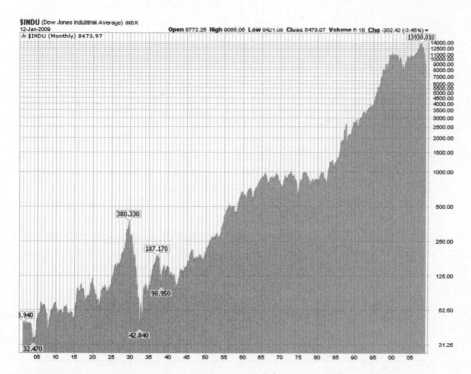

FIGURE 6.10 Dow Jones Industrial Average Chart Showing Manias, Panics and Crashes from the Year 1900 through the Year 2010

Source: © StockCharts.com. (www.StockCharts.com).

best match for the costs involved. Table 6.14 is an overview of some excellent front-end platforms that are available today.

MANIAS, PANICS, AND CRASHES

The nature of the financial markets is closely linked to mass psychology, and markets have a tendency to be moved either up or down by emotion on a large, global scale. Sometimes these moves can be very dramatic and swift as you can see on the chart in Figure 6.10, which shows the DJIA from the year 1900 all the way to the year 2010.

CHAPTER 7

Adapting to Changing Market Cycles

Just as most climates have four seasons to one degree or another, the markets have different environmental cycles. This means you need to quickly identify the changing cycles and then appropriately adapt to them.

If you live in New York City, for example, chances are you will not be going outside for a leisurely stroll down Fifth Avenue in shorts and a T-shirt and flip-flops in the month of February. Why is that? Because, if you've lived there for a while and experienced the local seasons, you've already identified that in February it will be pretty darn cold. To appropriately adapt, you will want to wear a heavy winter coat and maybe gloves and a scarf and earmuffs.

It is the same with the markets. You need to have "lived there for a while" and experienced a variety of market cycles so you know what "to wear," or rather how to adapt, so that you are financially comfortable. Instead of knowing to wear a winter coat in February, you will know that in a choppy, sideways, bracketed market you need to adapt your system and rules so that you do not get whipsawed and stopped out a lot. Or you may need to recognize a bull market changing to a bear market so that you can exit your position in a timely fashion to lock in profits.

FOUR MAJOR MARKET CYCLES

There are four major market cycles that you need to learn how to correctly identify. Each market cycle requires a different approach from your trading and investing system, and adapting to market cycles can improve your profitability dramatically.

Figures 7.1 through 7.4 show charts using the Applied Reality Trading (ART) system, which you will find out more about in Appendix B of this

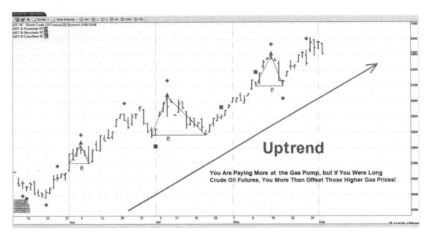

FIGURE 7.1   Trending Market Identified by the ART Software
Source: eSignal. Published by eSignal (www.esignal.com).

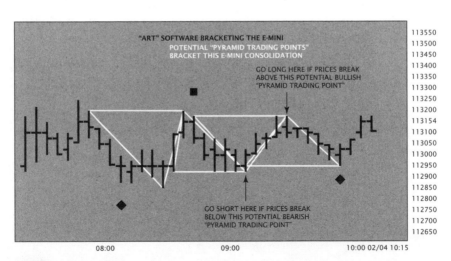

FIGURE 7.2   Bracketed Market Identified by the ART Software
Source: eSignal. Published by eSignal (www.esignal.com).

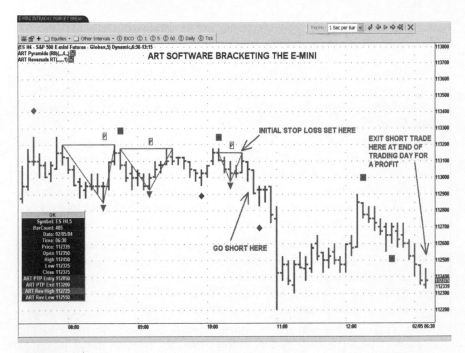

FIGURE 7.3 Market Breaking out of a Bracket Identified by the ART Software
Source: eSignal. Published by eSignal (www.esignal.com).

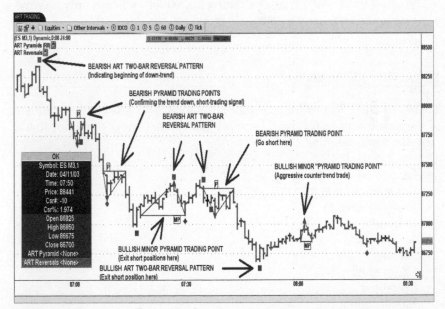

FIGURE 7.4 Market Correction Identified by Minor Pyramid Trading Point (MP) Triangles, Using the ART Software
Source: eSignal. Published by eSignal (www.esignal.com).

book. Software can very often enable you to effectively identify market cycles. Here are examples of the four major market cycles:

1. **Trending.** A trending market is moving consistently in one direction, up or down. (See Figure 7.1, which shows a bullish trend; notice how the triangles—Pyramid Trading Points®—are moving in an *up* or bullish trend.)

2. **Bracketed.** Also known as consolidated, this is when the market is stuck in a price range between identifiable resistance and support levels; on a chart it will look like a sideways horizontal band. (See Figure 7.2; notice how the triangles, potential Pyramid Trading Points, tell you this is a bracketed market when they form directly next to each other in a down, up, down, up sideways pattern.)

3. **Breaking out of a bracket.** This is a sharp change in price movement after the market has been consolidating. (See Figure 7.3, which shows the bracketed market you saw in Figure 7.2 break out to the downside; notice how the two down Pyramid Trading Point triangles from Figure 7.2 were confirmed and the two up triangles disappeared.)

4. **Corrective.** This is a short, sharp reverse in prices during a longer market trend. (See Figure 7.4, which shows the bearish trend indicated by the Pyramid Trading Point (P) triangles, which are all facing down; notice the two corrections in this trend marked by the Minor Pyramid Trading Point (MP) triangles facing up, which indicate only a correction in the trend, *not* a change in trend yet.)

IT'S ALL IN A NAME

There are many names for a bracketed market, and this can be confusing to the new trader or investor. Here is a list of the variety of names that all have the same meaning:

- Bracketed
- Consolidating
- Range-bound
- Sideways
- Nontrending
- Choppy
- Channeling
- Trendless
- Side-trending

- Sleepy
- Drunk
- Messy

You may even have some names that refer to bracketed markets not listed here, but this is a general list of the most common names.

USING TREND LINES TO IDENTIFY MARKET CYCLES

Trend lines are a terrific way for you to visualize the support and resistance of any current market cycle, whether it is trending up, trending down, or trending sideways. Visually you will be able to tell when the market movement breaks the trend line. See Figure 7.5 for an example of using a trend line drawn on the chart to clarify where the trend currently is. Trend lines assist you in identifying what market cycle you are in, and that is an important skill to master.

You can be conservative or aggressive in drawing your trend lines, and this will depend on your comfort level and what your strategy is. Aggressive trend lines have a tighter channel, and conservative trend lines have a wider channel in which the market moves.

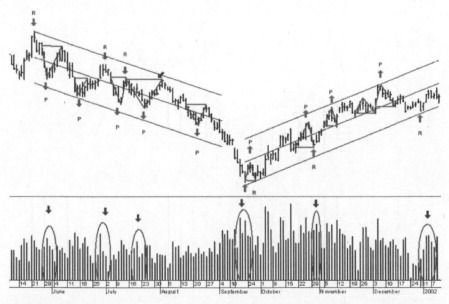

FIGURE 7.5 In a Downtrend and an Uptrend Using trend lines enables you to identify market cycles and changes in market cycles.

USING ELLIOTT WAVE ANALYSIS TO IDENTIFY MARKET CYCLES

Many traders use Elliott wave theory to identify waves, which is another way to identify market cycles. When using Elliot Wave, there are five waves in an up market and five waves in a down market. Each wave has its own relevance in determining your trading strategy. See Figure 7.6 for an illustration of a bullish pattern. Using Elliott waves is an advanced technique and requires that you have a thorough understanding of market waves and the ability to correctly determine which wave the market is in.

I use Elliott wave analysis extensively to map out and forecast potential future market movement. It serves as a road map for me in viewing the big picture of the markets. My analysis of the markets using this technique is always one of probabilities and not absolutes. With that mind-set I update my readings weekly to see where the market is moving and how the wave patterns are behaving from one week to the next.

Elliott wave analysis works for me as a filter, and for my actual entries and exits I use the Applied Reality Trading (ART) software, which gives me entries and exits based on the reality of price and volume in the current moment. Again, Elliott wave analysis is an advanced technique and you should exercise caution in utilizing it.

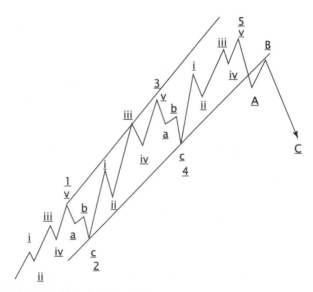

FIGURE 7.6 Bullish Elliott Wave Diagram

PITFALLS OF NOT IDENTIFYING MARKET CYCLES CORRECTLY

In my experience working with traders over the years, one of the most common reasons for failure is that traders are unable to identify market cycles correctly and do not realize the importance of identifying these cycles.

Sometimes when traders are able to identify a market cycle that their approach does not perform well in, it is difficult for them to sit on the sidelines and not take a trade. Often the best trade is no trade at all, but for some traders it can be uncomfortable to not be in the game. Patience is part of the psychological mind-set a trader needs in order to develop the ability to read market cycles effectively.

Effectively identifying market cycles is a skill that all successful traders have mastered. It is also essential to know what market cycles your system or approach will work well in and then have the discipline to stay out of the market when necessary.

Here are some common pitfalls of not identifying market cycles correctly:

- **Not identifying a bracketed market.** Here the pitfall is that you will get whipsawed by repeatedly entering the market and getting stopped out, resulting in paying a lot in commission fees to your broker and not capturing a profitable move in the market. Solution: Use trend lines and channel lines along with software to identify bracketed markets.
- **Misidentifying a reverse in trend.** The pitfall is that you might exit a perfectly good trend and miss out on significant profit potential as the market continues to move in the direction of your original position. Solution: Use scaling-out techniques for exiting the market so that you still have a portion of your position on the table and can profit from that if the trend is still in play.

Study market cycles and factor this concern into your trading strategy so you can effectively enter the market only when the conditions exist for your system to perform well.

CHAPTER 8

Education and Support

G etting a good education will build the foundation you need to perform well in the markets. This education will come from many areas in your life, not only from trading. It will come from your life experiences as well as your trading experiences, and all of this will play an important role in your trading success. You will be influenced by teachers, mentors, and coaches, and these various roles may overlap from time to time in your search for a well-rounded education.

The responsibility, though, falls totally on your shoulders to seek out the education you need. It is then also up to you to separate what information is useful and applies to you from what isn't useful and doesn't apply.

Take the initiative to find the people and institutions that can help you in your quest for knowledge, because knowledge is power.

A FEW CLASSIC TRADING BOOKS

There is no better way to start and to continue your education than by reading everything you can get your hands on that is related to trading. At first you should focus on the subjects that interest you most, and then you can branch out as you develop expertise in one or more areas.

I probably own just about every book ever written on trading, and when it comes down to getting your money's worth, buying books will probably give you the best initial value. Most libraries don't carry the books that we as traders need, so you will generally end up building up your own personal library. To cut back on the expense, buy used books and don't opt for express shipping.

Compared to expensive trading courses, getting a few classic books will give you a taste of a variety of approaches for a lot less money. You can implement these approaches and test them to see if they work for you. Then, if a particular book impacts you significantly, you can pursue that author's material, since the author will no doubt have a more in-depth course available.

In this day and age you can also find a lot of valuable information on the Internet, but as a whole, nothing can replace some of the old-time classic trading books that have stood the test of time. Be sure to get books that focus on the topics of money management and psychology. These two subjects apply to all traders, markets, and time frames. For a list of classic essential books, you can refer to Appendix D at the back of this book.

LEARNING STYLES

Everyone learns differently, and that is what makes the world go around. You will hear people say, "He's a visual thinker" or "I am a right-brain person," and it is true—we are all different. Many of us may even have disabilities that inhibit our learning, such as dyslexia, attention deficit disorder (ADD), or obsessive-compulsive disorder (OCD).

Whether our learning disabilities have been officially diagnosed or not, it is useful to know ourselves and know what works best when it comes to learning new material and absorbing it.

At your disposal you have your five senses, sight, hearing, taste, smell, and touch, and some people may even debate there is a sixth sense. Regardless of the actual number, it is usually optimal to reach out to all of your senses when learning. Here are some of the senses you can use in learning, along with ways to integrate them into your education:

- **Sight.** Reading, seeing diagrams and visuals, seeing and hearing videos.
- **Hearing.** Listening to audiotapes, seeing and hearing videos.
- **Touch.** Writing in workbooks.
- **Interaction.** Attending live webinars, seminars, and tutorials.

Maybe *interaction* is the sixth sense; you can decide. If you have a learning experience that enters into the realm of a live event via live webcast, live trade show, live seminar, or live one-on-one tutoring, you can see it adds another dimension to the process.

This extra dimension offers interaction and a connection with immediate feedback. The brain functions differently when challenged with feedback. It is just like the unpredictable feedback the brain encounters from the live markets. It is a much richer learning experience when you are able to have interaction in this way, because it makes the brain work in a more dynamic setting.

Determine which of these learning approaches work best for you. Then seek out the products and services that you will benefit from the most.

REPETITION, REPETITION, REPETITION

Another way to train the brain and to learn is through repetition. You can rewire your brain simply by doing the same process over and over and over. This is why even if you have bad trading habits (or no trading habits), you can rewire the synapses in your brain to improve your abilities.

Why do Olympic athletes do the same exercises endlessly over and over? It is because they are training their brains and their bodies to constantly improve and perfect their skills. Athletes call this *muscle memory*, and it works for traders, too.

You in effect can create an automatic reflex to succeed to the point where you don't even have to think about it. It's like Pavlov's dog, or the Pavlovian response; if you do enough conditioning through repetition, when the bell rings you will instantly react accordingly.

The secret is that you must repeat the *correct exercise* over and over—not the incorrect exercise. The brain can ingrain bad habits that are then difficult to break. So, how do you know you are repeating the correct exercises when trading? It is really all about baby steps; if you are constantly moving in a positive direction, even if it feels like small steps, then you want to keep repeating that behavior. If you are spiraling downward out of control, then you want to cease the behavior that caused the spiral.

You will know what is working and what is not. For example, if you didn't stick to your rules and you ignored a stop and blew your account out on one trade, you'll figure out that you need to stick to the rules. Then through repetition, repeating the process of sticking to the rules, you will condition yourself to do that automatically. If you feel that you are not able to determine what the correct exercises are, you may choose to work with a trading coach to assist you in setting up a plan.

PAPER TRADING IS AN ESSENTIAL LEARNING TOOL

One way to implement repetition and conditioning is to paper trade. That way, in a safe environment, just like a flight simulator for a pilot, you are repeating the same correct tasks over and over until you don't even need to think about them. The process becomes a natural part of you, and you are conditioned to succeed.

There is an ongoing debate in the trading community on the value of paper trading, and it is a fascinating one. All I can say is that if you can't be profitable paper trading you will never be profitable live trading with real money. It's that simple. See Chapter 10 for a complete outline on how to effectively paper trade.

DO IT YOUR WAY

All of our personalities are different, so for someone to tell you to do something exactly one particular way may not work for you. Instead, try to obtain the educational input that inspires you and helps you to succeed. Adapt that input to suit your personality and your style.

"Just Do It!"

Some traders spend a year or two learning how to trade before actually trading real money. Others have jumped right into trading the markets with a learn-as-you-go approach. There is no *right* or *wrong* way to do this.

As the Nike commercial used to say, the important thing is to:
"Just Do It!"

The Self-Taught Trader

Maybe you're one of those individuals who believe in teaching themselves, and if that is the case then go for it! There's nothing wrong with being a self-taught trader—look at the many successful entrepreneurs and leaders who never went to high school or college.

You may spend less time in the classroom and more time in the markets, learning as you trade. The only caution here is to make sure you're a good teacher and a good student. Implement discipline and accountability on your-self just as if you were a professor at a university. Establish benchmarks, and work to achieve them. Then evaluate your progress to be sure you are meeting your preset goals. And you must use risk control. See Chapter 12 for more information on implementing money management and controlling risk.

You may find that you will lose money in the markets while learning; just be sure that the money you have at risk is budgeted for this purpose and is money you can afford to lose. In effect, the live markets will be the

University of Trading, and just like any higher-education establishment, the cost of attendance can be significant.

The Teacher-Taught Trader

Or, maybe instead of being a self-taught trader, you might have the personality that prefers to work with many professional teachers before actually trading real money. You might need to be totally prepared. If you are this kind of trader, that's terrific.

Just try not to become a professional student and get addicted to educational gurus. Also, be sure to set up a time line on when you will begin paper trading, and when you will begin live trading. It is important to get in the market and see what it feels like to trade with real dollars.

The best of both worlds would be to blend the qualities of the self-taught trader and the teacher-taught trader together to create a balance. To be successful, you really need a little of both. It may be easier said than done, but if possible try to strike a balance between these two approaches.

YOU CAN LEARN FROM YOUR MISTAKES AND FAILURES

You can fail your way to the top. Trading is no different than any other profession in that you have to persevere to succeed and you have to be willing to take on risk. The inevitable result of taking on risk is to experience failure and to make mistakes. How you deal with failure and making mistakes will determine your longevity in any business, and it will determine your ability to do great things.

Many famous and successful people failed and made mistakes before they ever enjoyed success. So you see, sometimes failure is just the first step toward success. Just watch the Biography Channel for inspiration from great men and women throughout history.

Here are a few examples of successful failures:

- **Henry Ford** failed at five businesses that left him broke before he founded the Ford Motor Company.
- **Bill Gates** dropped out of Harvard and had a failed business with partner Paul Allen before creating the global empire that is now Microsoft.
- **Thomas Edison** was told by his teachers that he was "too stupid to learn anything," and he made more than a thousand attempts at inventing the light bulb before finally designing one that was commercially viable.

- **Orville and Wilbur Wright** battled depression and failed repeatedly before ever creating an airplane that could get airborne and stay there.
- **Vincent Van Gogh** sold only one painting during his lifetime, and while he had no commercial success, he created more than 800 known works that are masterpieces in every sense.
- **Michael Jordan**, arguably the greatest basketball player of all time, was actually cut from his high school basketball team.

In the end, making mistakes and failing are all part of the process of becoming successful. In an odd way, you can be thankful for your failures and mistakes if they teach you something. You might have missed valuable lessons if you'd never had the courage to fail, and as painful as failing can be, it is one of the very best learning opportunities that you will ever be given.

Be sure to view your mistakes, failures, and losses this way.

LIFE MENTORS, PROFESSIONAL MENTORS, AND TRADING COACHES

My first, and most important, mentor was my father. What I learned from him came not from his *teaching* but instead from my day-to-day observation of the examples he set. He was an attorney in New York City.

Since I had no desire to become a lawyer, my father was not a professional mentor for me; rather, he was a life mentor. He taught me my core values and helped me to shape my belief systems.

Two of the values he shared with me were his undying ability to persevere and his special way of creating a healthy balance in his life between work and play. He was also amazingly frugal, so his example when it came to money management and cutting costs influenced me later when I structured my trading business.

Another important mentor for me was Bill Williams, who has since retired from the trading business. Bill was a professional mentor to me and significantly influenced my trading when I studied with him many years ago. When I would watch him trade, he was relaxed and flowed with the market. He stayed focused on the present moment and taught me to want what the market wants.

The reason for mentioning both my father and Bill Williams is that every successful trader will be influenced by mentors, teachers, and coaches. It is important for you to seek out individuals who can guide you and support you in a way that enables you to grow to your full potential.

It is important to set up a one-on-one support system to provide you with a sounding board. For traders it is easy to be affected by the isolation of working alone in an office, usually with a computer and not much other human interaction. There are a number of things you can do to counteract this phenomenon, one of which is to identify a mentor or trading coach you can rely on for feedback and support.

Having this support network is a way for you to stay honest with yourself. The temptation to deny certain painful facts and realities is lessened when there is a mentor or coach to witness the process with you and guide you through challenges that may arise. It's valuable to have this kind of support, especially when starting out.

If you are looking for information on where to find an excellent trading coach to work with, e-mail me at Info@TradersCoach.com or call 858-695-0592 and I will refer you to my network of talented coaches who specialize in this industry. This kind of one-on-one customized support and education very often is the catalyst to move you to the next level.

CHAPTER 9

Writing a
Business Plan

This is where the rubber hits the road. Putting your ideas on paper in writing will help you see if your boat will float. And if there are holes in the plan, better to find out now and fix them before hitting the high seas. Often it is the simple things that can undo a trader's or investor's success.

Back-office basics like creating a work space that has no distractions and managing your record keeping to be sure your profit/loss (P/L) performance is always in line are essential items that are often overlooked.

When you are ready to lay out your own personal plan, you can use the blank template provided in this chapter. Essentially, the idea is for you to fill in the blanks and customize the template we've given you so that it suits your current situation and needs. Going forward, after preparing your first plan, update it every year to take into account changing market environments and your changing personal needs.

BUSINESS PLAN: BLANK TEMPLATE

This business plan blank template will be useful for you to organize your thoughts. You can customize it with your own information and tailor it to either a trader's plan or an investor's plan. Either photocopy the blank template from this book or write directly in the book; or for your convenience you can also download a free customizable template from the TradersCoach .com website by using the following link:

www.traderscoach.com/survivalguide.php

If you have any difficulty in accessing the link, you can also contact our office by calling 858-695-0592 (we are located in San Diego, California, in the United States) or by e-mailing us via info@traderscoach.com. At the TradersCoach.com link you will also find sample business plans to help you get started. These samples were prepared by students of ours who have allowed us to share their plans with you.

Anyone who is going to complete a business plan will probably have done a significant amount of trading and/or investing. At the very least, the person will have researched the topic extensively.

By filling in the blanks in the master template in this chapter, you may find that there are areas you might not have realized you need to address. This business plan template is a preflight checklist of sorts to ensure that you have addressed the primary areas necessary to be successful.

There will be a fair amount of decision making required to complete your plan. Let me give you a word of caution regarding the decision process. Try to give each plan item enough attention without getting stuck on any one individual item. Try to avoid the possibility of never completing the plan.

Depending on your personality, you may lean toward overthinking the plan and never finishing it. Or, instead, you might throw it together without much serious thought or substance. There is a happy medium that will suit you.

Historical Monthly Averages

You will see a section in this business plan template that covers *historical monthly averages*. Section 1:D outlines information that will assist you in estimating your future revenue probabilities. This data may be obtained from trading records you have taken from either your paper trading or live trading results.

What we are trying to do is develop a quantifiable history of your past performance, so that we can estimate your future performance. Of course, as you probably have heard many times, past performance does not guarantee future results when it comes to the financial markets and trading.

Market cycles change and human beings change, so the history we will be looking at is not a guarantee of what will happen in the future. But it is a good estimation tool. A minimum of three months of data is necessary as a starting sample size.

The more data you have to draw an average from, the more accurate your estimate and projection for the future will be. A longer historical trading period is more likely to cover a variety of market cycles and market events and how you, the trader, performed in each of these.

Individuals who are starting their trading business with no historical data will need to set up a plan that allows for a period of at least three months of paper trading to develop historical monthly averages. This type of business plan will need to provide for a period when there is no incoming revenue, and must have adequate financing to allow for that.

Make a Promise to Yourself

It is important to make a promise to yourself right now. If you are going to start designing this plan, then also promise yourself you are going to finish it and adhere to the plan. That commitment will go a long way toward ensuring your success.

FRONT MATTER: TITLE PAGE, TABLE OF CONTENTS, AND MISSION STATEMENT

The title page of your business plan is a quick snapshot of your business (see Form 9.1). It lists the name of your business, the date of the business plan, the owner of the business, and pertinent contact information. Following the

FORM 9.1 Business Plan Title Page—Template

Business Plan Title Page

Name of Business:	
Date:	
Contact Name:	
Contact Title:	
Address:	
Phone:	
E-Mail:	

Fill in your information in the blank form above.

FORM 9.2   Business Plan Table of Contents—Template

Business Plan Table of Contents

Mission Statement	Outline of the Business Mission
1. Summary	A. Business Concept B. Current Profile C. Key Success Factors D. Historical Monthly Averages E. Financial Situation F. Vision Statement
2. Strategy	A. Market Selection B. Entries and Exits C. Money Management Strategy D. Potential Threats and Risks E. Research and Development
3. Operations	A. Office Setup B. Order Execution C. Record Keeping
4. Financials	A. Starting Balance Sheet B. Cash Flow Forecasts C. Profit and Loss History D. Key Performance Ratios

title page is the table of contents (see Form 9.2). The business plan main topics are outlined on this single sheet and will be developed in more detail when you fill out the blank template in the following pages.

The next important section of your business plan is your mission statement (see Form 9.3), because this is where you can make the case for starting your own business. In a conversational tone, you will describe what your mission is and why you believe this will be a successful business. In very broad strokes, outline what the plan is and how to implement it. It is a summary of the concept of your business.

1. SUMMARY

The summary portion of your business plan covers all the working parts of your plan, including the business concept, current profile, key success factors, historical monthly averages, financial situation, and your vision statement.

FORM 9.3 Business Plan Mission Statement—Template

Business Plan Mission Statement

Fill in your information in the blank form above.

This portion of the plan defines where you have been, where you are now, and where you are planning to go. Here you will be entering information on your historical profit/loss performance and also identifying your vision for your future profit/loss performance goals.

1: A. Business Concept

1: A.1. Type of entity:

☐ Full-time business, corporation

☐ Part-time business, corporation

☐ Other: _____

1: A.2. Who is the business owner?
- ☐ Full-time trader
- ☐ Full-time investor
- ☐ Part-time trader
- ☐ Part-time investor
- ☐ Student of trading
- ☐ Student of investing
- ☐ Other: _____

1: A.3. Type of business plan:
- ☐ New business start-up
- ☐ Annual update of existing plan
- ☐ Change of strategic direction
- ☐ Cash flow shortage
- ☐ Other: _____

1: A.4. Other commitments and/or challenges of business owner:
(Check all that apply.)
- ☐ Employed full-time with another company.
- ☐ Employed part-time with another company.
- ☐ Enrolled full-time in school.
- ☐ Enrolled part-time in school.
- ☐ Author is a caregiver (for children, parents, or other).
- ☐ Other: _____
- ☐ Other: _____

1: A.5. Why is this business a good choice for the business owner? What skills does the owner have that are well suited for trading or investing?

_____

_____

_____

1: A.6. Why has the business owner decided to choose this business at this time and place? Why will it be fulfilling to the owner?

_____

_____

_____

1: A.7. Why does this business suit the needs of the business owner?

_____

_____

_____

1: A.8. What historical data supports the belief that this business will be successful?

_____

_____

_____

1: A.9. What measures will be instituted to improve the probability for success?

_____

_____

_____

1: A.10. Summary of short-term (12-month) goals for business, both financial and strategic:

_____

_____

_____

1: A.11. Summary of long-term (five-year) goals for business, both financial and strategic:

_____

_____

_____

1: B. Current Profile

1: B.1. Current net worth of business owner:

☐ $201,000–$300,000+ in debt

☐ $101,000–$200,000 in debt

☐ $51,000–$100,000 in debt

☐ $1,000–$50,000 in debt

☐ Zero net worth

☐ $1,000–$50,000 in assets

☐ $51,000–$100,000 in assets

☐ $101,000–$200,000 in assets

☐ $201,000–$300,000+ in assets

Net worth formula:
Total Assets – Total Liabilities = Net Worth
Net worth example:
Assets $995,000 – Liabilities $537,000 = Net worth $458,000

1: B.2. Age of business owner:

☐ 18–23 years old

☐ 24–30 years old

☐ 31–40 years old

☐ 41–50 years old

☐ 51–60 years old

☐ 61–70 years old

☐ 71–80 years old

☐ 81–90 years old

1: B.3. Tolerance for risk of business owner:

☐ High

☐ Medium

☐ Low

1: C. Key Success Factors

1: C.1. Business owner's duration of experience in trading or investing:

☐ One year

☐ Two years

☐ Three years

☐ Other: _____

1: C.2. Business owner's experience in trading or investing:

☐ Live trading experience—full-time

☐ Live trading experience—part-time

☐ Paper trading experience—full-time

☐ Paper trading experience—part-time

☐ Other: _____

1: C.3. List employees, including business owner, commitment of hours per week they will work for this business, and their job responsibilities:

☐ 1. Name: _____ Hours per week: _____
   Job responsibility: _____
   Relationship to business owner: __Business Owner__

☐ 2. Name: _____ Hours per week: _____
   Job responsibility: _____
   Relationship to business owner: _____

☐ 3. Name: _____ Hours per week: _____
   Job responsibility: _____
   Relationship to business owner: _____

☐ 4. Name: _____ Hours per week: _____
   Job responsibility: _____
   Relationship to business owner: _____

☐ **Total of all employees' hours per week:** _____

1: C.4. Total person-hours available for this business per week:

(Tally up number of hours per week in section 1: C.3.)

☐ 20 person-hours available per week

☐ 40 person-hours available per week

☐ Other: _____

1: C.5. Total person-hours available for this business per month:

(Take figure from section 1: C.4 and multiply it by 4. Example: 20 hours per week × 4 weeks = 80 hours per month.)

☐ 80 person-hours available per month

☐ 160 person-hours available per month

☐ Other: _____

1: C.6. Dollar value of dedicated checking account with operating cash for this business:

☐ $1,000

☐ $5,000

☐ $10,000

☐ $15,000

☐ $25,000

☐ Other: _____

1: C.7. List all trading, investing, and retirement accounts, value and account type of each, and broker used for each:

☐ 1. Account value: $_____ Account type: _____
        Broker: _____

☐ 2. Account value: $_____ Account type: _____
        Broker: _____

☐ 3. Account value: $_____ Account type: _____
        Broker: _____

☐ 4. Account value: $_____ Account type: _____
        Broker: _____

☐ 5. Account value: $_____ Account type: _____
        Broker: _____

☐ 6. Account value: $_____ Account type: _____
        Broker: _____

     Total value of all accounts: $_____

1: C.8. Total combined value of all trading and/or investing account(s):

(Tally all account values from section 1: C.7.)

☐ $ _____

1: C.9. Current business liabilities and available credit:

☐ 1. Credit Card Account Number: _____

Annual interest rate on account: _____%

Credit card type: _____

Creditor backing the debt: _____

Total credit line on account: $_____

Current principal balance owed: $_____

Minimum monthly payment due: $_____

☐ 2. Credit Card Account Number: _____

Annual interest rate on account: _____%

Credit card type: _____

Creditor backing the debt: _____

Total credit line on account: $_____

Current principal balance owed: $_____

Minimum monthly payment due: $_____

☐ 3. Business Loan Account Number: _____

Annual interest rate on account: _____%

Creditor backing the debt: _____

Total credit line on account: $_____

Current principal balance owed: $_____

Minimum monthly payment due: $_____

☐ 4. Cash Advance Account Number: _____

Annual interest rate on account: _____%

Creditor backing the debt: _____

Total credit line on account: $_____

Current principal balance owed: $_____

Minimum monthly payment due: $_____

☐ 5. Other business liabilities and/or available credit:

_____

_____

_____

_____

_____

_____

1: C.10. Existing equipment, technology, and other assets:
(Check all that apply.)

☐ Computer—laptop

☐ Computer—desktop

☐ Printer

☐ Backup battery

☐ Telephone—landline

☐ Telephone—cellular

☐ Fax

☐ Internet—hard wired

☐ Internet—WIFI

☐ Cable line

☐ DSL feed

☐ Copier machine

☐ Data feed

☐ News feed

☐ Trading software

☐ Record-keeping software

☐ Office space—outside home

☐ Office space—in home

☐ Office furniture

☐ Other: _____

☐ Other: _____

☐ Other: _____

1: C.11. Other supplemental reoccurring revenue (in addition to revenue from this business):

☐ Full-time job—monthly salary is: $_____

☐ Part-time job—monthly salary is: $_____

☐ Other monthly revenue—source: _____ $_____

☐ Other monthly revenue—source: _____ $_____

☐ Other monthly revenue—source: _____ $_____

Total supplemental reoccurring monthly revenue: $ _____

1: C.12. Motivation level of all personnel and business owner:

☐ Highly motivated, passionate about making this business successful.

☐ Moderately motivated; this is just another job.

☐ Not motivated; doesn't really feel that success is possible.

1: C.13. Perseverance level and problem-solving abilities of all personnel and business owner:

☐ Strong ability to persevere and problem solve.

☐ Moderate ability to persevere and problem solve.

☐ No ability to persevere and problem solve.

1: C.14. Work ethic of all personnel and business owner:

☐ Strong work ethic; enjoys hard work.

☐ Moderate work ethic; moderately lazy.

☐ Minimal work ethic; would rather be doing something else.

1: C.15. Probability of success for this business estimated by business owner:

☐ High success probability.

☐ Medium success probability.

☐ Low success probability.

1: D. Historical Monthly Averages

1: D.1. Number of months (sample size) used to calculate historical monthly average figures in this business plan:

☐ 3 months

☐ 6 months

☐ 9 months

☐ 12 months

☐ Other: _____

1: D.2. Number of person-hours worked per month to achieve these figures:

(Take figure in 1: C.5 and enter below.)

☐ 80 person-hours worked per month

☐ 160 person-hours worked per month

☐ Other: _____

1: D.3. Historical monthly averages are based on:
☐ Paper trading account
☐ Live trading account
☐ Paper investment portfolio
☐ Live investment portfolio
☐ Other: _____

1: D.4. Gross historical monthly average profit/loss from trading or investing:
☐ –($500)
☐ –($100)
☐ Breakeven
☐ +$100
☐ +$500
☐ +$1,000
☐ +$5,000
☐ +$10,000
☐ Other: _____

1: D.5. Per hour gross revenue:
☐ $20.00
☐ $40.00
☐ $80.00
☐ Other: _____

Per Hour Gross Revenue Formula
(Take figures from section 1: D.4 for revenue and section 1: D.2 for hours.)
Average Monthly Gross Revenue ÷ Person-Hours per Month = Per Hour Gross Revenue

Examples for one person full-time:
$10,000 ÷ 160 hours per month = $62.50 per hour
$5,000 ÷ 160 hours per month = $31.25 per hour

Examples for one person part-time:
$1,000 ÷ 40 hours per month = $25.00 per hour
$500 ÷ 40 hours per month = $12.50 per hour

1: E. Financial Situation

1: E.1. Total combined value of all trading or investing accounts:
(Enter figure from section 1: C.8 here.)

☐ $_____

1: E.2. Checking account operating cash dedicated to this business:
(Enter figure from section 1: C.6 here.)

☐ $_____

1: E.3. Monthly salary to business owner:

☐ $_____

1: E.4. Monthly estimated business expenses:
☐ Salary to employee: _____ $_____
☐ Salary to employee: _____ $_____
☐ Health insurance: $_____
☐ Office space—outside home: $_____
☐ Office space—in home: $_____
☐ Electric: $_____
☐ Other utilities: $_____
☐ Broker's commission fees: $_____
☐ Front-end platform fees: $_____
☐ Data feed: $_____
☐ Exchange fees: $_____
☐ Interest on debt: $_____
☐ Computer equipment: $_____
☐ Printer: $_____
☐ Telephone(s): $_____
☐ Internet: $_____
☐ Cable line: $_____
☐ DSL feed: $_____
☐ News feed: $_____
☐ Market entry and exit software: $_____

☐ Record-keeping software: $_____

☐ Bookkeeper services: $_____

☐ Clerical services: $_____

☐ Education: $_____

☐ Periodicals: $_____

☐ Travel and entertainment: $_____

☐ Other: _____ $_____

☐ Other: _____ $_____

☐ Other: _____ $_____

☐ Other: _____ $_____

☐ Other: _____ $_____

☐ Other: _____ $_____

Total monthly estimated expenses: $_____

1: E.5. Expenses—Total monthly estimated business expenses:

(Tally items listed in section 1: E.4 and enter here.)

☐ $_____

1: E.6. Gross Profit/Loss—Gross estimated per month from live trading account(s) for next fiscal year:

(Take gross historical monthly average profit/loss from section 1: D.4 and enter here.)

☐ Gross profit +$_____ per month

☐ Gross Loss –($_____) per month

☐ Gross – Breakeven

1: E.7. Net Profit/Loss—Net estimated per month from live trading accounts(s) for next fiscal year:

(Take gross historical monthly average profit/loss from section 1: D.4 and subtract dollar amount of expenses in section 1: E.5 to equal your net profit/loss.)

☐ Net Profit +$_____ per month

☐ Net Loss –($_____) per month

☐ Net – Breakeven

Net profit/loss formula:
Gross Profit/Loss – Expenses = Net Profit/Loss

Example for profitable net figures:
$1,000 – $600 = $400 net profit
Example for unprofitable net figures:
–($300) – ($500) = –($800) net loss

1: E.8. Funding needed for next fiscal year:

☐ No funding needed.

☐ Amount of funding needed for next 12 months: $_____

1: E.9. Potential source of funding for next fiscal year (if needed):

☐ Available savings: $_____

☐ Loan: _____ $_____

☐ Interest rate on debt: _____%

☐ Minimum monthly payment on debt: $_____

☐ Liquidation of current assets:

Specify asset: _____ $_____

Specify asset: _____ $_____

Specify asset: _____ $_____

Total potential funding: $_____

1: E.10. Projected "cash on hand" assets at conclusion of next fiscal year:

☐ $_____

1: F. Vision Statement

1: F.1. Where will the business be in six months to a year, both financially and structurally?

_____
_____
_____

1: F.2. Where will the business be in five years, both financially and structurally?

_____
_____
_____

1: F.3. Identify and define basic milestones for the coming months and years:

☐ Become profitable in paper account.   Target date: _____

☐ Become profitable in live account.   Target date: _____

☐ Increase monthly revenue by 10 percent.   Target date: _____

☐ Generate monthly revenue of $5,000.   Target date: _____

☐ Increase win ratio by 10 percent.   Target date: _____

☐ Increase payoff ratio by 10 percent.   Target date: _____

☐ Attain a win ratio of 50 percent.   Target date: _____

☐ Attain a payoff ratio of 3 to 1.   Target date: _____

☐ Reduce monthly expenses by 10 percent.   Target date: _____

☐ Increase monthly hours by 10 hours.   Target date: _____

☐ Decrease monthly hours by 10 hours.   Target date: _____

☐ Test a new trading strategy.   Target date: _____

☐ Test a new investment strategy.   Target date: _____

☐ Test a new risk control strategy.   Target date: _____

☐ Attend an educational seminar.   Target date: _____

☐ Implement a new record-keeping system.   Target date: _____

☐ Implement a new computer system.   Target date: _____

☐ Implement a new software system.   Target date: _____

☐ Other: _____   Target date: _____

☐ Other: _____   Target date: _____

☐ Other: _____   Target date: _____

☐ Other: _____   Target date: _____

☐ Other: _____   Target date: _____

☐ Other: _____   Target date: _____

2. STRATEGY

The strategy portion of your business plan identifies the markets you will be trading, what your specific entry and exit strategy will be, what your money management strategy will be, what potential threats and risks there are, and what research and development you will be doing.

Here you will specify the steps on how you will get from where you are now to where you want to be. This part of your plan is detailed and will be your guide to your day-to-day trading activities.

You may need to adjust and adapt your strategy from time to time, and this may require that you prepare an updated business plan. When market cycles change the profitability of your strategy can be affected, and you must always be testing, researching, and developing new and better ideas for the current market conditions.

2: A. Market Selection

2: A.1. What markets will be traded?

☐ Stocks—Specify symbols/exchanges:

_____

☐ Options—Specify symbols/exchanges:

_____

☐ Futures—Specify symbols/exchanges:

_____

☐ Forex—Specify symbols/exchanges:

_____

☐ Bonds—Specify symbols/exchanges:

_____

☐ Mutual funds—Specify symbols/exchanges:

_____

☐ Exchange-traded funds (ETFs)—Specify symbols/exchanges:

_____

☐ Indexes—Specify symbols/exchanges:

_____

☐ Other: _____ Specify symbols/exchanges:

_____

☐ Other: _____ Specify symbols/exchanges:

_____

2: A.2. What markets will be invested in?

☐ Stocks—Specify symbols/exchanges/etc:

_____

☐ Bonds—Specify symbols/exchanges/etc:

_____

☐ Mutual funds—Specify symbols/exchanges/etc:

_____

☐ Equity funds—Specify symbols/exchanges/etc:

_____

☐ Income funds—Specify symbols/exchanges/etc:
_____

☐ Treasury bills—Specify:
_____

☐ Certificates of deposit (CDs)—Specify:
_____

☐ Other : _____ Specify symbols/exchanges/etc:
_____

☐ Other : _____ Specify symbols/exchanges/etc:
_____

2: A.3. Why have these markets and specific instruments been selected?
_____
_____
_____

2: B. Entries and Exits

2: B.1. Average time frame that transactions will be held:
☐ Close out to cash every night (day trader).
☐ Hold transactions for one day to three months (position trader).
☐ Hold transactions for longer than three months (investor).
☐ Other: _____

2: B.2. Style of trading or investing:
☐ Trend trader
☐ Scalper
☐ Value investor
☐ Other: _____

2: B.3. Method to be used in selecting entries and exits:
☐ Fundamental analysis
☐ Technical analysis
☐ Combination of fundamental and technical analysis
☐ Other: _____

2: B.4. Fundamental techniques and tools to be used:

☐ News feeds—Specify: _____

☐ Economic reports—Specify: _____

☐ Scanning software—Specify: _____

☐ Adviser's reports—Specify: _____

☐ Other: _____ Specify: _____

☐ Other: _____ Specify: _____

☐ Other: _____ Specify: _____

☐ Other: _____ Specify: _____

☐ Other: _____ Specify: _____

2: B.5. Technical analysis techniques and tools to be used:

☐ Data feeds—Specify: _____

☐ Entry/exit software—Specify: _____

☐ Scanning software—Specify: _____

☐ Adviser's reports—Specify: _____

☐ Other: _____ Specify: _____

☐ Other: _____ Specify: _____

☐ Other: _____ Specify: _____

☐ Other: _____ Specify: _____

☐ Other: _____ Specify: _____

2: B.6. Uptrending market—setup entry/exit rules:

☐ _____

_____

☐ _____

_____

☐ _____

_____

☐ _____

_____

☐ _____

_____

☐ _____

_____

2: B.7. Downtrending market—setup entry/exit rules:

☐ _____

_____

☐ _____

_____

☐ _____

_____

☐ _____

_____

☐ _____

_____

☐ _____

_____

2: B.8. Bracketed market—setup entry/exit rules:

☐ _____

_____

☐ _____

_____

☐ _____

_____

☐ _____

_____

☐ _____

_____

☐ _____

_____

2: C. Money Management Strategy

2: C.1. When will trading be halted after losing money?

☐ Two losing trades in a row in one day.

☐ Three losing trades in a row in one day.

☐ $500 loss in one day.

☐ $1,000 loss in one day.

☐ Two losing trades in a row in one week.

☐ Three losing trades in a row in one week.

☐ $1,000 loss in one week.

☐ $2,000 loss in one week.

☐ 10 percent equity drawdown in trading account in one month.

☐ After a losing set of 25 trades where the result is a cumulative net loss.

☐ Other: _____

2: C.2. When will trading be halted after a profitable period?

☐ $500 profit in one day

☐ $1,000 profit in one day

☐ $2,000 profit in one day

☐ $1,000 profit in one week

☐ $2,000 profit in one week

☐ Never

☐ Other: _____

2: C.3. What percentage of trading account will be risked on each trade?

☐ 2 percent maximum risk on each trade.

☐ 1 percent maximum risk on each trade.

☐ Using average monthly win ratio and payoff ratio, mathematically calculate the optimal percent to risk using the optimal f formula.

☐ After a drawdown of 6 percent of trading account, reduce the percent to risk by 25 percent. For example, if normal risk amount is 2 percent on each trade, after a 6 percent drawdown only 1.5 percent will be risked.

☐ Other: _____

2: C.4. How will optimum trade size be determined?

☐ Use Trade Size Calculator software to calculate trade size for every trade.

☐ Manually calculate proper trade size using formula found in Chapter 12.

☐ Other: _____

2: C.5. What percent of trading account will be risked at any given time?

☐ 6 percent is the maximum active trading account risk. Example: There could be three live trades active, each with a separate risk of 2 percent. No new positions would be taken until one of the initial trades closed out.

☐ 10 percent is the maximum active trading account risk. Example: Five live trades could be active, each with a separate risk of 2 percent. No new positions would be taken until one of the initial trades closed out.

☐ Other: _____

2: C.6. What percentage of business owner's total net worth will be risked on trading?

☐ 10 percent of total net worth is the maximum amount to be risked in active trading account.

☐ Other: _____

2: C.7. When will a trade be exited?

☐ Will always determine initial stop-loss exit prior to entering the trade.

☐ Adhere to stop-loss exit when it is hit, and exit the market immediately.

☐ Use a stop-loss exit strategy that is based on market price activity, key support and resistance levels, volume, volatility dynamics, and/or fundamental rules (not on random and spontaneous decisions).

☐ Use trailing stops to lock in profit when the market moves in favor of the position.

☐ Use scaling-out rules to lock in profit and relieve psychological anxiety.

☐ Will not move stops for emotional reasons.

☐ When scaling into a position and increasing trade size, will adjust stop to allow for additional risk.

☐ When holding a position overnight, a day trader will adjust stop to allow for additional overnight risk.

☐ Set stops that breathe to avoid the expense of commissions caused by being whipsawed in a choppy market.

☐ Other: _____

☐ Other: _____

2: C.8. How will scaling out be implemented?

☐ 30 percent for the first scale-out, 30 percent for the second scale-out, and hold 40 percent of the trade until stopped out.

☐ One-third of position for the first scale-out, one-third of position for the second scale-out, and hold remaining one-third until stopped out.

☐ When market gaps in a profitable direction of the trade, creating a 50 percent gain. Example: If a long stock position at $20 per share gaps up to $30 per share, liquidate 30 percent of position to lock in profit.

☐ Other: _____

☐ Other: _____

2: C.9. How will scaling in be implemented?

☐ Only scale into a winning position.

☐ Do not double down.

☐ When scaling into a position, recalculate risk based on new trade size and adjust stop-loss exit to compensate for the added risk.

☐ Other: _____

2: C.10. How will portfolio be diversified?

☐ 2 percent per sector can be risked at any given time. Example: If a total of 6 percent of trading account is at risk, have 2 percent in the technology sector, 2 percent in the energy sector, and 2 percent in the currency sector.

☐ Other: _____

2: C.11. Establish record-keeping rules.

☐ Track every single trade every day.

☐ Write down the entry and exit price, and calculate the profit/loss.

☐ Write down emotions and feelings prior to, during, and after the trade is completed.

☐ Tabulate all totals for every day, week, month, and year.

☐ Determine adjustments that may improve performance for both your money management system and trading system based on the facts (not based on distortions). Avoiding the tabulation of totals can lead to distortions—so be sure to run the numbers every day.

☐ Fill out scorecard so that win ratio, payoff ratio, commission ratio, largest winning trade and largest losing trade, average winning trade and average losing trade, largest number of consecutive losses, average number of consecutive losses, largest trading account drawdown, average trading account drawdown, and percent of profit or loss is known every day on every account.

☐ Other: _____

2: D. Potential Threats and Risks

2: D.1. What are the most likely potential threats and risks to success?

☐ 1. Account drawdown.

☐ 2. Running out of operating capital.

☐ 3. Market risk. This type of risk could involve an event that would paralyze the markets. Examples: September 11, 2001; Pearl Harbor; Hurricane Katrina. Events include but are not limited to war, acts of God, weather, and financial collapses.

☐ 4. Lack of market liquidity.

☐ 5. Unprofitable system. Significant change in market dynamics rendering a previously profitable system suddenly not profitable.

☐ 6. Medical event. Risk of incapacitating one or more of the company's employees for a period of more than one week.

☐ 7. Internet interruption or reduction of Internet speed that would interfere with order execution, access to account status, and overall communication systems. Examples: Internet provider malfunction, unexpected shutdown of system, or excessive unexpected Internet traffic.

☐ 8. Energy supply interruption. This would interfere with order execution, access to account status, overall communication systems, and living and working necessities such as light. Example: brownouts, blackouts, and generator failures.

☐ 9. Task saturation. Example: losing focus due to burden overload.

☐ 10. Other threat or risk:

_____

_____

_____

☐ 11. Other threat or risk:

_____

_____

_____

☐ 12. Other threat or risk:

_____

_____

_____

2: D.2. Preventions and remedies for section 2:D.1 threats and risks:

☐ 1. Account drawdown.

Prevention: _____

Remedy: _____

☐ 2. Running out of operating capital.

Prevention: _____

Remedy: _____

☐ 3. Market risk.

Prevention: _____

Remedy: _____

☐ 4. Lack of market liquidity.

Prevention: _____

Remedy: _____

☐ 5. Unprofitable system.

Prevention: _____

Remedy: _____

☐ 6. Medical event.

Prevention: _____

Remedy: _____

☐ 7. Internet interruption.

Prevention: _____

Remedy: _____

☐ 8. Energy supply interruption.
Prevention: _____
Remedy: _____

☐ 9. Task saturation.
Prevention: _____
Remedy: _____

☐ 10. Other threat or risk: _____
Prevention: _____
Remedy: _____

☐ 11. Other threat or risk: _____
Prevention: _____
Remedy: _____

☐ 12. Other threat or risk: _____
Prevention: _____
Remedy: _____

2: E. Research and Development

2: E.1. What education will be planned for in the next fiscal year?

☐ Live seminar(s)
☐ Live webcasts
☐ Online course(s)
☐ Other: _____

3. OPERATIONS

The operations portion of your business plan is the nuts and bolts of your back-office basics and outlines how you will physically get the job done on a day-to-day basis. This includes details on your office setup, order execution plan, and record keeping.

3: A. Office Setup

3: A.1. Location of office:

☐ Home office space—dedicated space with door.
☐ Home office space—common area of home.

☐ Rented office space—dedicated space with door.

☐ Rented office space—common area such as cubicle.

☐ Other: _____

3: A.2. Describe level of distractions, or lack thereof, in office space and how this may or may not impact performance:

_____

_____

_____

3: A.3. Functionality of office and amenities available:

(Check all that apply.)

☐ Internet connection—hardwired

☐ Internet connection—wireless

☐ Computer—desktop

☐ Computer—laptop

☐ Electricity access (enough to handle all equipment)

☐ Cable feed

☐ DSL feed

☐ Television

☐ Phone/answering machine

☐ Live receptionist

☐ Fax machine

☐ Photocopier

☐ Personal filing storage cabinet

☐ Personal bookcase area

☐ Desk

☐ Chair—comfortable, ergonomic if possible

☐ Desk lighting

☐ Access to meeting room facilities

3: A.4. Primary trading computer capabilities:

(Check all that apply and fill in necessary blanks.)

☐ Desktop

☐ Laptop

☐ Year of issue: _____

☐ Random-access memory (RAM) amount: _____

☐ Central processing unit (CPU) type: _____

☐ Video card type: _____

☐ Monitors—How many? _____

☐ Monitors—What size? _____

☐ Battery backup in case of electrical blackout or brownout

☐ Ink-jet printer

☐ Laser printer

3: A.5. Backup secondary trading computer capabilities:

(Check all that apply and fill in necessary blanks.)

☐ Desktop

☐ Laptop

☐ Year of issue: _____

☐ Random-access memory (RAM) amount: _____

☐ Central processing unit (CPU) type: _____

☐ Video card type: _____

☐ Monitors—How many? _____

☐ Monitors—What size? _____

☐ Battery backup in case of electrical blackout or brownout

☐ Ink-jet printer

☐ Laser printer

3: A.6. Identify who will be your technical support service or technician; include name, phone, and e-mail of service provider:

_____

_____

_____

3: A.7. Office hours of operation for trading business:

☐ 9:00 A.M. to 5:00 P.M., Monday through Friday

☐ 6:00 A.M. to 2:00 P.M., Monday through Friday

☐ Other: _____

3: A.8. Lunch break schedule for trading business:

☐ 12:00 noon to 1:00 P.M., Monday through Friday

☐ 1:00 P.M. to 2:00 P.M., Monday through Friday

☐ Other: _____

3: A.9. Vacation and time off schedule for trading business:

☐ Two weeks off per year

☐ Three weeks off per year

☐ Four weeks off per year

☐ Other: _____

3: B. Order Execution

3: B.1. Process of placing entry and exit orders:

(Check all that apply.)

☐ Telephone order to broker.

☐ Automated order to broker.

☐ Manual order through broker platform.

☐ Manual order through front-end platform.

☐ Other: _____

3: B.2. Person(s) authorized to place entry and exit orders with broker:

☐ Name: _____

☐ Name: _____

☐ Name: _____

☐ Name: _____

☐ Name: _____

3: B.3. Complete list of brokers with phone numbers and e-mail addresses (this list corresponds to item 1: C.7 but has more contact information):

☐ 1. Account value: $_____ Account type: _____

Broker: _____

Contact name: _____

Phone: _____

E-mail: _____

Notes: _____

☐ 2. Account value: $_____ Account type: _____
       Broker: _____
       Contact name: _____
       Phone: _____
       E-mail: _____
       Notes: _____

☐ 3. Account value: $_____ Account type: _____
       Broker: _____
       Contact name: _____
       Phone: _____
       E-mail: _____
       Notes: _____

☐ 4. Account value: $_____ Account type: _____
       Broker: _____
       Contact name: _____
       Phone: _____
       E-mail: _____
       Notes: _____

☐ 5. Account value: $_____ Account type: _____
       Broker: _____
       Contact name: _____
       Phone: _____
       E-mail: _____
       Notes: _____

☐ 6. Account value: $_____ Account type: _____
       Broker: _____
       Contact name: _____
       Phone: _____
       E-mail: _____
       Notes: _____

3: B.4. Complete list of front-end platforms and data providers:

☐ 1. Vendor: _____ Account type: _____
Contact name: _____
Phone: _____
E-mail: _____
Notes: _____

☐ 2. Vendor: _____ Account type: _____
Contact name: _____
Phone: _____
E-mail: _____
Notes: _____

☐ 3. Vendor: _____ Account type: _____
Contact name: _____
Phone: _____
E-mail: _____
Notes: _____

☐ 4. Vendor: _____ Account type: _____
Contact name: _____
Phone: _____
E-mail: _____
Notes: _____

3: B.5. When, why, and how will you place certain types of orders?

(Check all that apply.)

☐ Market order: When, why, how: _____
☐ Limit order: When, why, how: _____
☐ Stop order: When, why, how: _____
☐ Trailing stop order: When, why, how: _____
☐ All or none order: When, why, how: _____
☐ Fill or kill order: When, why, how: _____
☐ Iceberg order: When, why, how: _____
☐ Other order: _____
When, why, how: _____
☐ Other order: _____
When, why, how: _____
☐ Other order: _____
When, why, how: _____

3: C. Record Keeping

Record keeping is crucial to the success of your business. In this section of your business plan, you will outline what data you will be recording. Form 9.4 and Form 9.5 are starting examples of what kind of data you will want to track and analyze. You can also find a complete set of record keeping ledgers in my book *A Trader's Money Management System* (John Wiley & Sons, 2008).

FORM 9.4 Daily Trade Ledger

Daily Trade Ledger Worksheet · Filled Orders								Date:
Open Trades Carried Forward								
Trade Number	Symbol	Position	Units	Bought $	Sold $	Gross $ P/L	Com* $	Net $ P/L
Daily Total:								
New Trades Filled Today								
Trade Number	Symbol	Position	Units	Bought $	Sold $	Gross $ P/L	Com* $	Net $ P/L
Daily Total:								
Grand Total:								

*Commission.

4. FINANCIALS

The financial portion of your business plan includes spreadsheets on your starting balance sheet, cash flow forecast, profit and loss history, and key performance ratios. See Form 9.6 through Form 9.10. The numbers part of the business equation is important to keep the machine working.

When your business is not staying in, or at least moving toward, profitable territory, it is a red flag. If you run the numbers with your business plan and find that the numbers are not sustainable with your current performance statistics or with your current resources, then adjustments will need to be made.

FORM 9.5 Weekly Trade Ledger

Weekly P/L History for Account #						Date:	
Broker Name:						Week (circle one):	
Account Notes:						1 2 3 4 5	
Day	Total Trades	Number Wins	Number Losses	Gross $ P/L	Com* $	Daily Net $ P/L	Running Acct. Bal.
Mon.							
Tue.							
Wed.							
Thu.							
Fri.							
Sat.							
Sun.							
Totals:							

*Commission

4: A. Starting Balance Sheet

FORM 9.6 Starting Balance Sheet—Template

Starting Business Balance Sheet	Date:
Description:	**Balance:**
Current Assets—from 1: C.6 and 1: C.7	
Checking account	
1. Broker account	
2. Broker account	
3. Broker account	
4. Broker account	
5. Broker account	
6. Broker account	
Assets total:	
Current Liabilities—from 1: C.9	
1. Loan:	
2. Credit card:	
3. Other:	
Liabilities total:	

4: B. Cash Flow Forecasts

FORM 9.7   Monthly Cash Flow Forecast—Template

Monthly Cash Flow Forecast

Starting cash position—from 1: E.2	$
Estimated gross profit/loss—from 1: E.6	$
Monthly Expenses:	
Salary to business owner—from 1: E.3	$
Fixed expenses—from 1: E.4	$
Net change in cash	$
Ending cash position	$

FORM 9.8   Annual Cash Flow Forecast—Template

Annual Cash Flow Forecast

Month	Starting Cash	Net Change	Ending Cash
Jan.			
Feb.			
Mar.			
Apr.			
May			
June			
July			
Aug.			
Sep.			
Oct.			
Nov.			
Dec.			

4: C. Profit and Loss History

FORM 9.9 Annual Trade Ledger—Profit and Loss History Report

Cumulative Annual P/L History for All Accounts						YEAR:	
Month	Total Trades	Number Wins	Number Losses	Gross $ P/L	Com* $	Monthly Net $ P/L	Running Acct. Bal.
Jan.							
Feb.							
Mar.							
Apr.							
May							
June							
July							
Aug.							
Sep.							
Oct.							
Nov.							
Dec.							
Totals:							

FORM 9.10 Monthly Trade Ledger—Individual Accounts

Monthly P/L History for Account # :						Month:	
Broker Name:						Year:	
Account Notes:							
Week	Total Trades	Number Wins	Number Losses	Gross $ P/L	Com* $	Weekly Net $ P/L	Running Acct. Bal.
1							
2							
3							
4							
5							
Totals:							

Prepare a separate monthly trade ledger for each of your brokerage accounts, including test accounts, paper trading accounts, and live trading accounts.
*Commission

4: D. Key Performance Ratios

Tracking your performance is crucial in maintaining consistent profitability. For more detail on payoff and win ratios you can refer to page 184 in this book.

Your *win ratio* represents your percentage of wins and your probability of winning. For example, if your win ratio is 40 percent, you have 40 percent winning trades and 60 percent losing trades.

Your *payoff ratio* is your average winning trade dollar amount divided by your average losing trade dollar amount. This represents how many dollars you earn compared to each dollar lost. For example , a payoff ratio of 3 to 1 would mean you earn three dollars for every dollar you lose.

4: D.1. Current payoff ratio: _____

4: D.2. Current win ratio: _____

BUSINESS PLAN TIPS

Once you have completed your business plan, stick to it. You can make notes on it and adapt it along the way if needed, but be always mindful of the plan. If you need accountability to stay on track, assign someone to be your conscience—someone you can check in with weekly or monthly to debrief with and evaluate your progress with. Select someone you feel comfortable with, such as a spouse, coach, mentor, or friend. The person doesn't necessarily need to be experienced in the financial field but they must be respectful of your goals and dedicated to helping you attain them.

Investors and position traders creating this kind of business plan will approach it differently than a trader in that they most likely will have an additional source of income or salary. For them the plan will serve as a way to be sure that they are on track with their investment portfolios in the face of market fluctuations and changing personal needs.

Often a knowledgeable financial adviser can be a good partner in preparing this kind of business plan, but ultimately it is your vision that is the key in shaping the outcome of the plan. You know your goals and needs better than anyone else, and if you lay out this plan you will be taking greater control of your financial destiny.

PART II

The Financial Pie

CHAPTER 10

The First Slice

Trading and Investing Rules

T he first slice of the "financial pie" (see Figure I.1 in the Introduction) and the first step for you, is to develop your *trading and investing rules*. This is not a solely independent part of trading success since it is completely dependent on your ability to master the other three slices of the pie, which are *scanning for opportunities, money management,* and *financial psychology.* All four of these pieces of the pie are equally essential in attaining trading success and profitability.

This chapter, The First Slice: Trading and Investing Rules, is designed to show you how to survive the development phase of building a system that is consistently profitable. Generally, traders tend to skip this part of the process. This chapter is *not* intended to give you the tools to create your profitable trading rules, since that is a vast and varied topic that is beyond the scope of this book. You will need instead to investigate this topic yourself, and there are many valid sources to go to for this, many of which are listed at the back of this book in Appendix D (Suggested Reading and Education).

You've probably heard the staggering statistic that 90 percent of all traders lose money in the markets, and only 5 percent actually are consistently profitable. The reason these statistics are so dramatic is because traders and investors enter the markets with real money and live trading accounts *before* they have developed profitable trading rules.

Human nature typically is such that we want instant and easy results. Most individuals are impatient and do not have the focus and determination to develop a successful system *before* trading with real money. They are like moths to the flame; wanting to get in the market with real money. And 90 percent of them get burned by the flame. You will need to resist this temptation if you want to survive.

DEVELOP AND TEST YOUR SYSTEM

Developing a profitable trading and investing system will require that you do your homework. If you already have a profitable system in place, then you are in terrific shape and can more or less skip this chapter.

But, if you are just starting out and have not yet developed a system, you will need to wholeheartedly dedicate yourself to this task. Many new traders have the illusion that they can purchase a software package, or a trading system or trading course, and hit the ground running with a profitable approach right off the bat.

What you will find if you are a novice, and what you already know if you are experienced, is that it is not that easy. If it were that easy, there wouldn't be a 90 percent failure among all traders. This is why, if you have the tenacity to apply yourself, you will have an edge in the market. In contrast, if you do not have the ability to persevere through this part of the process, you will be doomed to failure.

PERSEVERANCE IS THE HOLY GRAIL

What I've found in this business is that those who survive and prosper for the long term are the traders who can persevere through thick and thin and just keep going with new solutions and strategies. If there is a number-one quality that a trader needs to succeed, it is perseverance.

You've got to have the *drive* to come up with solutions that work and also *learn* from the solutions that don't work. You've got to look at every disappointment as an opportunity. This part of the process is really challenging, and frankly, not everyone has the ability to survive this part of the process.

Usually the traders who are not successful fail not because they aren't smart enough. They fail instead because they don't *persevere* enough to reach consistent profitability. For example, if Thomas Edison had given up his work on inventing the light bulb before he created the thousandth prototype, he would have missed success—because it took one thousand attempts before he finally created a working model of the light bulb we all know and use today.

This is why it is best for you to conduct a parallel test, meaning that until you have a profitable system developed, do not quit your day job to trade full-time. When you prepare your business plan (see Chapter 9), set your business up as a part-time venture. This is a very common path that traders take while they are developing a profitable approach. This path has a greater outcome of success, since you will not be faced with the added stress of worrying about meeting your monthly overhead expenses.

Think of your new trading company just as if it were a big corporation that has an entire department devoted to research and development. The only difference is that, unless you are teaming up with a partner, *you* will be the entire department. You'll be just like a scientist in a laboratory working on a new cure for some life-threatening disease, and when you find the cure, you will have hit pay dirt.

FAILURE IS NOT AN OPTION

So I'm visualizing you with your new trading company, working on your trading at night when you get home from your day job. You're tired, and you've been working steadily on your trading rules but your paper trading just took a turn for the worse and you've got a 20 percent drawdown in your practice account. You are feeling pretty discouraged, and are just about ready to quit.

This is a time when you will need to look for motivational support from either a trading coach, a trading buddy, or a trusted family member. It is during the times when you want to give up that you have to step back and gain perspective. You've got to have the feeling that "failure is not an option" and just "work the problem." You've got to have purpose and a reason for achieving this goal of creating a set of trading rules that are consistently profitable.

If you haven't already seen the movie *Apollo 13* about NASA's 1970 Apollo mission that almost did not make it home, you must see it. The remarkable teamwork of the ground crew working together to bring the three crew members aboard the ship home safely is a unique and miraculous true story.

"Houston, we have a problem . . ." is probably the most famous line of the movie. But my personal favorite line of the movie occurs when Gene Kranz, the flight director, says to his team very sternly when they are feeling discouraged, "Gentlemen, listen up! NASA has never lost a man in space, and I'll not let us lose a man in space on my watch. *Failure is not an option."* Gene Kranz was a motivator and had the right mind-set to create solutions when everyone else envisioned the likelihood of failure.

That sums up in a snapshot the mind-set you must have to succeed when faced with a challenge. You've got to have purpose and the will-power to motivate yourself to find the right solutions to the challenges that present themselves to you.

CREATING YOUR TRADING RULES PROFILE

Determining your *trading rules profile* is the first step in designing your rules. You must be able to fill in this profile before you can effectively develop rules that will be profitable for your situation.

Fill out your own custom profile by using the blank triangle chart in Figure 10.1. You can see that your profile consists of four important pieces of information: (1) signal type, (2) frequency, (3) style, and (4) market(s). This profile will be the cornerstone to your trading rules.

Next, look at Table 10.1 and Figures 10.2 through 10.7, which show six different profiles that are for example only. This table and these six sample illustrations can be used for reference to get a sense of what the spectrum of possibility is. Remember, where you start today is just the beginning. Your trading rules will be a work in progress and you may adapt any of the items in your profile, from changing the markets you trade to changing the frequency you trade.

TABLE 10.1 Sample Trading Rules Profiles

	Figure #	Signal Type	Frequency	Style	Markets
Profile A	10.2	Technical	Position trader	Trend	S&P E-mini and NASDAQ E-mini
Profile B	10.3	Technical	Day trader	Scalp	Forex and ETFs
Profile C	10.4	Fundamental	Investor	Trend	Stocks and mutual funds
Profile D	10.5	Fundamental	Position trader	Scalp	Stocks and ETFs
Profile E	10.6	Technical and fundamental	Investor	Trend	Bonds and indexes
Profile F	10.7	Technical and fundamental	Day trader	Scalp	Stocks and futures

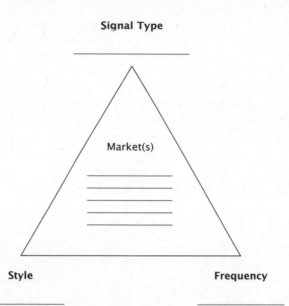

FIGURE 10.1   Blank Trading Rules Profile for You to Fill In

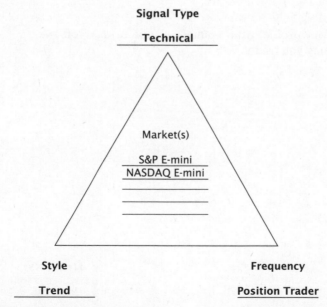

FIGURE 10.2   Sample Trading Rules Profile A

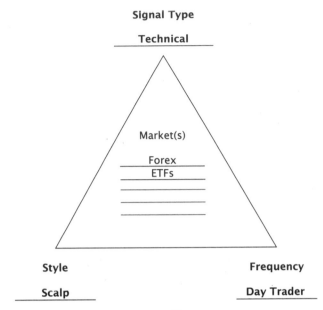

FIGURE 10.3   Sample Trading Rules Profile B

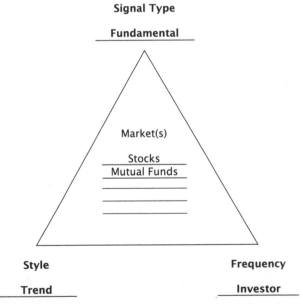

FIGURE 10.4   Sample Trading Rules Profile C

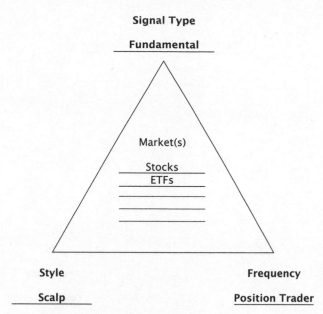

FIGURE 10.5 Sample Trading Rules Profile D

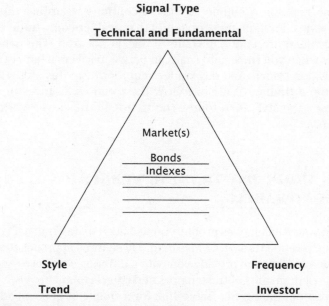

FIGURE 10.6 Sample Trading Rules Profile E

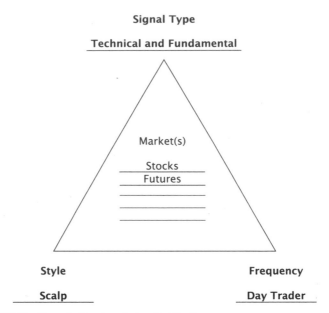

FIGURE 10.7   Sample Trading Rules Profile F

Let me mention a couple of misconceptions regarding trading and investing styles. First, many people feel that scalpers only trade the lower time frames and are only day traders, that is not true. The definition of scalping is when you trade, and scalp, in between reversal bars in *any* time frame. Position traders and day traders can both use this style. The same goes for trend trading. You can follow the trend as an investor or a day trader, again, the style is to follow the trend and this style works on any time frame.

A NOTE ABOUT DAY TRADING VERSUS POSITION TRADING

In creating your trading rules profile, you will need to determine if you will be day trading, position trading, or investing. These three approaches are different from one another and provide you with a differing set of pros and cons.

The most dramatic contrast in pros and cons is found between day trading and position trading. See Table 10.2 for a snapshot of some advantages and disadvantages of each. Carefully consider your personal situation and what will be the best approach for you at this time.

- **A day trader** is anyone who closes out a trading account to cash every night, and looks at shorter intraday time frames like the one-minute, five-minute, and 10-minute charts. Trades can last from minutes to hours.
- **A position trader** is anyone who can stay in a trade overnight, can assume overnight risk, does not need to convert to cash every night, and looks at longer time frames like the daily and weekly charts. Trades can last for days, weeks, or months.

As you can see in Table 10.2, there are a number of differences between day trading and position trading. You may encounter varying schools of thought regarding which path to take when you are a novice trader. Some believe that position trading is the best solution for new traders because the pace is slower and it is easier for the novice to process market information at this pace. Others will argue that the faster pace forces you to learn faster when you day trade.

The most significant difference between day trading and position trading is the speed at which your profit and loss can move and change. In day trading, the profit and loss feedback comes at you much faster and you need to be able to handle that emotionally. As a position trader, the pace is slower so it is easier to process the wins and losses from a psychological stand point.

Ultimately, you're the one to decide what is right for you at this time and place. You may have the personality that needs to be involved in faster action because of your nature, so you may prefer day trading. Or you may prefer to be involved in slower action and choose position trading. It comes down to knowing yourself and what will work for you.

I will say one thing about position trading as opposed to day trading, and that is you can make a very good living from position trading. By making fewer trades and capitalizing on overnight risk opportunities, you will lower your commission expenses and can very often come out with a better net profit at the end of the year.

However, when using margin, day traders in the futures markets can obtain more margin at a lower cost than traders in other markets. This is an advantage that gives you more opportunity to make a profit. As always, use caution when applying margin to your approach, and be sure to keep your risk in alignment with your account size. Check with your broker for current margin rates and restrictions.

TABLE 10.2 Pros and Cons of Being a Day Trader and Being a Position Trader

Day Traders		Position Traders	
They close all positions out to cash at night and use intraday time frame charts like the two-minute and five-minute. Trades can last from minutes to hours.		They hold positions overnight and use longer time frame charts like the daily, weekly, and monthly. Trades can last a day, a week, or months at a time.	
Pros	**Cons**	**Pros**	**Cons**
Have no exposure to overnight risk because all trades are closed out each night.	Cannot capitalize on overnight risk opportunities; all trades are closed out each night.	Can capitalize on overnight risk opportunities.	Have exposure to overnight risk because trades can be held for weeks or months at a time.
Can have a smaller trading account size since risk distance between entry and stop-loss exit is smaller.	Pay more in commissions because day traders place more trades than position traders do.	Pay less in commissions because position traders place fewer trades than day traders do.	Have to have a larger trading account size to accommodate overnight risk.
Place more trades than position traders, so they gain more experience in a shorter period of time.	Day trading requires more skill and experience to be profitable due to the advanced psychology required to manage fast-paced wins and losses.	Position trading is often considered the best time frame for new and novice traders because there is more time to psychologically process wins and losses.	Place fewer trades than day traders, so it takes a longer amount of time for them to gain experience.

HOLDING TRADES OVERNIGHT AND ASSUMING OVERNIGHT RISK

When holding trades overnight, you inherently are exposed to greater risk. For example, if you were trading a 15-minute time frame, your stop loss and position size will be based on the 15-minute chart. But let's say you are five minutes from the close of the day and the trade is profitable, and much more profit is possible if you hold the trade overnight based on the 15-minute chart.

Here are the five rules of engagement for an overnight trade:

1. The trade must currently be profitable.
2. The 15-minute chart must indicate a solid trend in place.
3. You must set a new stop loss based on the daily chart.
4. Reduce trade size so that risk remains no more than 2 percent of your trading account (based on the new adjusted stop from the daily chart).
5. Monitor the trade at the opening bell the next morning.

The key is to be sure to adjust all of your money management parameters to allow for the added risk of holding a trade overnight. And then you need to be ready to monitor the trade immediately at the opening bell.

MY DEFINITION OF SCALPING

There are many definitions of scalping the markets. Some traders believe that any form of day trading at all is considered scalping. This is not true, because you can day trade and scalp intraday charts like the one-minute and five-minute charts *but* you can also position trade and scalp charts like the daily, weekly, and monthly.

The distinction here is that the definition of scalping has nothing to do with the *time frame* of trading; it has everything to do with the *style* of trading. Scalping is a style of trading where you take quick profits that occur in between pivot points in channeling markets, regardless of whether the channel occurs on a one-minute day trading chart or on a daily position trading chart.

My definition: Scalping is any trading style that is *not* trend trading.

SAMPLE TRADING RULES TO START WITH

You will ultimately do your own research to determine what the most profitable rules are for you in your unique situation, in the market you are trading, and for the time frame you are trading. You will find that identifying effective commonsense rules is simple. Adhering to the rules can sometimes be more challenging than identifying them.

To kick off your research, here are some popular entry and exit rules that have stood the test of time:

- **Enter and go long when a bull market begins.** A bull market is defined as having higher highs and higher lows.
- **Enter and go short when a bear market begins.** A bear market is defined as having lower highs and lower lows.
- **Do not add in to a losing position.**
- **Exit upon a reversal in trend.**
- **Scale out upon a hyperbolic profitable move.** And wait for your stop to be hit before exiting the entire position.
- **Diversify your trades among sectors.**
- **Utilize stop-loss exits.**
- **Use trailing stops.** This will enable you to lock in profit as the position goes in your favor and will help you avoid having a winning position turn into a losing position.
- **Carefully calculate trade size to limit risk.** Generally, the trade size risk amount should be less than 2 percent of one's trading account size. That way if the trade gets stopped out the most you would lose would be 2 percent of your account. Example: Account $10,000 \times 2\% = \$200$.
- **Reduce trade size during a drawdown.**
- **Increase trade size during winning streaks.**
- **DOT—don't over trade.**
- **Carefully select the right orders to enter the market.** See list of order types in Chapter 6.

The key to success in implementing the aforementioned rules is identifying the various signals, such as bull market, bear market, reversal in trend, hyperbolic move, and so on. For this you will require information from either a technical source, a fundamental source, or a combination of these two.

There are many software providers, news feeds, and other tools that can enable you to obtain reliable signals. Part of your due diligence is to identify the best tools for your specific situation and utilize those tools.

COMBINING FUNDAMENTAL AND TECHNICAL SIGNALS IN YOUR TRADING RULES

When analyzing a financial market, we usually isolate our analysis into either fundamental or technical analysis. This is similar to when one talks about investors versus traders. Investors tend to rely on fundamental analysis, whereas traders tend to rely on technical analysis.

- **Fundamental analysis** is the analysis of published data that is widely recognized as being fundamentally factual. There is a variety of information available, including corporate data such as earnings, growth rate, price-earnings (P/E) ratio, and debt-equity ratio. Markets are also affected by economic reports such as unemployment, retail sales, and interest rates. For commodities and currency markets important data may include weather reports that affect crop prices, political developments that affect currencies, and so on.
- **Technical analysis** is the analysis of historical price and volume patterns in the financial markets. These historical patterns are used to determine probabilities of *future* price and volume activity. Basically, this analysis uses the past to predict probabilities of what the future will be. The analysis interprets actual buy and sell activity in the market, or current sentiment, and determines if the patterns are similar to prior patterns.

Up until the past 15 years or so, most analysis was fundamental simply because high-powered computers and technical analysis software were not readily available to a vast majority of individuals. Now the playing field has been leveled and even the individual investor has high-end tools.

These analysis tools—computers and financial analysis software—enable you to number crunch enormous amounts of data in a very short amount of time. So you can sort through mountains of fundamental data, technical data, or a combination of the two, and come up with the highest-probability trades.

This is all the more reason to acquaint yourself with both types of analysis and combine them for a powerful result.

TECHNICAL ANALYSIS SIGNALS

Technical analysis is a method of evaluating financial instruments by analyzing statistics generated by market activity, such as price and volume. The technical analyst is looking for patterns that occur in the current market that may be similar to previous historical patterns. This analysis is designed to identify high-probability setups based on patterns that may have resulted in a profitable outcome in the past.

Of course the standard disclaimer on every technical analysis product is that past performance does not guarantee future results, since the profitable outcome that may have been achieved in the past does not guarantee that a profitable outcome will be achieved in the future. The future is always an unknown quantity.

IIence, the job of the technical trader is to estimate probabilities of certain outcomes, and then enter trades that have the highest probabilities for success. Learning to accurately determine these probabilities can take years of experience to master.

One advantage of pure technical analysis over fundamental analysis is that the nature of the signal is based solely on reality and not on opinion or interpretation. Plus, the price and volume figures coming from the exchange cannot be altered or distorted by creative accounting. Until recent times, this did not seem like a huge factor, but with the current misdeeds of companies such as Enron and the like, it is now a consideration. Since companies can distort their reporting of earnings, debt, assets, liabilities, and such, fundamental analysis is flawed to the degree that you can't always believe what you hear, or what you read in your annual report.

With technical analysis, there can be delays in data delivery that can distort the reality of the data, but this factor will affect only day traders for the most part. By selecting high-end data providers, this delay in data can be reduced dramatically.

When reading technical analysis data from the markets, you will be looking at charts. These charts are made up of data that is plotted on an x-axis and a y-axis to show the movement of price, time, and volume. Charts illustrate how price, time, and volume look on paper and what kind of pattern they form.

Important Note: Charts can create optical illusions, depending how they are presented. For example, a more condensed chart will look more severe than a chart that is expanded. Pay attention to how you adjust your charts to be sure you are seeing the reality of the information. Go to Chapter 13 for more information and illustrations of this phenomenon.

Charts come in a variety of forms, including:

- Bar chart.
- Candlestick chart.
- Line chart.

In a bar chart, for example, each individual *price bar* tells a story. One price bar represents the interval of time that the price bar is illustrating. For example, a one-minute price bar shows you what happened for a 60-second period.

Here is the information you will see on this one price bar: (1) the open price, with a line to the left; (2) the close price, with a line to the right; (3) the high price, the top of the bar; and (4) the low price, the bottom of the bar. (See Figure 10.8.) The OHLC, or the open, high, low, and close of the bar, tells a complete story in a visually concise format.

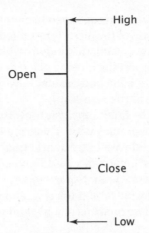

FIGURE 10.8 Price Bar
This is an illustration of a price bar showing the price open and close and the price high and low of this interval, the acronym for this is OHLC.

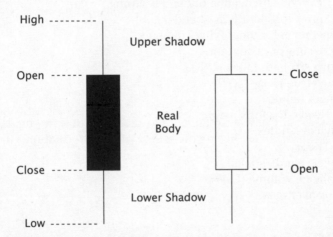

FIGURE 10.9 Candlestick
This is an illustration of a candlestick showing the price open and close and the price high and low of this interval.

In a candlestick chart, each individual *candlestick* tells a story. One candlestick represents the interval of time that the candlestick is illustrating. For example, a one-minute candlestick shows you what happened for a 60-second period. Just as with a price bar, you will see the open, close, high, and low price of that period. (See Figure 10.9.)

There are special names associated with each area of a candlestick, such as the body (black or white) and an upper and a lower shadow (wick).

The area between the open and the close is called the real body, and price excursions above and below the body are called shadows. If the candlestick closed higher than it opened, the body is white, with the opening price at the bottom of the body and the closing price at the top. If the candlestick closed lower than it opened, the body is black, with the opening price at the top and the closing price at the bottom.

There are a variety of technical analysis tools that can generate signals for you to carry out your trading rules with. There are hundreds if not thousands of choices you will be faced with in the marketplace. One word of caution is that you must match your personality and mind-set with the type of tool or tools that you decide to work with. Not every set of signals works for everyone, so testing will reveal what works for *you*, and that is *all* that matters.

Here are a few technical analysis signals and tools that can be the basis for your trading rules:

- Primary Pyramid Trading Point® for entries and exits and risk control.
- Minor Pyramid Trading Point® for scaling out and scalping.
- ART Reversals for scaling out and scalping.
- Trend lines for identifying trends.
- Channel lines for identifying channels.
- Price oscillator histogram.
- Relative strength index (RSI).
- Average true range (ATR).
- Bollinger bands.
- Elliott wave for forecasting.
- Fibonacci studies.
- Dow Theory.
- Japanese candlesticks.
- On balance volume (OBV).
- Moving averages.

FUNDAMENTAL ANALYSIS SIGNALS

Fundamental analysis means that you are basing your entries and exits on Federal Reserve reports, corporate annual reports, news, weather reports, and other public data that pertain to the current stability of the instrument you are trading.

Fundamental analysis is a completely different animal altogether than technical analysis. My approach to trading is primarily a technical approach, but fundamentals clearly play a significant role in many traders' sets of profitable rules. The key for you is to decide what your preference is—fundamental or technical, or a combination of the two—and then design your rules around this preference.

Here are a few illustrations of ways a fundamental approach can operate. Some of these fundamentals are used for long-term positions, and some are for short-term positions.

- Weather forecasts predict freezing temperatures in Florida this year, so you go long the commodity orange juice because the price will go up due to low supply and high demand.
- A cell phone maker's stock is downgraded; the value of its shares drops significantly, so you go short.
- There is unrest in the Middle East, which historically leads to higher prices in oil; you go long on crude oil.
- There are rumors that the CEO of XYZ Corporation will be indicted for illegal activity, so you short the XYZ Corporation.
- A tsunami hits Japan and creates devastation; the Japanese Yen drops dramatically.
- The U.S. unemployment report comes out with a rise in new jobs, and the economy looks like it is recovering; the stock market rallies.
- The Fed announces a major rise in interest rates, so you go long on bonds.
- Wal-Mart releases higher than expected quarterly earnings, so you go long on Wal-Mart.
- You research a company and find that its price-earnings growth (PEG) ratio is less than 1 (meaning it is undervalued), its return on equity is better than its competitors by 25 percent, and its debt-to-equity ratio is 10 percent, so you go long on that stock.
- Your individual retirement account (IRA) mutual fund holdings are not performing well; you research to find a mutual fund that has better historical performance numbers, and switch over to that fund.

It is crucial that you are accessing fundamental data the second it is released, so that you are in front of the herd when entering or exiting the market. In this regard, it is much like technical analysis in that it is important to have live, streaming, real-time data that is not delayed. The older the news or information, the less value it will have for you.

Here are some general types of data, reports, and information used in making fundamental analysis decisions:

- Weather reports and predictions.
- Federal reports on unemployment, gross domestic product (GDP) growth, and so on.
- Federal Reserve announcements on interest rates.
- Corporate annual reports.
- Quarterly corporate earnings reports.
- News services.
- Newspapers, such as the *Wall Street Journal* and the *New York Times*.

- Internet sites.
- On-site physical observations of weather, corporate sales activity, and so on.

Accurate presumptions and assumptions can get you into the market before the herd. In other words, if you can connect the dots and make accurate assumptions, you may be able to get a jump on a profitable trade. Say you are able to observe weather conditions and effects of such by actually living in Brazil; you may be able to get more accurate and more pertinent data and thereby make more accurate assumptions about making trades in the coffee commodities market.

VALUE INVESTING IN A BEAR MARKET

Value investing is a popular technique made famous by Benjamin Graham and Warren Buffett. Value investors all look extremely smart during a strong bull market, which we experienced for about 25 years from the early 1980s all the way until October 2007. The reason value investors looked smart during the bull market was because during this period, for the most part, if you put money in the stock market and waited a few years you were likely to make a comfortable profit.

Then the market cycle began to change, and companies that looked too big to fail started to collapse. The buy-and-hold or value investing strategy didn't work the way it had for so long; hence the "past performance does not guarantee future results" disclaimer comes to mind.

The world has entered a bear market in which the value investing or buy-and-hold strategy needs to be reassessed. In this new age, it is more important than ever to be educated and look at the big picture. If you are a value investor, you must always have your eye on the ball to be sure that the companies you have selected to invest in are performing the way you had planned. Do not fall prey to the devastation of a bear market; watch your portfolio carefully at all times.

THE IMPORTANCE OF PAPER TRADING

It's beneficial to be profitable by *paper trading* first before trading with real money. While paper trading will not have exactly the same psychological feel as trading with real money, it is a useful way to practice your trading skills in a risk-free environment so that you can focus on your financial approach and trading rules. Paper trading gives you time to hone your trading skills without losing money.

Those of you who are students of mine or have read my book *The ART of Trading* already know my position in favor of paper trading. Ironically, this topic is frequently debated and there are a few traders who have gone on record as opposing the entire idea. We'll go into the pros and cons of the subject in the following pages.

Every financial market is a championship arena, and trading is a zero-sum game. When you enter any financial market, you will be competing against some very skilled professionals. If you enter the market with your hard-earned money as a novice, you will be competing against traders who have more skill, more experience, and a larger account size. To give yourself a fighting chance, you need to enter the markets as a skilled professional. Anything less will make it impossible to succeed in trading on a consistent basis.

The safest way to develop your trading skills is by paper trading, which allows you to practice without the pressure of potentially losing money. If you cannot be profitable paper trading, how on earth do you plan to be profitable trading with real money and more stress?

As I mentioned earlier, some traders oppose paper trading; they believe that it is useless because you won't feel the psychological emotions that you experience when trading with real money. I strongly disagree with this. As a matter of fact, in the beginning you will find that, surprisingly enough, paper trading creates an emotional roller coaster similar to trading with real money. That is, it does if you approach paper trading with the same dedication.

The deeper psychological and emotional aspects of trading your hard-earned money can be worked on later after you have developed your trading skills. It is first better to have your approach developed through paper trading and then work on developing a deeper trading psychology over time.

Don't be impatient with your paper trading. Allow yourself time to develop your trading skills and approach. This is time very well spent, so there are no shortcuts here. Here are 10 steps for completing a thorough paper-trading test of your trading rules. Check off each one as you complete it.

Paper Trading 10-Step Plan

1. **Design your trading rules and your money management rules.** After you have designed your trading rules (technical, fundamental, or a combination of the two), then write them down on paper in a checklist format. Cover every aspect of your entries, exits, and overall methodology. In addition, get your money management rules written down in the same way.

2. **Start to paper trade.** Once you are clear on your rules, start paper trading on the same time frame, in the same financial market, and with

the account size you plan to work with when you use real money. If you have the time to day trade, it is best for you to paper trade your favorite market. Day trading will shorten your learning curve because you will trade more often and gain more experience for a given period of time. See whether trend trading, scalping, scaling in, or scaling out suits you best. Through trial and error in a safe paper-trading environment, you will be able to determine if you need to adapt your rules.

3. **Evaluate your performance.** Keep track of your paper-trading results and approach as if you were trading with real money. You can use The Trader's Assistant™ record-keeping system. You will find blank forms printed in my book *A Trader's Money Management System*, released by John Wiley & Sons in 2008.

4. **Group in lots of 25 trades.** Group your paper trades in lots of 25 trades each, and calculate your profit/loss, average win/loss, largest win/loss, number of winning trades, number of losing trades, number of consecutive winning trades, and number of consecutive losing trades. A group of 25 consecutive trades that has a profitable outcome is a profitable lot.

5. **Practice until profitable.** Analyze your paper-trading results and make adjustments until you are profitable and feel good about your trading.

6. **Have three profitable lots of 25 trades.** Before trading with real money, be sure you have a total of three consecutive profitable lots of 25 trades each while paper trading. And if you're a day trader, be sure to spread your day trading over enough days, weeks, or months so you experience uptrending, downtrending, and bracketed markets. You can achieve this by using a *playback* feature that is available on some front-end platforms.

7. **Keep trading in lots of 25 trades.** When trading with real money, keep using the 25-trade lot size to analyze your profit/loss, win/loss, and so on, and see how you are doing.

8. **Reevaluate your approach.** If you are not profitable trading with real money after trading one lot of 25 trades, stop trading and go back to paper trading again. If at this point you are immediately profitable paper trading, then chances are your psychology is the problem and you may need some additional help from a trading coach to uncover your psychological sabotage issues. But if your paper trading is not immediately profitable this time, then you may have just been lucky the first time and did not paper trade long enough to experience the different types of market cycles. Your trading approach needs to be adjusted. Until you have a qualified trading approach as proven

through how you paper trade, then you will not know if your problem lies in your trading approach or with your psychology.

9. **Experiencing drawdown.** If you experience six consecutive losing trades and/or a drawdown of more than 15 percent, the market cycle or volatility in the market and time frame you are trading has probably changed. You must adapt quickly and effectively to these changes.

10. **During an excessive drawdown, follow these steps.** (1) Stop trading with real money. Keep trading the same market and time frame and go back to paper trading. Wait until you have three winning lots of 25 paper trades before trading with real money again. (2) Make adjustments to your rules to see if doing so eliminates the losses you incurred in your recent drawdown. If so, paper trade again to validate your adjustments. (3) Change time frames until you find the time frame that works best.

Getting back to the traders I mentioned earlier who feel paper trading is not beneficial, it seems valuable at this time to address the most common objections to a paper-trading approach.

Here are the objections I hear most often:

- **Paper trading doesn't subject you to the same emotions.** You know that may be true to a point, yet it doesn't seem intelligent to use that as an argument. In medical school, would it make sense for surgeons to operate on live patients before they really know what they are doing? I don't think so. Trading is a life-or-death situation—your financial life or death, that is. Treat it with the respect it deserves, and paper trade until you know what you are doing.
- **You'll get addicted to paper trading.** I guess there are people who feel they'll be afraid to pull the trigger with real money if they paper trade too long. Here's the thing: If you know that your plan says you must have three sets of consecutive trades (25 trades in each set) that are profitable sets before you go live with real money, why be afraid to pull the trigger? If you prove to yourself you can be profitable, there is no problem. Then if you prove to yourself you can't be profitable, you'd better fix the problem.
- **Back-testing is the only way to test a system.** There are lots of ways to back-test. In essence, paper trading is one of the ways you can back-test. The eSignal platform has a great playback feature where you can take data from the day (or week or month or year) and play it back. You can in a sense paper trade a live market. Granted, technically it is not live, but if you play it forward one price bar at a time, you will experience it as if you were trading it live. The value of testing

your system in this way is that not only are you testing your system rules, but you are also testing your ability to follow those rules.

- **It's too much work.** Yes, it requires dedication and work to complete three sets of 25 profitable trades. But then again, anything of real value usually requires some work. The value acquired from this type of paper trading produces results. I've seen it time and time again. The question is: Are you under the illusion that trading profits will be quick and easy? And, if you enjoy the actual process of your trading, it won't seem like work since every step of progress will give you great satisfaction.

- **Paper trading is for sissies.** Well, no one has ever really said that to me, but the implication is there. You know, real men don't paper trade (or eat quiche); if you are man enough (or woman enough) to trade with real money, you can win in the markets, and so forth. It just seems like there is this macho thing where traders feel that "I'm tough enough to get my ass kicked, and that's how I'm going to learn." The reality is that even after profitably paper trading, chances are you'll get your ass kicked at some point or another anyway. The difference is that when you do, you'll have a better idea of why it happened and how to prevent it in the future.

All that matters right now is: What do you think about paper trading? My sincere hope is that you see the benefit and will implement a paper-trading plan to test your rules and see how they hold up prior to putting your money on the line.

And for the more advanced traders who already know from experience that they have a winning system, keep an open mind and paper trade through any challenging drawdowns. Test a new trading idea or approach by paper trading it to see if your drawdown might be the catalyst for a new way of trading.

SET UP MULTIPLE BROKERAGE ACCOUNTS TO MONITOR YOUR TRADING RESULTS

After your paper-trading phase when you are trading live, you will want to have separate accounts for each type of trading you are doing. For example, have three separate accounts for the following:

1. Day trading account.
2. Position trading account.
3. Investing account.

You may also decide that it helps to separate your accounts by market as well, such as separate accounts for futures, stocks, and forex, depending on how many markets you decide to trade. Because of the different needs of each type of market, from the margin parameters to the expiration of contracts, you will find having different accounts will organize your approach.

This separation of accounts will also assist you in analyzing results more easily between the different types of trading to determine which types are more profitable. You can also determine which time frames, markets, and approaches are more profitable. Look to see which market cycles each does better in as well.

Another benefit of this approach is that you will naturally be diversifying your portfolio among various markets and time frames, thereby lowering your risk.

CHAPTER 11

The Second Slice

Scanning for Opportunities

The second slice of the "financial pie" (see Figure I.1 in the Introduction of this book) is *scanning for opportunities*. The question "*How* do you find opportunities?" is going to be answered differently for each person, depending on what kind of trader you are and what markets you are trading. This chapter is designed to give you a starting point on how to most efficiently identify high-probability opportunities in the financial markets.

Your business plan and your trading rules will determine what you are going to scan or screen for, and the types of scans or screens you decide to use will in the end be implemented into your trading rules. These two areas are interconnected and work hand in hand.

When scanning, your goal is to begin with a broad universe of possible opportunities. You will then narrow down the universe to find the highest-probability opportunities. The idea is to be like a prospector who is sorting and sifting, looking for the nuggets of gold.

This is done by specifying conditions that need to be met. These conditions are based on your trading rules and historical performance results. Your previous successful trades and your trading rules will tell you what to look for and what are the best conditions that must be present in the market you are trading.

For example, if you are a trend trader and you have found that after a market has been in consolidation for a certain number of price bars it will most likely break out into a significant trend, either bullish or bearish, then you can scan the universe of stocks for this one condition and create a watch list. From this watch list you can then further narrow down your choices with other conditions based on your trading rules. This is a simple illustration of the basic idea of scanning for opportunities.

TECHNICAL SCANNING TECHNIQUES

There are many scanning techniques that technical traders will use for finding opportunities. These are standard scans that are available on a variety of front-end charting platforms; you can find a complete list of front-end platforms at the back of this book in Appendix C (Resources).

Examples of some popular technical scans are:

- Indicator-based conditions such as the Pyramid Trading Point®.
- Price-based conditions such as price crossing over the moving average.
- Volume-based conditions.
- Time-based conditions where you are only going to scan and trade during a specified time period.
- Bar data–based conditions such as comparing the last three bar highs or lows.
- Multiple conditions where you are scanning for two or more conditions at once, such as high volume combined with a bracketed market condition.
- Scanning multiple time frame charts such as one-minute, five-minute, 10-minute, daily, and weekly charts; can ensure that a trend is strongly in place on more than one time frame.
- Scanning for bracketed markets.

Popular Scanning Tools

There are a number of effective technical and fundamental scanning tools available to you that will save you time and enable you to take advantage of emerging opportunities more quickly. Here is a list of tools and companies that offer scanning features:

- TradersCoach.com, ART Scanner.
- eSignal.
- NinjaTrader, Market Analyzer.
- TradeStation, Radar Screen.
- Worden Brothers.

Do some research to determine what these companies offer and see if what they offer matches what you are looking for. The time you save by not having to do manual scans may justify the cost of purchasing software to assist you with this. The key is to determine specifically which scans you will be using, so that you are not subscribing to services you ultimately do not need.

Looking for Bracketed Markets Is a Technical Approach Used to Scan for Opportunities

Looking for a market that has been bracketed for an extended period of time is an excellent technical analysis scanning technique. You can do a scan to find such markets, which will have a high probability for a breakout trend. As the bracket becomes longer and narrower, it becomes more unstable and ready for a breakout. For trend traders, this scan creates a watch list of trades that could move at any time. The ART scanner has the ability to scan for bracketed markets that have a high probability of breaking out.

The value of using software tools for scanning is that they do all the heavy lifting. There was a time when scans of this nature had to be done manually, which can be a laborious task.

It is well worth the cost of buying the right software to expedite your scanning and speed up your action and reaction time, making you more able to get in and get out quickly when there are markets on the move. Of course, scanning software also saves your valuable time, which translates into saving you money.

Look at Figure 11.1 and Figure 11.2, which show screen shots of the ART Scanner finding bracketed markets. Figure 11.1 is a scan that was produced on the TradeStation platform using its RadarScreen feature. Figure 11.2 is a scan that was produced on the NinjaTrader platform using its Market Analyzer feature. Note how both platforms are able to do the same job, but each one displays the information in a slightly different way. Ultimately, it is your job to decide which platform suits you best.

FUNDAMENTAL SCANNING TECHNIQUES

There are many pieces of information that traders using fundamentals work with to find opportunities. Some of these fundamental scans are available as standard tools in a number of front-end platforms.

Symbol	Interval	Last	Net Chg	Net %Chg	High	Low	Volume Today	ART Scanner
AMAT	Weekly	13.80	-0.29	-2.06%	13.93	13.72	21,091,253	Bull P, Bull 1B
MSFT	Daily	24.14	-0.35	-1.43%	24.25	24.03	52,703,425	Bull P, Bull 1B, Bear Breakout
INTC	Daily	22.85	-0.37	-1.59%	23.03	22.76	64,894,030	Bull P, Bear 2B, Bracketed
AMD(D)	Daily	8.49	-0.13	-1.51%	8.69	8.45	16,884,857	Bull P, Bull 2B, Bracketed
ESH11	2 Min	1291.00	3.29	0.26%	0.00	0.00	0	Bull P, Bull 2B, Bracketed
QQQ	2 Min	56.90	-0.86	-1.50%	57.15	56.65	43,678,437	Unconfirmed Bear P, Bull P, Bear 2B, Bracketed
DIA(D)	2 Min	123.39	-1.46	-1.17%	123.88	123.03	5,912,935	Bear P, Bear 1B, Bracketed
SBUX	Daily	36.44	-0.17	-0.46%	36.75	35.94	6,055,433	Bull P, Bear 2B, Bracketed
AAPL	Daily	334.50	-0.72	-0.21%	335.98	329.42	13,661,031	Bear P, Bull 1B, Bracketed
GE(D)	Daily	19.36	-0.26	-1.33%	19.48	19.13	39,042,352	Bull MP, Bull 1B, Bracketed, Bear Breakout
F(D)	Daily	14.80	-0.20	-1.33%	14.93	14.65	49,541,838	Bear P, Bear 1B, Bracketed, Bear Breakout
BAC(D)	Daily	11.40	-0.18	-1.55%	11.52	11.38	122,145,885	Bear P, Bull 1B, Bear Breakout
GLD(D)	Daily	147.60	0.11	0.07%	147.95	146.97	15,946,475	Unconfirmed Bull P, Unconfirmed Bear P, Unconfirmed Bull P, Bull P, Bull 2B, Bracketed
C(D)	Daily	40.10	-0.92	-2.24%	40.64	40.06	34,732,735	Bear P, Bull 1B
CAG(D)	Daily	25.44	-0.08	-0.32%	25.54	25.30	2,581,931	Bull P, Bear 2B, Bracketed
YHOO	Daily	16.06	-0.24	-1.47%	16.17	16.00	19,252,089	Bear MP, Bull 2B
GOOG	Daily	518.39	-5.64	-1.08%	520.00	513.40	2,252,638	Bear P, Bull 1B, Bracketed
XOM(D)	Daily	80.61	-0.96	-1.18%	81.01	80.07	16,300,482	Bull P, Bear 2B, Bracketed
URE(D)	Daily	58.96	-1.51	-2.50%	59.73	59.00	556,501	Bull P, Bear 2B, Bracketed, Bear Breakout
CRUS	Daily	15.78	-0.17	-1.07%	16.03	15.70	2,554,918	Bear P, Bear 2B
SONC	Daily	11.32	-0.25	-2.16%	11.50	11.22	428,616	Unconfirmed Bull P, Bull P, Bull 2B
URRE	Daily	1.55	-0.03	-1.90%	1.58	1.53	804,850	Bear P, Bull 2B
URZ(D)	Daily	2.87	-0.09	-3.04%	2.92	2.80	331,296	Bear P, Bull 2B
CVI(D)	Daily	19.47	-0.65	-3.23%	19.80	19.14	1,515,638	Bear P, Bull 2B
IDTI	Daily	8.05	-0.35	-4.17%	8.32	8.13	1,130,773	Unconfirmed Bull P, Bull P, Bull 2B
JEF(D)	Daily	22.50	-0.46	-2.00%	22.79	22.47	1,005,932	Bear P, Bull 1B, Bracketed
TREX(D)	Daily	28.22	-0.46	-1.60%	28.76	28.03	121,147	Bear MP, Bull 2B
EURCHF	Daily	1.24507	0.00387	0.31%	1.24673	1.24013	0	Bear P, Bull 2B, Bracketed
EURUSD	Daily	1.40647	0.00183	0.13%	1.40806	1.40017	0	Bull P, Bear 1B, Bracketed, Bear Breakout
GBPUSD	Daily	1.61056	-0.00164	-0.10%	1.61259	1.60578	0	Bear P, Bull 1B, Bracketed
USDJPY	Daily	81.846	-0.134	-0.16%	82.076	81.761	0	Bull P, Bull 2B, Bracketed
ESH11	1 Min	1291.00	3.29	0.26%	0.00	0.00	0	Bull P, Bull 2B, Bracketed
ESH11	5 Min	1291.00	3.29	0.26%	0.00	0.00	0	Unconfirmed Bull P, Bull P, Bull 2B, Bracketed
YHOO	Daily	16.06	-0.24	-1.47%	16.17	16.00	19,252,089	Bear MP, Bull 2B
YHOO	3 Min	16.06	-0.24	-1.47%	16.17	16.00	19,252,089	Bear MP, Bull 2B, Bracketed
GOOG	Daily	518.39	-5.64	-1.08%	520.00	513.40	2,252,638	Bear P, Bull 1B, Bracketed
YHOO	Weekly	16.06	-0.24	-1.47%	16.17	16.00	19,252,089	Bear P, Bear 1B
$NDU	Daily	12381.26	-130.74	-1.04%	12511.36	12331.77	914,113	Bear MP, Bull 2B, Bracketed
HD(D)	Daily	36.82	-0.23	-0.62%	37.00	36.53	9,676,393	Bull MP, Bull 1B, Bracketed
IBM(D)	Daily	168.28	-1.88	-1.10%	168.69	167.07	5,150,032	Bear MP, Bull 2B, Bracketed
BA(D)	Daily	78.03	-1.49	-1.92%	76.76	75.77	3,589,447	Bear P, Bull 2B, Bracketed
SCCO(D)	Daily	33.83	-1.22	-3.48%	34.24	33.51	2,256,237	Bear P, Bear 2B
UTX(D)	Daily	86.09	-1.41	-1.61%	86.52	85.78	4,121,189	Bull P, Bull 1B, Bracketed, Bear Breakout
INTC	Daily	22.85	-0.37	-1.59%	23.03	22.76	64,894,030	Bull P, Bear 2B, Bracketed
VZ(D)	Daily	36.85	-0.30	-0.81%	36.93	36.64	9,106,061	Bear MP, Bull 1B, Bracketed
MCD(D)	Daily	82.50	0.17	0.21%	82.70	81.49	6,554,343	Bear P, Bear 1B, Bracketed
MMM(D)	Daily	92.47	-1.09	-1.17%	92.88	91.76	2,990,188	Bear MP, Bear 2B, Bracketed, Bear Breakout
T(D)	Daily	31.08	-0.24	-0.77%	31.16	30.94	18,118,320	Unconfirmed Bull P, Bear MP, Bull 1B, Bracketed
MRK(D)	Daily	36.90	-0.16	-0.43%	36.99	36.62	12,602,065	Bull P, Bear 2B, Bracketed
XOM(D)	Daily	80.61	-0.96	-1.18%	81.01	80.07	16,300,482	Bull P, Bear 2B, Bracketed
MRK(D)	Daily	36.90	-0.16	-0.43%	36.99	36.62	12,602,065	Bull P, Bear 2B, Bracketed
HD(D)	Daily	36.82	-0.23	-0.62%	37.00	36.53	9,676,393	Bull MP, Bull 1B, Bracketed

FIGURE 11.1 TradeStation Scan Example

This is a screen shot showing a scan of instruments that are in a bracketed market and are exhibiting high volume. This scan was produced using the ART Scanner on the TradeStation platform using the RadarScreen feature.

Source: Created with TradeStation. © TradeStation Technologies, Inc. All rights reserved.

Examples of some popular fundamental scans are:

- Price-to-earnings (P/E) ratio.
- Debt-to-equity ratio.
- Price-earnings growth (PEG) ratio.
- Return on equity.
- Earnings growth.
- Revenue growth.
- Historical volatility.
- Calendar year high.
- Calendar year low.

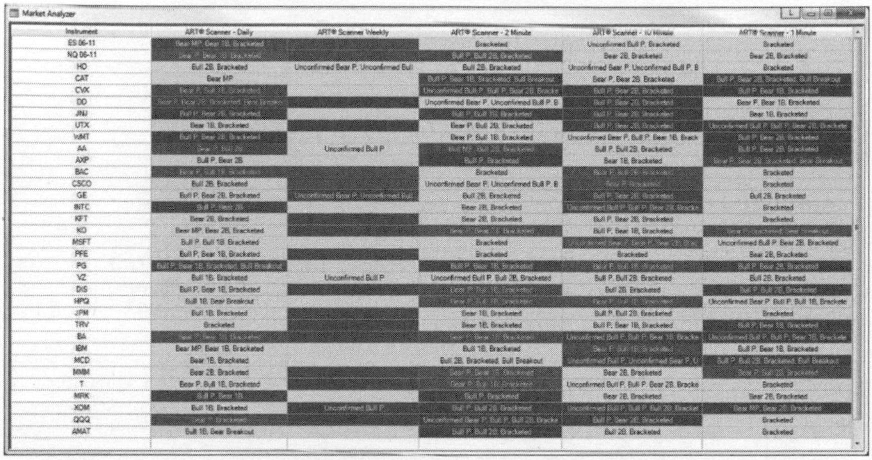

FIGURE 11.2 NinjaTrader Scan Example

This is a screen shot showing a scan of instruments that are in a bracketed market and are exhibiting high volume. This scan was produced using the ART Scanner on the NinjaTrader platform using the Market Analyzer feature.

Source: NinjaTrader (www.NinjaTrader.com).

Corporations release quarterly data. This data is poured into your front-end platform or other scanning service to give you the end result of your scan. It is a massive amount of data, considering that on just one stock exchange, the New York Stock Exchange, there are more than 3,000 companies listed. And each company must report an extensive amount of information—earnings, debt, growth, and more. With today's computer power you can scan for the criteria you are looking for quickly and efficiently.

Governmental Financial Reports May Assist You in Scanning for Opportunities

The ever-changing financial landscape of the country may also assist you in scanning for fundamental trading opportunities. A change in market trend may be indicated by some late-breaking news report from a Federal Open Market Committee (FOMC) meeting or from the U.S. Department of Labor. Shifts in the economy are tracked and reported by the many governmental agencies that are assigned the task of monitoring a country's financial health and growth. See Figure 11.3 for some of the economic reports that are released in the United States that provide vital U.S. economic data that you can implement into your trading strategy.

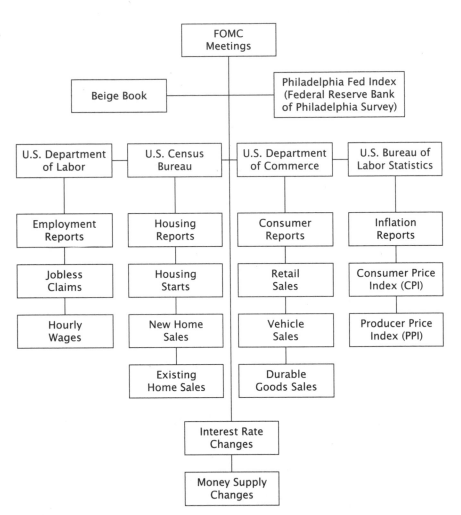

FIGURE 11.3 U.S. Economic Reports
There are eight Federal Open Market Committee (FOMC) meetings held in the United States each year, and this illustration shows some of the fundamental data that is released following these meetings in addition to economic data that is released from other governmental agencies.

U.S. Federal Reserve System

The U.S. Federal Reserve System, also known as the Federal Reserve and the Fed, is the central banking system for the United States. It was created in 1913 with the enactment of the Federal Reserve Act in response to a series of financial panics, including a severe panic in 1907. Over time, the responsibility of the Fed has expanded and changed.

The current structure of the U.S. Federal Reserve System is composed of the following:

- **The Federal Reserve Board** (or the seven members of the Board of Governors), appointed by the U.S. President, publishes the Beige Book.
- **The 12 Federal Reserve Banks** are located in major cities throughout the country: 1st District, Boston; 2nd District, New York; 3rd District, Philadelphia; 4th District, Cleveland, Ohio; 5th District, Richmond, Virginia; 6th District, Atlanta, Georgia; 7th District, Chicago; 8th District, St. Louis; 9th District, Minneapolis; 10th District, Kansas City, Missouri; 11th District, Dallas; and 12th District, San Francisco.
- **The Federal Open Market Committee (FOMC)** consists of the seven members of the Federal Reserve Board and also the 12 regional Federal Reserve Bank presidents.
- **Privately owned U.S. member banks.**
- **Various advisory councils.**

According to the Federal Reserve Board, the Federal Reserve is independent within the government in that its decisions do not have to be ratified by the President or anyone else in the executive or legislative branch of government.

However, its authority is derived from the U.S. Congress and is subject to congressional oversight. In addition, the members of the Federal Reserve Board, including its chairman and vice chairman, are chosen by the President and confirmed by Congress.

The three most recent Fed chairmen have been:

- **Ben Bernanke**, February 1, 2006, to the present.
- **Alan Greenspan**, August 11, 1987, to January 31, 2006.
- **Paul Volcker**, August 6, 1979, to August 11, 1987.

A useful website link with FOMC calendars, statements, and minutes is: www.federalreserve.gov/monetarypolicy/fomccalendars.htm

Beige Book

The Beige Book, also known as the Summary of Commentary on Current Economic Conditions, is a report published by the U.S. Federal Reserve Board eight times a year. The report is published two weeks in advance of the meetings of the Federal Open Market Committee (FOMC).

Each report is a gathering of anecdotal information on current economic conditions by each Federal Reserve Bank in its district from bank and branch directors and interviews with key business contacts, economists, and market experts.

Federal Open Market Committee Decides Monetary Policy in the United States

The Federal Open Market Committee, consisting of the seven members of the Federal Reserve Board and the 12 regional Federal Reserve Bank presidents, makes key decisions about interest rates and the growth of the U.S. money supply.

The Committee meets eight times a year, approximately once every six weeks. Attendance at these meetings is restricted because of the confidential nature of the information discussed. Before each regularly scheduled meeting of the FOMC, the Federal Reserve Board publishes a report known as the Beige Book. This report comes out two weeks before the FOMC meeting.

Sector, Industry Group, and Individual Company Analysis

The terms *industry* and *sector* are often used interchangeably to describe a group of companies that operate in the same segment of the economy or share a similar business type. Despite this tendency to confuse the two, they have distinctly different meanings to the trader or investor.

The difference pertains to their scope; a sector refers to the larger segment of the economy, whereas an industry group describes a smaller and more specific set of companies or businesses. Once we understand the meanings of these terms, we can then look at Table 11.1 to see how they relate to each other from a macro to a micro analysis approach. The macro vision of sectors works its way down to the micro vision of an individual company.

Top-Down Approach Is a Fundamental Technique Used to Scan for Opportunities

Top-down analysis looks at the big picture from the sector standpoint, then moves down and looks at the industry group, and then finally looks at the individual company. Moving from left to right in Table 11.1, you can clearly see how this plays out.

Code	Sector	Subcode	Industry Group	Company
10	Energy	1010	Energy	Exxon Mobil
15	Materials	1510	Materials	DuPont
20	Industrials	2010	Capital Goods	3M
		2020	Professional Services	Emerson Electric
		2030	Transportation	Boeing
25	Consumer Discretionary	2510	Automobiles	Ford
		2520	Consumer Apparel	Coach
		2530	Consumer Services	H&R Block
		2540	Media	Time Warner
		2550	Retailing	McDonald's
30	Consumer Staples	3010	Food & Staples Retailing	Wal-Mart
		3020	Food, Bev., & Tobacco	Coca-Cola
		3030	Household Products	Kimberly-Clark
35	Health Care	3510	Equipment & Services	Aetna
		3520	Pharmaceuticals	Johnson & Johnson
40	Financials	4010	Banks	Bank of America
		4020	Diversified Financials	American Express
		4030	Insurance	Aflac
		4040	Real Estate	Century 21
45	Information Technology	4510	Software & Services	Microsoft
		4520	Hardware & Equipment	Hewlett-Packard
		4530	Semiconductors	Intel
50	Telecommunication	5010	Telecommunication	AT&T
55	Utilities	5510	Utilities	San Diego Gas & Electric

TABLE 11.1 Global Industry Classification Standard (GICS) Table Illustrating How Stock Sectors, Industries, and Individual Companies Can Be Observed from a Macro to a Micro Level

Notes: The Global Industry Classification Standard (GICS) system is used to classify companies listed on the Standard & Poor's (S&P) 500 index. This table is intended for educational purposes only. Information is subject to change. Readers are advised to consult with their broker or data provider for current information.

For example, if you looked at the following from this table you would see:

- **Sector:** Information Technology.
- **Subcode:** 4530.
- **Industry Group:** Semiconductors.
- **Company:** Intel.

Figure 11.4 shows how you can use software to scan with the top-down approach. The strategy is to first find a sector that, for example, is possibly not performing well. Then you continue down to find an individual industry group that is not performing well, and then find one individual company within that group that *is* performing well despite the sector's downturn. When the sector turns around, that one company is likely to break out from the crowd and do very well.

Sector analysis can be used for commodities as well.

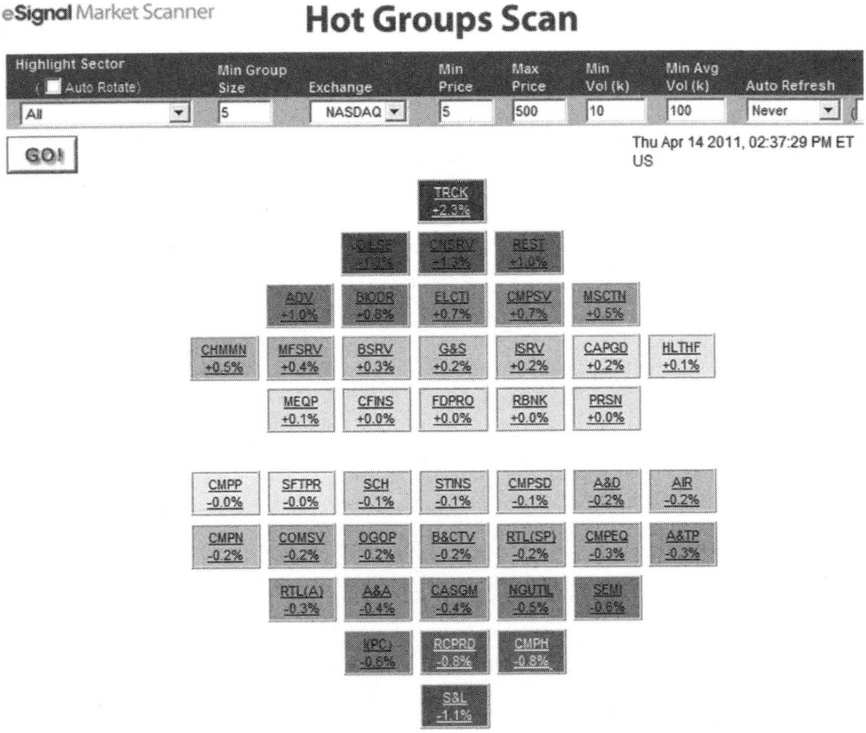

FIGURE 11.4 Hot Groups Scan
This screen shot of a top-down scan was produced using the eSignal platform.
Source: eSignal (www.esignal.com).

OPPORTUNITY IS ALWAYS ABUNDANT IN THE MARKETS

The most important principle of opportunity is to be sure that you are viewing the financial markets in the most beneficial way. You will need to be sure that you are approaching whatever market you trade as one that is abundant in opportunity. This is an important mind-set that will open you up to the idea that you are not operating from a position of weakness but instead from a position of strength and abundance.

As you will see, there is an infinite number of possibilities available to you with regard to what type of financial market to trade and what worldwide exchange to trade through. Look at the tables throughout this chapter to see the vast array of markets you can choose from.

Each market has its own personality and requirements, and you will need to align yourself with the right market for you at this time and place in your development. As you grow and gain experience, you will no doubt expand your awareness of new markets. The tables are intended to give you a broad view and sample of the many market possibilities available.

This idea of approaching the market with a sense of abundance may seem like a minor point, but in reality it is crucial in any businessperson's ability to find opportunity, success, and consistent profitability.

STOCKS

The primary purpose for any company to sell its stock is to raise necessary capital for development or expansion. A stock market or equity market is a public entity for the trading of company stock in shares, and derivatives of stock, at an agreed price; these are securities listed on a stock exchange.

There are stock market exchanges in virtually every developed country throughout the world. The biggest markets reside in the United States, United Kingdom, Japan, India, China, Canada, France, South Korea, and the Netherlands.

Here is a listing of 18 of the world's largest stock exchanges:

1. New York Stock Exchange (NYSE), United States.
2. NASDAQ, United States.
3. Toronto Stock Exchange (TSX), Canada.
4. Euronext, Amsterdam, Netherlands.
5. London Stock Exchange (LSE), United Kingdom.

6. Euronext, Paris, France.

7. Frankfurt Stock Exchange, Germany.

8. Nigerian Stock Exchange (NSE), Nigeria.

9. Johannesburg Stock Exchange (JSE), South Africa.

10. Singapore Exchange (SGX), Singapore.

11. Tokyo Stock Exchange (TSE), Japan.

12. Hong Kong Stock Exchange (HKEX), Hong Kong.

13. Shanghai Stock Exchange (SSE), China.

14. Bombay Stock Exchange (BSE), India.

15. Mexican Stock Exchange (BMV), Mexico.

16. BM&F Bovespa, Brazil.

17. Korea Exchange (KRX), South Korea.

18. Australian Securities Exchange (ASX), Australia.

As you can see from this list of worldwide stock exchanges, there are global opportunities in the stock market and you can select the specific exchanges and instruments that will work best for you. You may find that selecting a stock market and exchange that is in your time zone will assist you in trading during normal business hours.

Dow Jones Industrial Average

The Dow Jones Industrial Average (DJIA or Dow) was started in 1896 by *Wall Street Journal* editor Charles Dow and is now owned by the CME Group. The Dow has come to be known as a barometer of the overall health of the U.S. economy, and also the world economy. The original group of companies listed on the DJIA in 1896 consisted of 12 stocks.

General Electric (GE) is the only stock from the original 12 that remains on the current list today. Over the years and decades stocks have been removed from the Dow and new ones have been added. Even GE was dropped in 1898, only to be reinstated nine years later. The original list of 12 stocks grew over the years to 20 and then to the current list of 30 stocks. This increase in the number of stocks listed on the index was a reflection of the expanding U.S. economy.

You can see what the current stocks on the DJIA index are by looking at Table 11.2. The sector and industry classification system used for the DJIA is the Industry Classification Benchmark (ICB). The ICB system is similar to but different from the GICS system, seen in Table 11.1, that is used to classify the S&P 500 index.

If you are interested in stocks and have not yet visited the DJIA website, it is well worth your time to visit. It has extensive historical information

TABLE 11.2 Dow Jones Industrial Average (DJIA) List of 30 Stocks with Industry Classifications, and Stock Symbols

	Company	Industry	Symbol
1	3M	Conglomerate	MMM
2	Alcoa	Aluminum	AA
3	American Express	Consumer Finance	AXP
4	AT&T	Telecommunication	T
5	Bank of America	Banking	BAC
6	Boeing	Aerospace & Defense	BA
7	Caterpillar	Construction Equipment	CAT
8	Chevron	Oil & Gas	CVX
9	Cisco Systems	Computer Networking	CSCO
10	Coca-Cola	Beverages	KO
11	DuPont	Chemical Industry	DD
12	Exxon Mobil	Oil & Gas	XOM
13	General Electric	Conglomerate	GE
14	Hewlett-Packard	Technology	HPQ
15	Home Depot	Home Improvement	HD
16	Intel	Semiconductors	INTC
17	IBM	Computers & Technology	IBM
18	Johnson & Johnson	Pharmaceuticals	JNJ
19	JPMorgan Chase	Banking	JPM
20	Kraft Foods	Food Processing	KFT
21	McDonald's	Fast Food	MCD
22	Merck	Pharmaceuticals	MRK
23	Microsoft	Software	MSFT
24	Pfizer	Pharmaceuticals	PFE
25	Procter & Gamble	Consumer Goods	PG
26	Travelers	Insurance	TRV
27	United Technology	Conglomerate	UTX
28	Verizon	Telecommunication	VZ
29	Wal-Mart	Retail	WMT
30	Walt Disney	Broadcasting & Entertainment	DIS

The DJIA uses the Industry Classification Benchmark, ICB, system to identify the industry for each company listed. This table is intended for educational purposes only. Information is subject to change. Readers are advised to consult with their broker or data provider for current information.

about the U.S. stock market over the past 100 years and is, in a word, fascinating. The website link is:

www.djaverages.com/

The steady rise of the DJIA over the past 100 years, despite significant downturns from time to time, has led many investors to adopt a buy-and-hold strategy, believing they could consistently gain 10 percent on their money per year over time provided they stayed in the market long enough. See Table 11.3

TABLE 11.3 Time Line of the DJIA Index Value since Its First Year in 1896 until 2011

Date	DJIA @ Market Close
05-26-1896	40.94
12-18-1899	**58.27**
03-14-1907	**76.23**
02-01-1917	**88.52**
10-01-1928	252.16
08-01-1929	380.33
10-28-1929	**260.64**
10-29-1929	**230.07**
11-04-1929	238.95
11-06-1929	**232.13**
12-31-1929	248.48
12-01-1930	164.58
07-08-1932	41.22
08-01-1932	73.16
08-12-1932	**63.11**
06-01-1933	98.14
07-21-1933	**88.71**
12-02-1935	144.13
12-02-1940	131.13
12-03-1945	192.91
12-01-1950	235.42
12-01-1955	488.40
12-01-1960	615.89
12-01-1965	969.26
12-01-1970	838.92
12-01-1975	852.41
12-01-1980	963.99
12-02-1985	1,546.67
09-01-1987	2,596.28
10-19-1987	**1,738.74**
10-21-1987	2,027.85
10-26-1987	**1,793.93**
12-03-1990	2,633.66
12-01-1995	5,117.12
12-01-2000	10,787.99
12-01-2005	10,717.50
10-01-2007	13,930.01
09-02-2008	10,850.66
10-15-2008	**8,577.91**
12-01-2010	11,577.51
05-13-2011	12,595.75

Note: Significant market decline dates are indicated in bold. Much of the data in this table is taken from the DJIA website and the Yahoo! Finance website; the website links are, respectively: DJIA—www.djaverages.com; Yahoo—http://finance.yahoo.com/q/hp?s=%5EDJI.

for a time line of the value of the Dow over the years. The Yahoo! website has a thorough listing of all Dow numbers from 1929 until the present. The website link is:

http://finance.yahoo.com/q/hp?s=%5EDJI

Also see the Dow 1900 to the present monthly chart from StockCharts .com by going to the website link:

http://stockcharts.com/charts/historical/djia1900.html

Today, in the year 2011, during the current worldwide economic volatility, investors have become less enamored of the blind buy-and-hold strategy, finding that the market can at times wield its strength and take a sharp, quick downturn at any time.

Investors today are becoming more aware of watching their portfolios closely in a new way. Smart investors worldwide are becoming more proactive and are learning about how the market moves so that they can protect themselves from dramatic market shifts. There are more people than ever entering and exiting the market (trading) when there are indications that the market is going to have a correction.

OPTIONS

An option is a derivative financial instrument that establishes a contract between two parties concerning the buying or selling of an asset at a reference price. The buyer of the option gains the right, but not the obligation, to engage in some specific transaction on the asset, while the seller incurs the obligation to fulfill the transaction if so requested by the buyer.

The price of an option is derived from the difference between the reference price and the value of the *underlying* asset (commonly a stock, bond, currency, or futures contract) plus a premium based on the time remaining until the expiration of the option.

An option that conveys the right to buy something is referred to as a *call*; an option that conveys the right to sell is referred to as a *put*. The reference price at which the underlying asset may be traded is called the *strike price* or exercise price. The process of activating an option and thereby trading the underlying asset at the agreed-upon price is referred to as *exercising* it. Most options have an *expiration date*. If the option is not exercised by the expiration date, it becomes void and worthless.

In return for granting the option, called writing the option, the originator of the option collects a payment (the *premium*) from the buyer. The writer of an option must make good on delivering (or receiving) the underlying asset or its cash equivalent if the option is exercised.

An option can usually be sold by its original buyer to another party. Many options are created in standard form and traded on an anonymous options exchange among members of the general public, whereas other over-the-counter options are customized ad hoc to the desires of the buyer, usually by an investment bank.

Here are a number of options that can be traded:

- Stock options.
- Commodity options.
- Bond options.
- Index options.
- Exchange-traded fund (ETF) options.
- Credit options.
- Options on futures contracts.

Options Contract Codes and Symbols

Options contracts are identified with symbols and codes that are different from, say, stocks. These codes and symbols consist of four parts:

1. Instrument.
2. Contract month.
3. Contract year.
4. Strike price.

If you are interested in trading options, my recommendation is that you read Larry McMillan's books on options, since he is the authority and you will learn what you need to know about developing a successful option strategy with his material.

McMillan's material can be difficult to absorb for the beginner because it is very high-level. If you find that his books are in any way overwhelming, then you should go to his website and order one of his video courses or newsletters, which make these concepts easier to comprehend. The website link is:

www.optionstrategist.com

An additional excellent resource on options trading is the Traders Coach.com Options online home study course. You can find out more about this course by logging on to this website link:

www.traderscoach.com/survivalguide.php

FUTURES

A futures *contract* is a standardized contract between two parties to exchange a specified asset of standardized quantity and quality for a price agreed upon today, the futures price or the strike price. But the delivery is to occur at a specified *future date*, the delivery date. The contracts are traded on a futures exchange.

The party agreeing to buy the underlying asset in the future (the buyer of the contract) is said to be long, and the party agreeing to sell the asset in the future (the seller of the contract) is said to be short. The terminology reflects the expectations of the parties. The buyer hopes the asset price is going to increase, whereas the seller hopes for a decrease.

In many cases, the underlying asset to a futures contract may not be traditional commodities at all; that is, for financial futures, the underlying asset or item can be currencies, securities, or financial instruments, as well as intangible assets or referenced items such as stock indexes and interest rates.

While the futures contract specifies an exchange to take place in the future, the purpose of the futures exchange is to minimize the risk of default by either party. Thus the exchange requires both parties to put up an initial amount of cash, the margin. Additionally, since the futures price will generally change daily, the difference in the prior agreed-upon price and the daily futures price is settled daily also.

The exchange will draw money out of one party's margin account and put it into the other's so that each party has the appropriate daily loss or profit. If the margin account goes below a certain value, then a margin call is made and the account owner must replenish the account. This process is known as *marking to market*. Thus on the delivery date the amount exchanged is not the specified price on the contract but the *spot* value. This is because any gain or loss has already been previously settled by marking to market.

Unlike an option, both parties of a futures contract must fulfill the contract on the delivery date. The seller delivers the underlying asset to the buyer, or, if it is a cash-settled futures contract, then cash is transferred from the futures trader who sustained a loss to the one who made a profit. To exit the commitment prior to the settlement date, the holder of a futures position can close out the contract obligations by taking the opposite position on another futures contract on the same asset and settlement date. The difference in futures prices is then a profit or a loss.

Futures Contract Codes and Symbols

Futures contracts are identified with symbols and codes that are different from, say, stocks. These codes and symbols consist of three parts (see Figure 11.5):

1. Instrument—root symbol.
2. Contract month.
3. Contract year.

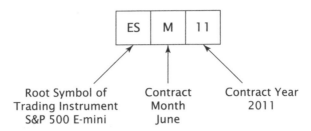

FIGURE 11.5 Illustration of Futures Contract Codes: Root Symbol, Month, and Year

These symbols are constantly changing as time passes; the only part of the symbol that is a constant is the root symbol. When looking at a futures contract code or symbol, the contract month is represented by an alpha code, and you will need to know which months are represented by which alpha codes.

See Table 11.4 for a list of alpha codes for each month from January to December. For example, January is represented by the letter F and December is represented by the letter Z. The contract year is represented by the last two digits of the year; for example, the year 2011 is represented by "11."

Tables 11.5 through 11.10 list various types of futures contracts, along with their exchanges, contract sizes, and root symbols.

TABLE 11.4	Alpha Codes for Each Month of the Year for a Futures Contract
Futures Contract Month	**Alpha Code**
January	F
February	G
March	H
April	J
May	K
June	M
July	N
August	Q
September	U
October	V
November	X
December	Z

TABLE 11.5 Futures: Agricultural

Commodity	Exchange	Contract Size	Root Symbol
Corn	CBOT	5,000 bu.	C/ZC
Corn	Euronext	50 tons	EME
Oats	CBOT	5,000 bu.	O/ZO
Rough Rice	CBOT	2,000 cwt.	RR
Soybeans	CBOT	5,000 bu.	S/ZS
Rapeseed	Euronext	50 tons	ECO
Soybean Meal	CBOT	100 short tons	SM/ZM
Soybean Oil	CBOT	60,000 lbs.	BO/ZB
Wheat	CBOT	5,000 bu.	W/ZW
Cocoa	ICE	10 tons	CC
Coffee *C*	ICE	37,500 lbs.	KC
Cotton No.2	ICE	50,000 lbs.	CT
Sugar No.11	ICE	112,000 lbs.	SB
Sugar No.14	ICE	112,000 lbs.	SE
Frozen Orange Juice	ICE	15,000 lbs.	FCOJ-A

This table is intended for educational purposes only. Information is subject to change. Readers are advised to consult with their broker or data provider for current information.

TABLE 11.6 Futures: Livestock and Meat

Commodity	Exchange	Contract Size	Root Symbol
Lean Hogs	CME	40,000 lbs. (20 tons)	LH
Frozen Pork Bellies	CME	40,000 lbs. (20 tons)	PB
Live Cattle	CME	40,000 lbs. (20 tons)	LC
Feeder Cattle	CME	50,000 lbs. (25 tons)	FC

This table is intended for educational purposes only. Information is subject to change. Readers are advised to consult with their broker or data provider for current information.

TABLE 11.7 Futures: Energy

Commodity	Exchange	Contract Size	Root Symbol
WTI Crude Oil	NYMEX	42,000 U.S. gals.	CL
Brent Crude	ICE	42,000 U.S. gals.	B
Ethanol	CBOT	29,000 U.S. gals.	ZK
Natural Gas	NYMEX	10,000 mm Btu	NG
Heating Oil	NYMEX	42,000 U.S. gals.	HO
Gulf Coast Gasoline	NYMEX	42,000 U.S. gals.	LR
RBOB Gasoline	NYMEX	42,000 U.S. gals.	RB
Propane	NYMEX	42,000 U.S. gals.	PN

This table is intended for educational purposes only. Information is subject to change. Readers are advised to consult with their broker or data provider for current information.

TABLE 11.8 Futures: Metals

Commodity	Exchange	Contract Size	Root Symbol
Gold	NYMEX	Troy ounce	GC
Platinum	NYMEX	Troy ounce	PL
Palladium	NYMEX	Troy ounce	PA
Silver	NYMEX	Troy ounce	SI
Copper	LME	Metric ton	HG

This table is intended for educational purposes only. Information is subject to change. Readers are advised to consult with their broker or data provider for current information.

TABLE 11.9 Futures: Currencies

Commodity	Contract Size	Root Symbol
U.S. Dollar Index	1,000 × U.S. Dollar Index	DX
British Pound	62,500 BP	B6
Australian Dollar	100,000 AD	AD
Canadian Dollar	100,000 CD	CD
Euro Currency	125,000 euros	EC
Japanese Yen	12,500,000 JY	JY
Mexican Peso	500,000 MP	PM
Swiss Franc	125,000 Swiss francs	SF

This table is intended for educational purposes only. Information is subject to change. Readers are advised to consult with their broker or data provider for current information.

TABLE 11.10 Futures: Financials

Commodity	Contract Size	Root Symbol
E-mini S&P 500	$50 × S&P 500 Index	ES
E-mini NASDAQ-100	$20 × NASDAQ100 Index	NQ
E-mini Dow	$5 × DJIA	YM

This table is intended for educational purposes only. Information is subject to change. Readers are advised to consult with their broker or data provider for current information.

FOREX

The forex market is currently the largest and most liquid market in the world, with average daily currency trading volumes exceeding $2 trillion per day. And this bustling market is trading 24 hours per day most days of the week worldwide. Basically, when one currency market is closing another one is opening.

See Table 11.11 for the major currencies that are traded. You will see that each currency is identified by its ISO code which is designated by the International Standardization Organization (ISO). For example the United States dollar has an ISO code of USD.

Another benefit to the forex market is the exceptional leverage available. For example, a trader with $1,000 in an account can control a position of $100,000, which is referred to as having 100:1 leverage. As mentioned in Chapter 6, use caution when implementing leverage and apply risk control to manage your trade size.

Trading Currency Pairs

The *major* currency pairs all involve the U.S. dollar on one side of the trade, such as AUD/USD. (See Table 11.12.) The U.S. dollar is the central currency against which other currencies are traded. In a recent triennial survey of the global foreign exchange market in 2004, the Bank for International Settlements (BIS) found that the U.S. dollar was on one side of 88 percent of all reported forex market transactions.

Cross-currency pairs do *not* involve the U.S. dollar on either side; an example is GBP/CHF, which is a sterling cross.

Some other cross-currency pair types include:

- Euro crosses, such as EUR/CHF.
- Yen crosses, such as CAD/JPY.
- Sterling crosses, GBP/NZD.

When trading in currency pairs, currencies are always quoted in relation to another currency. The value of one currency is reflected through the value of the other. For example, if you want to know the exchange rate between the euro and the U.S. dollar, the quote could be:

EUR/USD = 1.4362

The currency on the left, EUR, is the base currency and the currency on the right, USD, is the *quote* or counter currency. The value of the base currency is always one unit, and the quoted currency is what the one unit equals in the other currency. In this example:

1 EUR = 1.4362 US Dollars

Meaning of Base Currency and Counter Currency

When you look at currency pairs, you will see that one currency is listed first and then another is listed second; for example, EUR/USD lists the euro first and the U.S. dollar second.

The first currency listed in this code is known as the *base currency*, and the second listed in this code is known as the *counter currency*. This evolved over the years to reflect the traditionally strong currencies versus traditionally weak currencies, with the strong currency coming first.

The base currency (the stronger currency, listed first) is what you're buying or selling when you buy or sell the pair. It's also the face amount of the trade. So if you buy 100,000 EUR/JPY, you've just bought 100,000 euros and sold the equivalent amount in Japanese yen. Your profits and losses will be denominated in the base currency.

PIPs Are The Unit Of Movement In Forex

A pip is the unit of movement in the forex market. Most currency pairs are quoted using five digits. The placement of the decimal point depends on whether it's a JPY currency pair or not. If it is a JPY pair, there are two digits behind the decimal point. For all other currency pairs, there are four digits behind the decimal point.

TABLE 11.11 Major Forex Currencies

Country	Currency Name	ISO Code
United States	U.S. dollar	USD
Eurozone	Euro	EUR
Canada	Canadian dollar	CAD
Japan	Yen	JPY
United Kingdom	Pound sterling	GBP
Switzerland	Swiss franc	CHF
Australia	Australian dollar	AUD
New Zealand	New Zealand dollar	NZD

TABLE 11.12 Major Forex Currency Pairs

Description	Nickname	ISO Code
Euro/U.S. dollar	Fiber	EUR/USD
U.S. dollar/Japanese yen	N/A	USD/JPY
British pound/U.S. dollar	Sterling	GBP/USD
U.S. dollar/Swiss franc	Swissy	USD/CHF
U.S. dollar/Canadian dollar	Loonie	USD/CAD
Australian dollar/U.S. dollar	Matie *or* Aussie	AUD/USD
New Zealand dollar/U.S. dollar	Kiwi	NZD/USD

It is the last digit that is considered the pip. For example on the EUR/USD market if the price moves from 1.4362 to 1.4392 it has just gone up by 30 pips. In the USD/JPY market if the price moves from 83.31 to 83.51 it has just gone up by 20 pips.

EXCHANGE-TRADED FUNDS

An exchange-traded fund (ETF) is an investment fund traded on stock exchanges, much like stocks. An ETF holds assets such as stocks, commodities, or bonds, and trades close to its net asset value (NAV) over the course of the trading day. Most ETFs track an index, such as the S&P 500. ETFs are attractive as investments because of their low costs, tax efficiency, and stock-like features. See Table 11.13 for some of the more popular ETF markets.

TABLE 11.13   Major ETFs

ETF Name	Category	Symbol
Energy Select Sector SPDR	Commodity-linked	XLE
Ultra Oil & Gas Pro Shares	Commodity-linked	DIG
Power Shares DB U.S. Dollar Index Bullish	Currency	UUP
Currency Shares Japanese Yen Trust	Currency	FXY
Financial Select Sector SPDR	Equity sector	XLF
Ultra Financials Pro Shares	Equity sector	UYG
iShares JPMorgan Emerging Markets Bond Fund	Fixed income	EMB
iShares iBoxx $ HY Corp Bond Fund	Fixed income	HYG
iShares MSCI Emerging Markets Index	Emerging markets	EEM
iShares FTSE/Xinhua China 25 Index	Emerging markets	FXI
SPDR S&P 500	Large-cap equity index	SPY
PowerShares QQQ NASDAQ-100—NDX	Large-cap equity index	QQQ
SPDR S&P MidCap 400	Mid-cap equity index	MDY
SPDR S&P Retail	Mid-cap equity index	XRT
iShares Russell 2000 Index	Small-cap equity index	IWM
Direxion Small Cap Bull 3x Shares	Small-cap equity index	TNA

This table is intended for educational purposes only. Information is subject to change. Readers are advised to consult with their broker or data provider for current information.

CHAPTER 12

The Third Slice

Money Management

T he third slice of the "financial pie" (see Figure I.1 in the Introduction) is *money management*. If you improve this one area of your trading approach, you'll have the greatest chance of delivering the quickest results to your bottom line in the shortest amount of time. Plus, money management concepts are pretty simple and easy to implement.

But, despite the fact that these approaches are relatively straightforward, many traders still don't implement money management techniques. This happens for one of three basic reasons: (1) they haven't learned these concepts yet; (2) they have learned the concepts but lack the discipline and trader's mind-set to adhere to them; or (3) they don't believe they need these concepts, because their ego makes them feel they are far superior and therefore impervious to risk.

To make these concepts work, you will need to believe that you actually do need a money management plan. Believing that you need a plan is really the first crucial step. Everything after that tends to fall into place. Sadly, it is usually a staggering financial loss that will drive this point home to a trader.

WHAT CAN MONEY MANAGEMENT DO FOR YOU?

Money management to me is like a wonder drug. It does so many things that can enhance even a mediocre system. I've watched many students experience the thrill of finally attaining consistent profitability just because they improved their ability to control risk by adhering to a money management plan.

In a nutshell, here are some things that money management can do:

- Allows you to be wrong and not go bust.
- Helps you minimize risk and maximize profit.
- Takes into account that every trade can be a potential loss.
- Separates the professionals from the novices.
- Relieves anxiety when you know that risk is controlled.

Sometimes, money management can transform an anxiety-ridden trader into a consistent, well-balanced trader. It may take some getting used to for certain individuals, since the adrenaline rush of taking on excessive risk is part of the enjoyment of trading for a number of traders.

For me, my preference is to get an adrenaline rush from making a steady and consistent profit. Once you get a taste of that, you will become a believer in using a money management plan.

THREE WAYS TO CONTROL RISK

As a trader you have three ways to manage your risk. You are in the driver's seat and you will be making decisions on the following:

1. Entry (where to get in).
2. Exit (where to get out—be sure to take into account market liquidity).
3. Trade Size (in shares or contracts).

All three of these decisions are critical to your bottom line, and lacking the skill or knowledge to effectively execute and carry out a well-thought-out plan that incorporates all three of these variables will result in financial loss.

RISK FACTORS TO DEVELOP YOUR PLAN AROUND

There is a variety of risk factors in the financial markets, all of which you must plan for. By knowing the potential risks, you are more able to defend against them.

Here's a basic list of six risks to start with:

1. **Trade risk.** This is the calculated risk you take on each individual trade. Your defense against this risk is to always set a stop-loss exit

prior to entering a trade. A good rule of thumb is to never risk more than 2 percent of the capital in your trading account on any one trade. Once you identify your stop-loss exit, you can properly customize your trade size based on this information.

2. **Market risk.** The inherent risk of being in the markets is called market risk. This type of risk involves the entire gamut of risk possible when in the markets. Market risk can be far greater than trade risk. This type of risk encompasses catastrophic world events and market crashes that create complete paralysis in the markets. Events causing market gaps in price against your trade are also considered market risk. Your defense against this risk is to not trade with more than 10 percent of your net worth.

3. **Margin risk.** This involves risk where you can lose more than the dollar amount in your margined trading account. Because you are leveraged, you then *owe* the brokerage firm money if the trade goes against you. Your defense against this type of risk is to use caution with margin and implement stops and proper trade size at all times.

4. **Liquidity risk.** If there are no buyers when you want to sell, you will experience the inconvenience of liquidity risk. In addition to the inconvenience, this type of risk can be costly when the price is going straight down to zero and you are not able to get out, much like the experience of Enron shareholders in the year 2001. One defense against this type of risk is to diversify among a spectrum of market sectors.

5. **Overnight risk.** For day traders, overnight risk presents a concern in that what can happen overnight when the markets are closed can dramatically impact the value of their position. There is the potential to have a gap open where the price is miles away from where it closed the day before. This gap possibility can negatively impact your account value. One defense for this is simply to not hold trades overnight; instead, convert your positions to cash at the end of the day.

6. **Volatility risk.** There is the risk of a bumpy market that may tend to stop you out of trades repeatedly, creating a significant drawdown. This occurs when your stop-loss exits are not in alignment with the market and are not able to breathe with current fluctuations. Defense against this risk is to use an entry/exit system that takes into account the current market dynamics.

Risk is inevitable in the markets and there is an art to managing the possibilities. It is not a matter of fearing the risk, instead focus on playing the what-if scenario so that you can adequately prepare yourself.

STOP-LOSS EXITS CAN SAVE THE DAY

The topic of where to set stop-loss exits generally falls under the heading of "trading system." You must carefully coordinate your exits with your entries, and this is a trading skill that you will develop with experience. The theory of stop selection is a separate topic from money management, but the two are so connected that it is important to give you an outline of stop theory as part of our discussion.

There are many stops that you can incorporate into your system, and the following six are the ones I find most valuable:

1. **Initial stop.** This is the first stop set at the beginning of your trade. It is identified before you enter the market. The initial stop is also used to calculate your position size. It is the largest loss you will take in the current trade. See Figure 12.1 where the first up triangle on the bottom left-hand side of the chart is bullish and the initial stop is placed at the base leg of the Pyramid Trading Point, marked with a "P."

2. **Trailing stop.** A trailing stop develops as the market develops. This stop enables you to lock in profit as the market moves in your favor. See Figure 12.1 where the three up triangles marked "P" follow the initial stop loss that we set on the very first up triangle. These following three up triangles lock in profit as the bullish trend moves in our favor, and these stops are placed at the base leg of each new up triangle. We exit the market when the market goes against us and our stop is hit on the up triangle in the upper right-hand corner of the chart.

3. **Resistance stop.** This is a form of trailing stop used in trends. It is placed just under countertrend pullbacks in a trend.

4. **Three-bar trailing stop.** This type of trailing stop is used in a trend if the market seems to be losing momentum and you anticipate a reversal in trend.

5. **One-bar trailing stop.** This type of trailing stop is used when prices have reached your profit target zone or when you have a breakaway market and want to lock in profits, usually after three to five price bars moving strongly in your favor.

6. **Trend line stop.** This stop is set using a trend line placed under the lows in an uptrend or on top of the highs in a downtrend. You want to get out when prices close on the other side of the trend line. See Figure 12.2.

Other stops used are generally a form of one of these six stops or a derivative of them. Setting stops will require judgment by you, the trader.

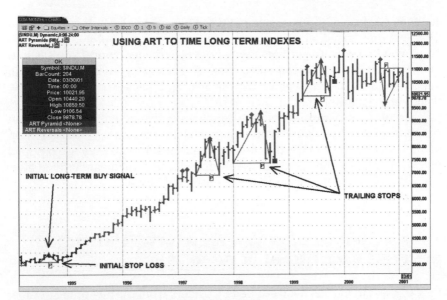

FIGURE 12.1 Initial Stop and Trailing Stops
The ART software identifies the initial stops and the subsequent trailing stops.
Source: eSignal. (www.esignal.com).

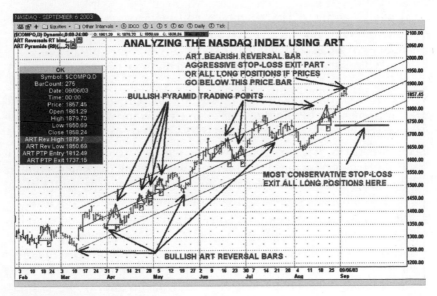

FIGURE 12.2 Trend Line Stop
Illustration of a trend line stop.
Source: eSignal. (www.esignal.com).

Judgment is based on experience and the type of trader you are. You will set your stops based on your psychology and comfort level.

If you find you are getting stopped out too frequently or if you seem to be getting out of trends too early, then chances are you are trading from a fearful mind-set. Try to let go of your fear and place stops at reasonable places in the market.

Position your stops in relation to market price activity; don't pick an arbitrary place to set your stop. Many traders incorrectly choose a stop so their loss is the same exact dollar amount each time they are stopped out. By doing this, they are completely disregarding the meaningful market support and resistance areas where stops should be set.

YOUR SURVIVAL DEPENDS ON HAVING A HEALTHY RESPECT FOR THE RISK OF RUIN

Risk of ruin (ROR) has been studied by traders from the beginning of time, and is the mathematical basis for most money management systems. The theory is based on a formula that will tell you what the chances are that in using a particular set of trading rules you are likely to go completely bankrupt and to be ruined.

Ideally, you want to design a money management system that will protect you from ruin and will give you zero percent likely chance (this is not a guarantee) of going completely bankrupt.

The ROR mathematical formula is based on three components:

1. **Win ratio.** Your win ratio represents your percentage of wins and your probability of winning. For example, if your win ratio is 40 percent, you have 40 percent winning trades and 60 percent losing trades.

2. **Payoff ratio.** This is your average winning trade dollar amount divided by your average losing trade dollar amount (how many dollars you earn compared to each dollar lost). For example, a payoff ratio of 3 to 1 would mean you earn three dollars for every dollar you lose.

3. **Percent of capital exposed to trading.** A general rule of thumb is that you risk no more than 2 percent of your trading account value on any one trade. You can determine the optimal, or more exact percent of capital to risk by referring to the risk of ruin tables or by using the optimal f formula in this chapter. Advanced traders may at times decide to risk more than 2 percent, and novice traders may choose to risk less than 1 percent. This amount will need to change as your performance ratios change.

Your trading system governs the first two items in the risk of ruin formula (win ratio and payoff ratio), and your money management system controls the third item (percent of capital exposed). The risk of ruin decreases as the payoff ratio and/or win ratio increases. The larger the percent of capital risked, the higher the chances for risk of ruin. So, in essence, if your known quantity is your win ratio and your payoff ratio, then the unknown quantity, is going to be the percent of capital you decide to expose when trading. Will it be 1 percent, 2 percent, or 3 percent? Or will the percent you select be a custom number that will change as your trading results change?

For our purposes, we are assuming that you already have a system that gives you an edge and provides you with a payoff ratio that is better than 1 to 1. You can estimate what your risk of ruin is by identifying what your payoff ratio and win ratio are and by referring to the risk of ruin tables.

You will find risk of ruin tables in three books that I know of, which are *Beyond Technical Analysis* by Tushar Chande; *A Trader's Money Management System*, which is my book; and *Money Management Strategies for Futures Traders* by Nauzer Balsara.

Tushar Chande, *Beyond Technical Analysis*, *2nd Edition* (John Wiley & Sons, 2001), has the following tables:

- 1 percent capital at risk.
- 1.5 percent capital at risk.
- 2 percent capital at risk.

Bennett McDowell, *A Trader's Money Management System* (John Wiley & Sons, 2008), has this table:

- 10 percent capital at risk.

Nauzer Balsara, *Money Management Strategies for Futures Traders* (John Wiley & Sons, 1992), has the following tables:

- 10 percent capital at risk.
- 20 percent capital at risk.
- 25 percent capital at risk.
- 33.33 percent capital at risk.
- 50 percent capital at risk.
- 100 percent capital at risk.

It is quite revealing to see how your probabilities in these tables can go from 100 percent likely chance of ruin to 0.0 percent. So with a little planning and thought you can dramatically increase your odds of survival just by having respect for the ROR formula. You do not need to be a mathematical genius, and you don't need to know how to do the calculations yourself; just understand the principles and the impact your risk choices make. It's as simple as adjusting the percent of your capital you put at risk—either lower or higher, depending on your current performance statistics.

As Tushar Chande explains in his book *Beyond Technical Analysis*, "These calculations (risk of ruin) assume that the payoff ratio and probability of winning are constant. In reality, these numbers keep changing in time, and any estimates you have today will probably change in a few months. Thus, it is better to consider a range of payoff ratios and winning percentages when you consider your risk of ruin."

Keeping in mind that the past does not predict the future, it is imperative that you constantly monitor your current win and payoff ratios to adjust the percentage of risk you take with every new trade. Determining how to analyze this data in and of itself can be a part of your personal money management plan.

OPTIMAL *f* FORMULA: INFORMATION SIMILAR TO THE RISK OF RUIN TABLES

Optimal *f* is the optimal fraction of capital to be risked on a trade. This formula was originally developed by John L. Kelly Jr. of Bell Labs in the early 1940s, and is sometimes referred to as the Kelly formula. Edward O. Thorp in *The Mathematics of Gambling* modified the fixed-fraction formula to account for the average payoff ratio, A, in addition to the average probability of success, p. The figures you calculate using this formula are more aggressive than using the risk of ruin tables.

In his book *Money Management Strategies for Futures Traders*, Professor Nauzer J. Balsara defines the formula for determining the optimal fraction, f, of capital to be risked on a trade as:

$$f = \frac{[(A + 1) \times p] - 1}{A}$$

In this formula the definitions are as follows:

- f is the optimal fraction (percentage to be risked).
- A is the average payoff ratio (dollars won for every dollar lost).
- p is the average win ratio (probability of success).

Here is an actual example of the formula in use:

- f is the unknown quantity (the optimal fraction or percentage to be risked).
- A is an average payoff ratio of 2 to 1.
- p is an average win ratio of 35 percent.

The equation looks like this:

$$f = \frac{[(2+1) \times 0.35] - 1}{2} = \frac{1.05 - 1}{2} = \frac{0.05}{2} = 0.025$$

This gives a value of 0.025 for f; to get a percentage, multiply f result by 100. Thus 2.5 percent is the optimal percentage of your trading account to risk on a trade based on this historical payoff ratio and win ratio data and the optimal f formula.

COMPARING OPTIMAL *f* EQUATION RESULTS TO THE RISK OF RUIN TABLES

The optimal f equation results give you a higher risk percentage than the risk of ruin tables do when striving for a zero percent likely chance of ruin. Let's look at the following example:

- f is the unknown quantity (the optimal fraction or percentage to be risked).
- A is an average payoff ratio of 2 to 1.
- p is an average win ratio of 40 percent.

The equation looks like this:

$$f = \frac{[(2+1) \times 0.40] - 1}{2} = \frac{1.20 - 1}{2} = \frac{0.20}{2} = 0.10$$

This gives you a value of 0.10 for f. To get a percentage, multiply f result by 100.

So, in this example, the optimal f formula calculates that for a trader with a payoff ratio of 2 to 1 and a win ratio of 40 percent winning trades, the optimal amount of capital to risk is 10 percent. When we refer to Balsara's risk of ruin table for 10 percent of capital at risk, the calculation for this scenario gives us a risk of ruin probability of 14.3 percent.

The only reason for bringing this point up is to make you aware of the difference between the two approaches for determining your percentage of risk. Using the optimal f formula, you should understand that it does *not* calculate a risk percentage that gives you a zero percent probability of ruin (this is a probability, *not* a guarantee).

Optimal f is a more aggressive approach than when using the risk of ruin tables. When using the risk of ruin tables you can select a percent to risk that gives you a zero percent probability of ruin, keep in mind this is not a guarantee.

THE 2 PERCENT RISK AMOUNT FORMULA

Hypothetically let's say that your optimal f formula and/or your risk of ruin tables tell you that the optimum percent for you to risk on each trade should be 2 percent. Here is how you will calculate that Formula:

Formula:

$$\text{Account Size} \times 2\% = \text{Risk Amount}$$

Example:

$$\$25,000 \times 2\% = \$500$$

This means that if you have a $25,000 trading account and you are going to calculate a 2 percent risk amount on that account, you will be able to risk $500 and not subject yourself to risk of ruin. This means that if a trade goes against you and you are stopped out, the most you will lose is $500, including commission.

USING THE TRADE SIZE FORMULA

After you know what dollar amount you can afford to put at risk, the next step is to carefully calculate your trade size to fit within this framework. It is a bit like reverse engineering the trade by taking on only as large a trade as your risk parameters allow you to.

It is imperative that you do not decide on your trade size randomly. When students tell me that they always trade in lots of 1,000 shares, I know they are not calculating the exact optimal trade size. If they were doing the calculations, the trade size would vary depending on the market dynamics. In addition to this, you must know your entry and your exit before you get into a live trade. For example:

Formula:

[Risk Amount – Commission] ÷ Difference between Entry and Exit
   = Trade Size

Example:

$$[\$500 - \$80] \div \$1.50 = 280 \text{ shares}$$

Details:

- Trading account size: $25,000.
- 2 percent risk allowance: $500.
- MSFT trade entry value: $60 per share.
- MSFT initial stop: $58.50 per share.
- Difference between entry and stop: $1.50.
- Commission: $80 round-trip.
- Maximum trade size: 280 shares.

Your trading system says to go long now at $60 per share. Your initial stop-loss exit is at $58.50, and the difference between your entry at $60 and your initial stop loss exit at $58.50 is $1.50. How many shares (trade size) can you buy when your risk is $1.50 per share and your 2 percent account risk is $500? The answer is: $500 − $80 (commission) = $420. Then, $420 divided by $1.50 (difference between entry and stop amount) = 280 shares.

TRADE SIZE FORMULA USING LEVERAGE

The trade size formula takes into consideration the entry price, the initial stop-loss exit price, commission cost, and the dollar amount that can be risked on this trade. Therefore, it is possible to use leverage (margin) to produce the maximum trade size based on this formula.

Trade Size Formula:

[Risk Amount − Commission] ÷ Difference between Entry and Stop = Trade Size

Example:

$$[\$1,000 - \$51.22] \div \$1.26 = 753 \text{ shares}$$

Details:

- Trading account size: $50,000.
- Amount of margin: 150 percent.
- Trading account size (using margin): $75,000.
- 2 percent risk allowance (on $50,000): $1,000.
- IBM trade entry value: $91.49 per share.
- IBM initial stop: $90.23 per share.

- Difference between entry and stop: $1.26.
- Commission: $51.22.
- Maximum trade size: 753 shares.
- Initial purchase of 753 shares @ $91.49 = $68,891.97 IBM.
- Actual dollar amount of margin @ entry: $18,891.97 IBM.

For example, if we entered an IBM stock trade @ $91.49 and our initial stop-loss exit was set @ $90.23, then our maximum trade size would be 753 shares based on an account size of $50,000 using 150 percent margin and a commission cost of $51.22. Our actual dollar margin amount would be $18,891.97, but our risk on the trade, if stopped out, would be $1,000, or 2 percent of $50,000. Here, we are using margin while keeping the trade risk within 2 percent.

USING THE TRADE SIZE CALCULATOR

You can certainly manually calculate your trade size as in the examples we just looked at. But here is a case in which it is easier and faster to use software for this purpose.

Take a look at Figure 12.3 to see an example of using the Trade Size Calculator software to determine your trade size. Here you will see that the specifics of the trade are as follows:

- Account size: $50,000.
- Percent of capital at risk: 2 percent.
- Trade entry price: $26.99.
- Initial trade exit price: $25.45.
- Risk amount per share: $1.54.
- Commission: $10 round-trip.

In Figure 12.3 you can see that the risk amount is the distance between the trade entry price and the initial stop-loss exit price. That amount of risk comes to $1.54 per share and is indicated by an arrow pointing to the entry and the arrow pointing to the initial stop-loss exit. After entering the specifics of the trade into the calculator, the results rendered are:

- Maximum trade size: 642 shares.
- Dollar risk: $998.68.

You can manually determine the proper trade size using the formula in this chapter, but, as you can see, it is quick and easy to use the calculator.

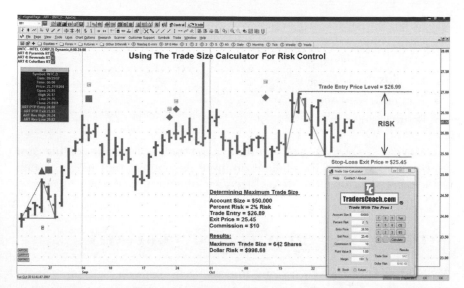

FIGURE 12.3 Trade Size Calculator Example
Illustration of the Trade Size Calculator Determining Proper Trade Size.
Source: eSignal. (www.esignal.com).

You can use your 10-trial of the software by going to Appendix A. There you will see how to download your software from the TradersCoach.com website.

GOOD RECORD KEEPING AND PERFORMANCE ANALYSIS ARE ESSENTIAL

Record keeping and performance analysis form an essential part of any successful trader's plan. Without the accountability factor, the temptation to go rogue is far too great. With proper records you will know where you stand at any given point in your career and you will be able to analyze your results.

In *A Trader's Money Management System*, (John Wiley & Sons, 2008), the book I wrote on money management, there is a complete set of record-keeping forms that help you to stay on track. The system takes you from the micro level all the way to the macro level and includes the following nine forms:

1. Stock Trade Posting Card.
2. Option Trade Posting Card.
3. Future Trade Posting Card.

4. Daily Worksheet.

5. Daily Trade Ledger.

6. Weekly Trade Ledger.

7. Monthly Trade Ledger.

8. Annual Trade Ledger.

9. Score Card.

You can see how to track your individual trades on a trade posting card at the micro level and then take it on up to the annual trade ledger, which is the macro level and the big-picture view of your annual performance.

WITHOUT RISK, THERE IS NO OPPORTUNITY . . .

My students are used to hearing me say, that "Without risk, there is no opportunity . . . ," because for me that saying is a cornerstone of any trading business. You must embrace risk and have confidence in your ability to manage that risk and deliver a consistent profit.

Just like the confident circus performer, you know how to walk the tightrope and you are confident in an area where others are not. This is how business owners are rewarded for taking on risk when others are not willing to or are not physically able to. Taking on risk is inherently more stressful and requires more skill than not taking on risk; therefore risk takers are handsomely rewarded for their efforts and vision when they do succeed.

The mind-set to develop is that risk is not something to fear. Risk is something to expertly manage and exploit for your own gain. Because you are more skilled at managing risk, you will have an edge over the average market participant. This is something to remember and to implement into your trading psychology.

CHAPTER 13

The Fourth Slice

Financial Psychology

Psychology is probably the most elusive piece of the trading pie for many traders. As we discussed in the Introduction, there are four pieces to the trading pie that you must master to be successful. These trading pie pieces are: *trading and investing rules, scanning for opportunities, money management*, and last but not least, *financial psychology*.

This topic of psychology is abstract and nonlinear, and that may be the reason it is so challenging to master. Human emotions and their resulting reactions to inputs vary dramatically from person to person. The factors affecting each trader's psychology can be complicated and diverse, and I will say that successful traders tend to truly know themselves better than the average person does.

The process of trading forces individuals to look inward to confront issues that along the way they discover are holding them back from being profitable. Successful traders are introspective if for no other reason than they must look inside to maintain discipline and consistency in their approach. Knowing themselves and their natural tendencies, for better or worse, is the only way to achieve consistency and discipline in all facets of their job.

The surprising fact is that even the most successful and developed traders face new psychological issues as they continually move up from one profit plateau to another. Working on your psyche will be a lifelong endeavor, but a rewarding one. My advice is that you continually explore and cultivate strengthening your psychology, since with every new plateau you will face a new and different set of emotional challenges.

This chapter is not designed to be the end-all solution for finding every answer to mastering and maintaining your own personal financial psychology. It is meant to outline areas of study and basic principles that one should be aware of in order to tame the emotional beast that lies within us all.

THE TRADER'S MIND-SET

The goal is for a trader to develop and maintain what I call the trader's mind-set in order to become consistently profitable. There are certain qualities of this state of mind that can help you to know if you are on the right track.

The 20 qualities of the trader's mind-set are:

1. Not caring about the money.
2. Acceptance of the risk in trading and investing.
3. Winning and losing trades accepted equally from an emotional standpoint.
4. Enjoyment of the process.
5. No feeling of being victimized by the markets.
6. Always looking to improve skills.
7. Trading and investing account profits now accumulating and flowing in as skills improve.
8. Being open minded, keeping opinions to a minimum.
9. No anger.
10. Learning from every trade or position.
11. Using one chosen approach or system and not being influenced by the market or other traders.
12. No need to conquer or control the market.
13. Feeling confident and in control.
14. A sense of not forcing the markets.
15. Trading with money you can afford to risk.
16. Taking full responsibility for all trading results.
17. A sense of calmness when trading.
18. Ability to focus on the present reality.
19. Not caring which way the market breaks or moves.
20. Aligning trades in the direction of the market, flowing with the market.

You will find that during times of stress or conflict or change, even if you have once mastered and exhibited all of these 20 trader's mind-set qualities, you may take a step or two backward. Both novice traders learning to develop these qualities and experienced traders working toward keeping on track must be aware that developing and maintaining the trader's mind-set is a critical requirement to achieving consistent profitability.

EVEN GOOD CHANGE CAN BE STRESSFUL AND EMOTIONALLY CHALLENGING

Having outlined the 20 qualities of the trader's mind-set, we have to address the possibility that achieving these healthy traits and maintaining them can be difficult during certain periods in our lives. One basic lesson in psychology is that significant change can be disruptive to one's emotional stability. For this reason, even after you have attained the trader's mind-set, there likely will be times when you will have setbacks.

Having setbacks to a strong and healthy trader's mind-set can happen for these eight reasons:

1. You are pushing the envelope and working your way up to a higher profit plateau, which causes stress by changing your underlying structure.
2. You are experiencing physical illness yourself or caring for a loved one with a physical illness.
3. You've had a change in environment, such as moving to a new office or home.
4. Death of a loved one.
5. Birth of a loved one.
6. You've had a change in relationship status, such as a new marriage or a divorce.
7. You are experiencing financial burdens, loss of a job, or unexpected catastrophe.
8. You are experiencing financial windfalls and success, such as inheriting money, winning money, or becoming more successful with your trading.

Significant life changes can be disorienting phenomena for the human race. And as we get older we have even less tolerance for dramatic life changes. This applies to all types of change—good change and bad change.

For example, sometimes when people win a multimillion-dollar lottery jackpot (which is a good change), they experience extreme amounts of stress and discomfort. After the newness and shock of the winnings wear off, they very often say that they were happier before they won the money.

The change in lottery winners' financial standing affects their emotional stability. They may feel guilt over winning the money, fear over losing the money, distrust of friends and family members who may want to share in their new money, and just plain old discomfort over the newness of the money. Two friends of mine won $2 million a few years ago, and have since lost all the winnings and become divorced. It seems unbelievable, but to watch them go through the process was a learning experience for me.

And, if you think about it, this lottery example is similar to when a novice losing trader transforms into a winning trader, or when a moderately winning trader transforms into a substantially winning trader. The newness can be disorienting, and you have to guard against slipping into a self-destructive mode. You may be saying, "That would never happen to me," but believe me, it can happen.

LOOKING AT 15 DESTRUCTIVE PSYCHOLOGICAL TRADING ISSUES AND THEIR CAUSES

This list of 15 issues is useful in troubleshooting common problems that many traders experience. You may experience a combination of these, or you may find that you are facing challenges that are not on this list. The key is to confront any emotional issues that arise head-on so that you can eliminate them before they have a chance to negatively affect your profits.

1. **Fear of being stopped out or fear of taking a loss.** The usual reason for this is that the trader fears failure and feels like he or she cannot take another loss. The trader's ego is at stake.

2. **Getting out of trades too early.** The trader is relieving anxiety by closing a position. Fear of position reversing, and then feeling let down. Need for instant gratification.

3. **Wishing and hoping.** The trader does not want to take control or take responsibility for the trade. Inability to accept the present reality of the marketplace.

4. **Anger after a losing trade.** There is a feeling of being a victim of the markets. Unrealistic expectations. Caring too much about a specific trade. Tying your self-worth to your success in the markets. Needing approval from the markets.

5. **Trading with money you cannot afford to lose or trading with borrowed money.** Trading seen as last hope at success. Trying to be

successful at something. Fear of losing your chance at opportunity. No discipline. Greed. Desperation.

6. **Adding onto a losing position (doubling down).** Not wanting to admit your trade is wrong. Hoping it will come back. Ego at stake.

7. **Compulsive trading.** Drawn to the excitement of the markets. Addiction and gambling issues are present. Needing to feel you are always in the game. Difficulty when not trading, such as on weekends. Obsessed with trading.

8. **Excessive joy after a winning trade.** Tying self-worth to the markets. Feeling unrealistically in control of the markets.

9. **Stagnant or poor trading account profits—limiting profits.** Feeling you don't deserve to be successful. You don't deserve money or profits. Usually psychological issues such as poor self-esteem.

10. **Not following your trading system.** You don't believe it really works. You did not test it well. It does not match your personality. You want more excitement in your trading. You don't trust your own ability to choose a successful system.

11. **Overthinking the trade or second-guessing your trading.** Fear of loss or being wrong. Perfectionist personality. Wanting a sure thing where sure things don't exist. Not understanding that loss is a part of trading and the outcome of each trade is unknown. Not accepting there is risk in trading. Not accepting the unknown.

12. **Not trading the correct trade size.** Dreaming the trade will be only profitable. Not fully recognizing the risk and not understanding the importance of money management. Refusing to take responsibility for managing your risk. Too lazy to calculate proper trade size.

13. **Trading too much.** Need to conquer the market. Greed. Trying to get even with the market for a previous loss. The excitement of trading (similar to item 7, compulsive trading).

14. **Afraid to trade.** No trading system in place. Not comfortable with risk and the unknown. Fear of total loss. Fear of ridicule. Need for control. No confidence in your trading system or yourself.

15. **Irritable after the trading day.** Emotional roller coaster due to anger, fear, and greed. Putting too much attention on trading results and not enough on the process and learning the skill of trading. Focusing on the money too much. Unrealistic trading expectations.

Confrontation is generally uncomfortable and requires a certain amount of courage and determination. But confrontation is needed sooner rather than later when dealing with psychological issues.

OPTICAL ILLUSIONS SHOW HOW OUR MINDS CAN MISLEAD US

There is perception and reality, and sometimes it is hard to distinguish between the two. Take a look at Figures 13.1, 13.2, and 13.3. They illustrate how our minds can play tricks on us and how the brain does not always visually process information in a way that allows us to see reality. Instead, what we are seeing is our perception or an illusion.

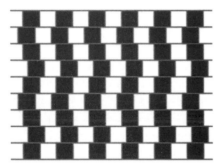

FIGURE 13.1 Café Wall Illusion
Get your ruler out, because those seemingly wavy, bent lines are in fact perfectly straight. This phenomenon was first described in 1973 by Richard Gregory, a professor of neuropsychology at the University of Bristol.

FIGURE 13.2 Scintillating Grid Illusion
Discovered by E. Lingelbach in 1994, this illusion is considered a variation of the Hermann grid illusion that was reported by Ludimar Hermann in 1870. Try to count the black dots. You will find that there really aren't any black dots, even though your brain may think otherwise.

FIGURE 13.3 Chubb Illusion
This illusion was observed by Chubb and colleagues in 1989. Fold the page of this book to lay the two inner squares of this image next to each other. You will find that they are exactly the same shade, even though the right inner square seems lighter than the left inner square.

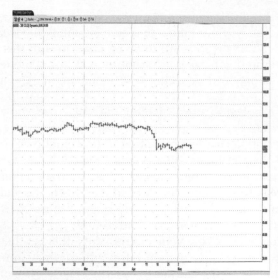

FIGURE 13.4 Sizing Example 1
This daily chart looks like a calm, meandering, sideways market.

Source: eSignal. Published by eSignal (www.esignal.com).

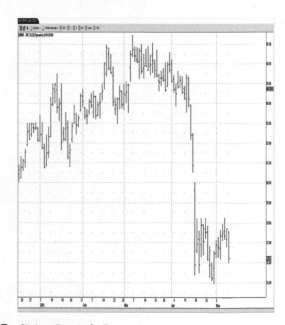

FIGURE 13.5 Sizing Example 2
This daily chart looks like a dramatic gap to the downside. (*Note:* It is basically the same chart as Figure 13.4 except that it is sized differently.)

Source: eSignal. Published by eSignal (www.esignal.com).

These optical illusions occur because of the way the neurons in our brain interact. The way our minds perceive stimuli both visually and intellectually is not always reality. We must be conscious of this fact to guard against misinterpreting market information and losing money by reacting to an illusion as opposed to seeing and understanding the market reality for what it is.

Now take a look at Figure 13.4 and Figure 13.5 to see how these optical illusions can relate to your trading performance. Our sensory perception of the same information can deliver quite different emotions.

The daily chart in Figure 13.4 seems to show a fairly calm sideways market with not much action to speak of. In contrast, Figure 13.5 shows a dramatic break to the downside with a gap down; it seems like a completely different chart. The reality is that both of these charts contain the same information; they are just sized differently.

Use caution when sizing your charts, since this can have a dramatic impact on how you perceive market information, which in turn can affect how you enter and exit the market.

Epilogue

W e've come full circle, and tying it all together brings us back to Chapter 1, which is titled It's a Jungle Out There! Surviving and prospering consistently in the trading business requires that you be prepared to battle the elements in the jungle at all times. It means never becoming too comfortable or too confident. It means expecting the unexpected and always watching your back. And it means getting tough when the going gets tough.

Being a trader is the equivalent to having your own business and living the life of an entrepreneur. In essence, to one degree or another, it is sometimes living life on the edge. You will need to handle the ups and downs of your trading business every day, just like animals in the jungle face the challenges they encounter. But your reward for doing so will be more control over your destiny and your financial freedom.

This approach is a stark contrast to the civilized world's illusion of security, which is based on working in a corporate job from nine to five every day. The reality, of course, in the day job scenario is: There is *no guaranteed security* in a corporate job. A corporate job can evaporate at any time, without warning.

Or your job industry could change, technology could change, or the political landscape could change, and your once-valuable skills may no longer have value in the current marketplace. The illusion of having security by working for someone else is just that.

It is an illusion.

So the premise of this book is more than being a survival guide for traders; in effect it is a survival guide for life. This is a survival guide for your financial life, that is. The more control you take over your own finances and your own independent trading career, the more financial freedom you will have for the long term.

Hopefully, this book has enabled you to view your finances in a new way that opens up the door of opportunity so that you can begin to set up a structure to generate consistent revenue from your trading. I wish you the best in all your endeavors in life and in your trading and investing career.

Online Bonus— Survival Guide Central

Your purchase of this book entitles you to the free use of a special online headquarters for trading information that provides you with free education, software trials and more. The name of this online feature is *Survival Guide Central, SGC* and it can be accessed by clicking on the following link:

www.traderscoach.com/survivalguide.php

Survival Guide Central has a wealth of cutting edge, up to the minute information. Here is a sample of some of the features and benefits you will find on this landing page:

- Current updated information for many of the sections of this book, *Survival Guide for Traders*, including all the appendixes, trading resource information, tables from Chapter 6, and much more.
- Business plan template in a printable PDF file from Chapter 9.
- Live, free webcasts with a variety of industry experts who will teach you about options, forex, stocks, futures, money management, psychology, Elliott Wave, Gann, candlesticks, taxes, and more.
- Trading journal and other free e-book downloads.
- Registration forms and instructions on how to register for your software trials.
- ART Charts in four color that you can view and print out.
- Videos you can view with step-by-step instructions on everything from how to load your software to how to use the ART signals.

- Live free webcasts that you can attend to learn more about the ART software and how to utilize all of its features.

TEN DAY TRIAL ON TRADERSCOACH.COM SOFTWARE PRODUCTS

With the purchase of this book, you are entitled to a 10-day trial on a number of different TradersCoach.com software products. To register for a software trial on the Applied Reality Trading® (ART®) trading software, follow the Quick-Start steps in this appendix.

QUICK-START: FOR YOUR APPLIED REALITY TRADING SOFTWARE TRIAL

Applied Reality Trading—the ART system—is the total solution giving you exact entries, exits, and risk control. The system is based on the realities of the market and is designed to add structure and discipline to your trading and investing, thus reducing stress and anxiety. ART indicates exact entries and exits based on key support and resistance levels as well as taking into consideration market volatility.

This book comes with a 10-day free trial of the ART software. The trial period does not begin and your ART software does not become activated until you register your software on the TradersCoach.com website. When you sign up for your trial, you are entitled to discounted rates on ownership of the ART software. You can register for your trial using the following link:
www.traderscoach.com/survivalguide.php

We want you to get up and running as soon as possible, so follow these five steps, which will speed you along on the path to benefiting from the ART software. If you need any help or have any questions, you can always contact us via this e-mail address: Info@TradersCoach.com.

Step 1: Select Your Market and Time Frame

Decide on which financial market you will start in, such as stocks, futures, options, or forex. Also, determine what time frame suits your needs.

Regarding time frames: If you are investing, you may be able to work with longer time frames and will use end-of-day data such as daily, weekly, and monthly charts. If you want to day trade, you will use shorter time frames, and will require real-time data such as one-minute, five-minute, and 10-minute charts.

Once you have determined what market and time frame you will start with you will be able to decide on the ART platform that is compatible with your trading and investing needs.

Step 2: Select Your ART Platform, Data Feed, and Broker

Go to Appendix C (Resources), and review the available ART platforms that are compatible with the ART software. You may also go to www.Traders Coach.com to see if there have been any new ART platforms added since the time of this book's printing.

Your decision about which platform to select will depend on what market you would like to work in, the time frame you choose, which broker you plan to use, and which data feed you select. (If you already have an account opened with one of the ART platforms that is meeting your needs, you can skip to Quick-Start Step 4.)

In Appendix C (Resources) there is also a list of possible brokers and data feeds. Keep in mind that some brokerage firms supply free live, streaming data if you meet certain requirements, so you may obtain brokerage services and data from the same source.

Remember, not all brokers service all financial markets. For, example, if you plan to trade the forex market, not every broker will be able to place trades for you and provide forex data, as the foreign exchange is a specialized market. When researching, be sure to ask all broker and data feed vendors what markets they specialize in before choosing your ART platform. Then, select the platform that is going to support the market you will be working in.

Step 3: Open an Account with Your Platform

Contact the company that has the platform that you will be plugging the ART software into. That company will activate your account to the specifications you request. Remember, some of the platforms available are free, so you will want to ask questions to learn about what services each platform provides and what the costs are, if any. We have not listed service options or costs, since these will change over time. To get the most accurate current information, call the phone numbers provided in Appendix C (Resources).

When you open your platform account, you will receive account information, passwords, and so on that you will need when you register your ART software.

Step 4: Register Your ART Software

Once you have your platform account open, go to www.TradersCoach.com to register your ART software. You will need certain information from this book and your new platform account information, so be sure to have these items handy while you are registering. You can register your ART software with the following link:

www.traderscoach.com/survivalguide.php

Your purchase of this book entitles you to a free 10-day trial of the ART software. Following your trial, you will be offered a very special price on ownership of the ART software so that you can continue to benefit from the ART system.

Step 5: Get Started!

You are now ready to start trading and investing with ART. Remember to paper trade using the methods described in this book, and when you have mastered the ART software, go into the market and use the science of technical analysis combined with the art of reality-based trading and investing to begin looking at your trading and finances in a whole new way. Enjoy, and if you have any questions, contact one of our service representatives via Info@TradersCoach.com.

ART SOFTWARE TECHNICAL SUPPORT

Once you have registered for your ART software, your technical support will begin. The technical support that you receive for 10 days is designed to troubleshoot technical issues only. For trading and investing methodology issues, you may want to consult *The ART of Trading*, by Bennett McDowell (John Wiley & Sons, 2008), which if studied will answer many of your questions in detail.

This ART trial is a very special free offer, which means that technical support will be limited. Please visit this link for technical support:

www.traderscoach.com/survivalguide.php

EQUIPMENT AND SYSTEM REQUIREMENTS FOR THE ART SOFTWARE

To utilize the ART software trial that purchase of this book entitles you to, the recommended equipment and system minimums are:

- Operating System: Windows XP; Windows Vista; Windows 7 or greater
- CPU Processor Chip: i7; i5 or greater.
- Monitor: 1,024 × 768 resolution;
- RAM: 2 GB. (*Note:* If you plan to work with multiple charts or have other programs open at the same time, you will need 6 GB RAM.)
- Available hard disk space: 250 MB.
- Internet connectivity: DSL; cable modem; ISDN; T1 or T3.
- Internet Browser: Microsoft Internet Explorer 8.0+.
- Data: Live data feed from the financial markets.

Computer technology is constantly changing, so these requirements likely will change in the months and years to come. For an update on the computer requirements, you can visit the following link, which will have current information:

www.traderscoach.com/survivalguide.php

HOW TO CONTACT US

As always, we are dedicated to assisting you to become the most profitable trader you can be. We welcome the opportunity to work together with you to find the best possible solutions for your trading needs. Contact us at any time if you are looking to brainstorm on your trading approach and want to fine tune it for greater success.

And, of course, if you have any questions, you are welcome to call, phone, e-mail, or fax us:

- Phone: 858-695-0592
- Phone: 800-695-6188 Toll Free In United States and Canada
- Fax: 858-695-1397
- E-mail: Info@TradersCoach.com
- Forum: Plus, you can visit the TradersCoach.com forum to ask questions and interact with other traders. The forum link is:

www.traderscoach.websitetoolbox.com

WWW.TRADERSCOACH.COM/SURVIVALGUIDE.PHP

This link, www.traderscoach.com/survivalguide.php, combined with your purchase of this book is your free access ticket to *Survival Guide Central,*

SGC. This feature will enable you to keep your copy of the *Survival Guide for Traders* current for years to come. Plus, you will have access to a printable version of the business plan found in Chapter 9. Just visit this link and you will find these features along with access to the free software trials that the purchase of this book entitles you to. Be sure to have a copy of your *Survival Guide* handy when visiting this link, as you will be asked a security question to ensure that you are a current owner of this book before gaining free access to *Survival Guide Central*. If you have any questions or need assistance in registering for this special online feature, you can call us at 858-695-0592 or e-mail us via Info@TradersCoach.com.

ART Basics

Here you will find the ART software basics so you can get started and determine whether the ART software matches your personality and trading style in order to give you an edge in the markets. In addition to this appendix, another essential resource complete with videos, free ART software trial information, current ART charts, and commentary can be found at the following link:

www.traderscoach.com/survivalguide.php

If you would like to take your understanding of ART to an even higher level, it's recommended that you purchase and study *The ART of Trading*, by Bennett McDowell (John Wiley & Sons, 2008). This manual has much more in-depth information on how to customize the ART software for your needs and has an extensive "Advanced Techniques" section of nine chapters, which in itself can advance your ART skills immensely.

THERE ARE FOUR ART SIGNALS

The ART signals can be used to create an infinite number of strategies and these signals can be combined for powerful entry, exit, and risk control approaches. No two traders use the ART system in exactly the same way. This is because the open architecture and flexibility of the system allows each trader to customize it to their own unique trading personality and style. The four ART signals are as follows:

Primary Pyramid Trading Point—P

The Primary Pyramid Trading Point is a trend identifier that keeps you in a trend long enough to maximize profits. Pyramid Trading Points look like triangles and indicate trend direction. Bullish entries are confirmed once prices meet trend definitions such as higher highs (key resistance) and higher lows (key support). Bearish entries are confirmed on lower lows (key resistance) and lower highs (key support). Volatility is determined by the velocity of the left-hand side of the triangle as compared to the velocity of the right-hand side of the triangle.

The point or *apex* of the triangle always shows you the direction of the trend and represents *resistance*. The *base leg*, or flat part of the triangle, always represents *support*. See Figure B1 and Figure B2.

Minor Pyramid Trading Point—MP

The Minor Pyramid Trading Point signal indicates only a correction in the primary trend (the primary trend is always identified by a Primary Pyramid Trading Point). So the Minor Pyramid Trading Point is used as a signal to scale into or scale out of a trend. It may also be used to scalp the market or to indicate the beginning of a change in trend.

ART One-Bar Reversal—1B

The One-Bar Reversal signal indicates market pivot points representing significant short-term tops and bottoms of market swings. ART Reversals are high-probability signals used for scalping, scaling out of trends, and scaling into trades, as well as for countertrend trading. You can use ART Reversals in a variety of ways to complement your trading style.

ART Two-Bar Reversal—2B

This signal is similar in meaning to the ART One-Bar Reversal but requires two price bars in the pattern to identify market swing pivot points.

ART SIGNALS HAVE LABELS AND ICONS

You will note that each ART signal has a unique label and icon to identify it on your chart (see Table B.1). The variations on how and when to use these four ART trading signals are unlimited. Your experience and beliefs will determine how you decide to mix and match these signals to create your own custom ART trading system. By studying the ART methodology you

TABLE B.1 The ART Trading Signals

Signal Description	Label	Icon
Primary Pyramid Trading Point	P	Triangle ▲ or ▼
Minor Pyramid Trading Point	MP	Triangle ▲ or ▼
ART One-Bar Reversal	1B	Diamond ◆
ART Two-Bar Reversal	2B	Square ■

TABLE B.2 The ART Trading Signals (and Icons for TradeStation Users)

Signal Description	Label	Icon
Primary Pyramid Trading Point	P	Triangle ▲ or ▼
Minor Pyramid Trading Point	MP	Triangle ▲ or ▼
ART One-Bar Reversal	1B	Circle ●
ART Two-Bar Reversal	2B	Circle ●

will develop your own unique approach. Through paper trading, you will test your trading approach and discover what works best for you.

Note to TradeStation Users

The charts in this appendix were created using the eSignal platform and have slightly different icons than the TradeStation platform (the labels are the same). The only difference is that the ART Reversals have circle icons on the TradeStation chart instead of squares and diamonds. (See Table B.2.)

ART COLOR MEANINGS

The colors of each of the three ART studies enable you to quickly identify what the market is doing with each and every new price bar or candlestick. The three ART studies are: (1) Pyramid Trading Points; (2) ART color bars; and (3) ART reversals. There are default color meanings for the ART studies, but these defaults can be changed to suit your personal preference. The default color meanings of each of the three ART studies are as follows:

Color Meanings for Pyramid Trading Points

▲ = **Yellow up triangle** indicates a potential bullish Pyramid Trading Point (when voided it will disappear).

▼ = **Yellow down triangle** indicates a potential bearish Pyramid Trading Point (when voided it will disappear).

▲ = **Green up triangle** indicates a confirmed bullish Pyramid Trading Point.

▼ = **Red down triangle** indicates a confirmed bearish Pyramid Trading Point.

Color Meanings for ART Reversals

♦ = **Green diamond** indicates a bullish ART One-Bar Reversal.

♦ = **Red diamond** indicates a bearish ART One-Bar Reversal.

♦ = **Gray diamond** indicates a voided bullish or bearish ART One-Bar Reversal.

■ = **Green square** indicates a bullish ART Two-Bar Reversal.

■ = **Red square** indicates a bearish ART Two-Bar Reversal.

■ = **Gray square** indicates a voided bullish or bearish ART Two-Bar Reversal.

Color Meanings for ART Charts

• **Yellow** indicates a preconfirmed or prevoided potential Pyramid Trading Point.

• **Green** indicates a bullish ART trading signal.

• **Red** indicates a bearish ART trading signal.

• **Gray** indicates a voided ART Reversal.

• **Black** indicates a neutral price bar.

Note: These are the default colors for the ART software system. You can change the defaults by referring to your *ART Trading Software User's Manual* and following the "User Input" instructions.

EXACT ENTRIES AND EXITS GIVE YOU STRUCTURE AND DISCIPLINE

Because Applied Reality Trading indicates exact entries and exits that are easily seen on your chart, you know at all times whether you should be in the market or out of the market. The ART signals enable you to avoid random trades and investments and help eliminate emotional trading and investing. You want to avoid emotional behavior since it leads to poor results.

The ART signals allow you to trade and invest confidently. They lower your stress and anxiety, which allows you to remain calm and to make rational, objective, and sound decisions. We call this adding structure to your finances.

By adding structure, you can overcome psychological barriers that may be keeping you from attaining financial success. For example, those experiencing fear and emotional discomfort while trading and investing usually lack structure and/or confidence in their actions. ART not only deals with these issues but also enables you to reach higher levels of financial mastery.

Today, more than ever before, traders have an overwhelming amount of information available to absorb, analyze, and process. Too much market information can cause you unnecessary stress and can impair your judgment. By the time you absorb and process this excessive information, you may miss some fantastic opportunities. Keeping easily visible on your chart the signals that depict exact entries and exits, ART eliminates this information analysis paralysis.

PYRAMID TRADING POINT

A significant change in the market, represented by price action, is defined as a Pyramid Trading Point (PTP), which looks like a triangular Egyptian pyramid, hence the name. ART Reversal bars are commonly found at the apex (pointed peak) of a Pyramid Trading Point.

P = Primary Pyramid Trading Point

The Primary Pyramid Trading Point identifies the *primary* trend direction. It will appear on your chart with a P symbol near the base leg (flat base) of the triangle. A *confirmed* Primary PTP is formed when prices exceed the apex (pointed peak) of the triangle. When it is confirmed, it will appear as either red (for a downtrend) or green (for an uptrend). A potential Primary PTP will appear as the color yellow until it is confirmed.

This signal is important and can tell you trend direction, trend entry points, trend exit points, trend exhaustion, and how to behave in a bracketed market to avoid whipsaw drawdowns.

MP = Minor Pyramid Trading Point

The Minor Pyramid Trading Point is used to identify a trend *correction* or *reversal*. It does not identify a primary trend. It is often the first PTP that forms in the opposite direction of the primary trend. It will appear on your chart with an MP symbol near the base leg (flat base) of the triangle. When it is confirmed, it will appear as either red (for a downtrend) or green (for an uptrend). A potential Minor PTP will appear as the color yellow until it is confirmed.

Important Note: A Minor PTP occurs only when prices have still not exceeded the base leg of the most recent Pyramid Trading Point of the primary trend. Its position in relation to *the most recent PTP of the primary trend* is what distinguishes it as minor instead of primary.

PTP = Pyramid Trading Point

We use the abbreviation PTP to refer to a Pyramid Trading Point in an effort to streamline the text.

Five Ways the Primary PTP Can Help You

1. Identify trend direction.
2. Select trend entry points.
3. Select trend exit points.
4. Determine trend exhaustion or key trend reversals.
5. Identify a bracketed market.

Five Ways the Minor PTP Can Help You

1. Identify market corrections and consolidations in primary trends.
2. Scale out of trends.
3. Countertrend trade.
4. Scalp trade.
5. Identify possible trend reversals.

POTENTIAL VERSUS CONFIRMED PYRAMID TRADING POINT

It's important to understand the difference between a *potential* and a *confirmed* PTP. A potential PTP will appear yellow on your chart and will not change color until it has been confirmed. Once the PTP has been confirmed, it will change color to either red for a bearish downtrend or green for a bullish uptrend. The definitions of potential PTP and confirmed PTP follow.

- **Potential Pyramid Trading Point.** A potential PTP may occur when prices have not yet exceeded the pointed peak or apex of the triangle. A number of charts in this appendix show potential pyramids in a row; they will appear *yellow* on a live color chart generated by the software. The reason a pyramid is considered potential is because price activity has not yet broken beyond the apex of the triangle.
- **Confirmed Pyramid Trading Point.** When prices exceed the pointed peak or apex of the triangle, the pyramid will become confirmed and will appear *red* or *green* on a live color chart generated by the software.

The ART software will give you a voice alert (if you select this feature) only when the PTP has been confirmed. The value of watching your monitor to check for yellow potential PTP signals is that you will have a heads-up that a signal may be forming and you will have time to calculate your trade size prior to the signal confirmation.

Important Note: If the yellow PTP signal is voided (not confirmed), it will disappear from your chart. Another note is that sometimes in fast-moving markets a confirmed PTP signal will appear without warning (no yellow potential PTP). Once you have been using the software and are comfortable with it, this information will become second nature and you will respond automatically to the various changing signals.

PYRAMID TRADING POINT RULES FOR TREND ENTRIES AND EXITS

The ART software uses sophisticated algorithms to identify high-probability entries into and exits out of the market based on current price and volume activity. By using the Pyramid Trading Point signals, you can clearly identify entries and exits using the following information and the rules in Figure B.1 and Figure B.2. In Figure B.3 you can see how the ART software places bullish and bearish PTP signals on your chart so you can easily see the changing trend direction at all times.

Trend Entries

When drawn, a Pyramid Trading Point becomes confirmed only when prices exceed the apex of the Pyramid Trading Point, triggering the trade entry. Until the apex is exceeded, the Pyramid Trading Point is considered to be a potential Pyramid Trading Point and will remain yellow in color.

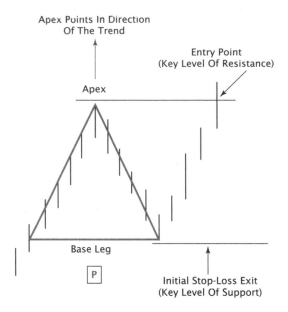

FIGURE B.1 Bullish Pyramid Trading Point Diagram
Entry and exit rules: The apex always points in the direction of the trend; enter one tick above the apex; initial stop-loss exit is one tick below the base leg if the market goes against you.

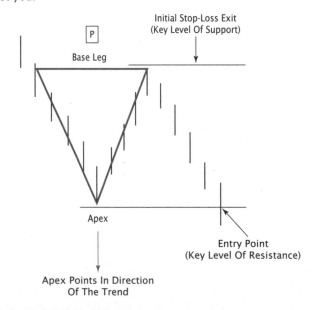

FIGURE B.2 Bearish Pyramid Trading Point Diagram
Entry and exit rules: The apex always points in the direction of the trend; enter one tick below the apex; initial stop-loss exit is one tick above the base leg if the market goes against you.

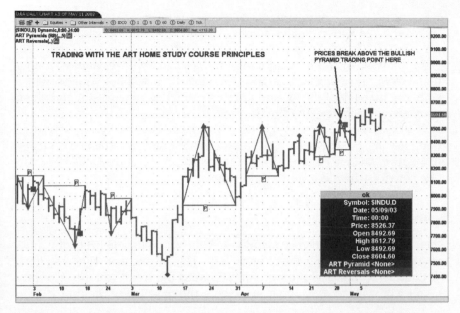

FIGURE B.3 Bullish and Bearish Pyramid Trading Points
This chart illustrates bullish (triangles pointing upward) and bearish (triangles pointing downward) Pyramid Trading Points. On a color chart the bullish PTP signals would be colored green and the bearish PTP signals would be colored red.
Source: eSignal (www.esignal.com).

When the apex of a primary Pyramid Trading Point is exceeded, this signals that a primary trend is in place. An entry signal is triggered when prices exceed the apex by one or two ticks. The logic behind this signal is that some new information has come into the market, causing prices to end their correction. This establishes the base leg of a Pyramid Trading Point. When prices move past the apex of the Pyramid Trading Point, this triggers your entry signal.

With a bullish Pyramid Trading Point (see Figure B.1), positive information has come into the market, causing prices to go higher and exceed the apex. With a bearish Pyramid Trading Point (see Figure B.2), negative information has come into the market, causing prices to go lower and below the apex. You do not care what the information is, because you know price action is a real truth and that is what triggers the ART entry signal.

Initial-Stop Trend Exits

Most trading systems use a moving average to determine an exit signal. Moving averages are usually derivatives of price and therefore do not represent the true realities of the market. Furthermore, moving averages can be adjusted with variables such as simple versus compounded moving averages.

In contrast to the moving average approach, with Pyramid Trading Points you are trading with market realities. You will set your stop-loss exit at the base leg of the pyramid. An exit signal is generated if and when prices reverse one tick past the base leg.

If prices reverse and go against you by passing the Pyramid Trading Point base leg, then some new information has come into the market causing the reversal (see Figure B.1 and Figure B.2). We exit the trade based on price activity, which is a truth of the market.

Trailing-Stop Trend Exits

When a trend is going in your favor, you will want to lock in profits by moving your stop accordingly (see Figure B.4). This means that when you have a second PTP appear in the same direction as the trend you are currently in, you will want to move your stop from the base leg of the first PTP in

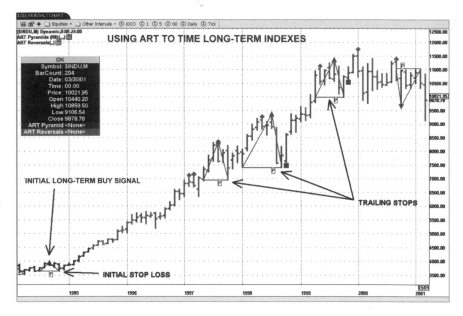

FIGURE B.4 Trailing Stops
The bullish Pyramid Trading Points clearly identify the uptrend and the levels at which to place specific trailing stops to lock in profits as the trend moves in your favor.
Source: eSignal (www.esignal.com).

the trend to the base leg of the second PTP in the trend. As additional PTP signals appear, you will want to repeat this trailing-stop method until the trend is exhausted or reverses.

Scaling-Out Trend Exits

A favorite technique of mine is scaling out of positions (see Figure B.5). When there is a sharp, fast, hyperbolic move in the direction of your trend, it is useful to lock in profit by taking a portion of your position off the table. This technique also reduces anxiety and any fears related to the possibility of the position turning against you. This approach makes it easier emotionally to leave the rest of your position on the table until you get stopped out.

You will need to lay out your personal rules for scaling out prior to initiating a live position to be sure that you do not emotionally bail out of your trend prematurely. One of the most common causes for low payoff

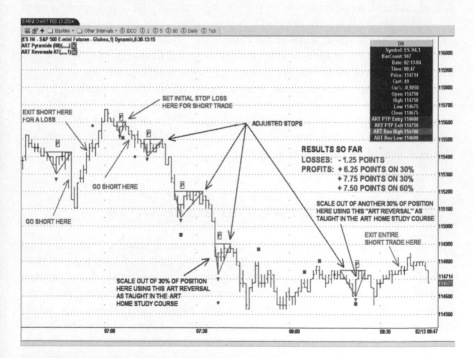

FIGURE B.5 Scaling Out of Positions with ART

Scaling out of a position locks in profit when the ART system tells you there is a high probability that the trend is nearing exhaustion. Generally a trend will reverse after four or five Primary PTP signals in the same direction.

Source: eSignal (www.esignal.com).

ratios is that the trader abandons trend positions before they reach their full profit potential.

With the ART software, some traders will use a signal like an ART Reversal bar or a Minor PTP combined with a significant move in their favor to signal scaling out of a position. For this method to be effective, you must have a large-enough position in play to make it work. For example, if you have three contracts on, you could scale out one contract easily and leave the remaining two contracts in play. If you have only one contract in play, you cannot effectively scale out.

MOMENTUM AND NEW INFORMATION

When a Pyramid Trading Point forms on your chart, momentum has changed, which causes the Pyramid Trading Point. Maybe a news-related item came out, or momentum in the existing trend just dried up. The next thing to realize about the Pyramid Trading Point is that if prices exceed a pivot, whether to the upside or the downside, some new information came into the market for traders and investors to feel differently. Maybe momentum has returned, or the smart money knows something we don't.

Whatever the reason, all we know is that the market is pushing prices beyond the old behavior that stopped it before. When this happens, we need to recognize that something is going on. This alone may be a reason to enter a position. Your reasons for entry into the market will be further strengthened with high volume.

PYRAMID TRADING POINT REQUIREMENTS

The minimum requirements for a bullish Pyramid Trading Point are two previous bars with higher highs and higher lows, and the following two bars of lower highs and lower lows. The minimum requirements for a bearish Pyramid Trading Point are two previous bars with lower highs and lower lows, and the following two bars of higher highs and higher lows. When prices pull back more than the minimum requirements, you can draw the base leg of the Pyramid Trading Point.

The ART trading software takes into consideration minimum Pyramid Trading Point requirements along with other momentum characteristics when identifying a Pyramid Trading Point. The ART software looks for the highest-probability Pyramid Trading Point and may pass on some even though they meet the minimum requirements.

In most cases the ART charting software will draw a *yellow*-colored Pyramid Trading Point icon before the signal is confirmed so that you know its strength and have time to calculate your correct trade size.

IDENTIFYING TREND DIRECTION

The Pyramid Trading Point looks like a triangle when drawn on a chart. The apex of the triangle always points in the direction of the trend (either bullish or bearish). Using the Pyramid Trading Point makes trend trading easier. It is hard to miss the trend if you know how to properly use the Pyramid Trading Point. Figure B.6 shows you how the Pyramid Trading Point triangles point in the direction of the trend. The bearish Pyramid Trading Point points downward in the direction of the downtrend, and the bullish Pyramid Trading Point points upward in the direction of the uptrend.

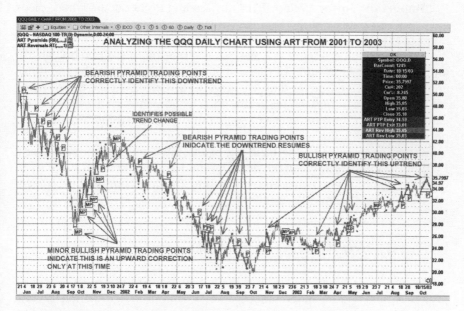

FIGURE B.6 Pyramid Trading Points Identify Trend Direction
Note that the Primary PTP (P) signals identify primary trends, and the Minor PTP (MP) signals identify corrections in the trend or reversals in the trend.
Source: eSignal (www.esignal.com).

IDENTIFYING TREND EXHAUSTION AND TREND REVERSALS

The Pyramid Trading Point can be used to gauge when a trend may exhaust itself. Most trends end after four, five, or six consecutive primary Pyramid Trading Points in the same direction, which indicate a mature trend nearing its end. On rare occasions, significant and exceptional trends may have eight or more consecutive Pyramid Trading Points in the same direction before the trend changes. The most significant trends occur when traders on other time frames are participating in the trend as well.

IDENTIFYING TREND CORRECTIONS USING THE MINOR PYRAMID TRADING POINT

Using the rules and definitions of a Minor Pyramid Trading Point, we can quickly distinguish between the primary trend and a minor trend correction. The Minor PTP is often the first Pyramid Trading Point that forms in the opposite direction of the primary trend.

Important Note: A Minor Pyramid Trading Point occurs when prices have still not exceeded the base leg of the most recent Pyramid Trading Point of the primary trend.

When looking at Figure B.7, we can see that there are two bullish MP Minor PTP signals. Neither of these signals is telling us that the trend has completely reversed; so far they are merely corrections of the trend. When we look at other factors on the chart, such as how mature the trend is, we can determine if it makes sense to scale out or exit the trend based on our personal rules.

When prices exceed the base leg of the most recent dominant-trend Pyramid Trading Point, then the next Pyramid Trading Point that occurs in the direction of the existing Minor Pyramid Trading Point will be considered a Primary Pyramid Trading Point.

IDENTIFYING BRACKETED MARKETS

There are times when a market will remain bracketed for an extended period of time and meander along sideways with no real direction. Significant trends occur when a market breaks out from a channel or bracket like this. That can be a terrific opportunity, and the Pyramid Trading Point can help you catch these significant trends emerging from bracketed markets. Figure B.8 illustrates a classic bracketed market with multiple yellow Pyramid Trading Points appearing in bullish and bearish positions side by side.

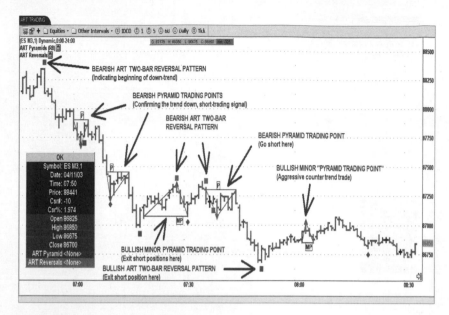

Figure B.7 Minor Pyramid Trading Points (MP) Identify Trend Corrections
Source: eSignal (www.esignal.com).

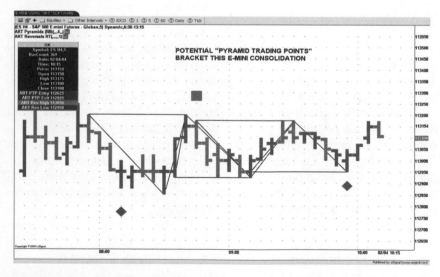

FIGURE B.8 ART Software Bracketing the E-Mini
This chart shows multiple yellow potential Pyramid Trading Points side by side in a classic bracketed market being identified by the ART software.
Source: eSignal (www.esignal.com).

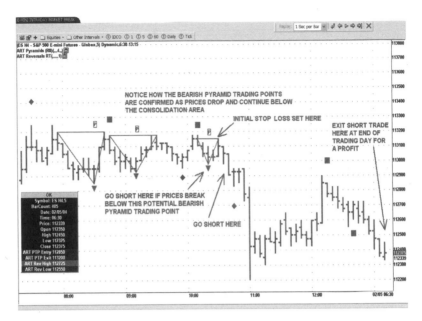

FIGURE B.9   ART Software Confirming Bearish Pyramids
When the bracketed market from Figure B.8 breaks to the downside, the bearish triangles are confirmed and turn red; the yellow bullish triangles disappear.
Source: eSignal (www.esignal.com).

When the market for Figure B.8 does break to the downside (see Figure B.9), the bullish yellow pyramids disappear and the bearish pyramids are confirmed (they turn red). This classic bracketed PTP pattern effectively prevents you from getting whipsawed by consolidating markets.

It is said that markets trend approximately 35 percent of the time, meaning that 65 percent of the time they are bracketed or trendless. It is common for inexperienced traders and investors to get whipsawed during these trendless periods, causing significant drawdowns. When you see this classic yellow pyramid pattern, it is important to recognize it as both a time to stay out of the market and also a time to be ready to jump in when the market does break in one direction or the other.

CUSTOMIZING THE ART SOFTWARE TO TAILOR IT TO YOUR TRADING NEEDS

The ART trading software has many features that can be adjusted to suit your needs and to suit changing market conditions such as market volatility.

You will want to refer to the *ART Trading Software User's Manual* that you download from the TradersCoach.com website to give you the step-by-step instructions on how to change the default settings that are set up in the software when you first receive it. Two of the most popular features are the MinScore and the Audio Technology.

Adjusting the MinScore for a Pyramid Trading Point

The MinScore is used to calculate the score of the conditions that make up the peaks and valleys used to identify the Pyramid Trading Point patterns. This is a numeric setting with a range of values from 1 to 8 (the default value is 5). This setting controls how well-formed the pyramids must be before they are selected as Pyramid Trading Points.

Increasing the MinScore value will cause the ART software to identify only the higher-scoring peaks and valleys. Under perfect conditions, with a MinScore value of 8 (the highest setting), the highs and lows of these bars would ascend smoothly up and down, as shown in Figure B.10.

Lowering this value will cause the ART Pyramid Trading Point system to identify lesser-scoring peaks and valleys (see Figure B.11). For example,

Perfect Pyramid

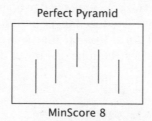

MinScore 8

FIGURE B.10   Perfect Pyramid with a MinScore Setting of 8
This setting allows for the most selective pyramids with a higher probability for success than others with lower MinScores.

Less Than Perfect Pyramids

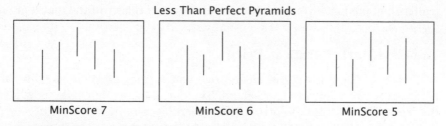

MinScore 7   MinScore 6   MinScore 5

Figure B.11   Less Perfect Pyramids with MinScores of 7, 6, and 5
Notice how the shape of the pyramid gets progressively more ragged as the highs and lows fall out of line. These settings allow for less selective pyramids than a MinScore of 8 does.

setting the MinScore to 1 (the lowest setting) will result in Pyramid Trading Points being identified that are less constrictive in nature. Because these are lesser-scoring PTP signals, there will be more of them and they will have a lower probability of success than the higher-scoring MinScore PTP signals.

The MinScore setting controls the minimum score and therefore how well-formed a Pyramid Trading Point must be before it is selected by the software. A MinScore value of 1 is very tolerant and will allow many small pyramids to form with lower probabilities of success. MinScore values of 4, 5, or 6 seem to work best. Values of 7 and 8 are very selective. These lead to fewer pyramids but with higher probabilities of success.

Adjusting the Audio Technology for Your Pyramid Trading Point

One of the most popular features of the ART trading software is that you can set specific voices and tones to signal to you that there is a "Pyramid Trading Point entry now" or a "Pyramid Trading Point exit now." You will actually hear either a man's voice, a woman's voice, or a tone that tells you when to enter and exit a trade.

The value of this feature is that you can multitask yet avoid missing important entries and exits, and you don't need to constantly keep your eyes on the computer screen. This will reduce fatigue and stress for you. Refer to your *ART Trading Software User's Manual* that you will download when you register your ART trial for instructions on how to adjust the audio features.

PRICE BARS AND VOLUME

In the pages that follow, you will learn that ART has a different definition of a bullish and bearish price bar than most systems do, and you'll see how volume can have great meaning, depending on its intensity. These two truths combined give you the ultimate undistorted reality of the markets.

The First Market Truth Is Price

ART uses an open, high, low, close price bar. A price bar tells us what is going on between buyers and sellers. The current price bar tells us what the reality is now—not tomorrow, not yesterday, nor one minute ago.

Price bars not only tell us the price of the market we are looking at, but also tell more about who is in control in the market. An individual price bar can also indicate the possibility of a reversal in the trend. Comparing the current price bar with the previous one tells us how the market is doing now compared to one price bar ago.

New information coming into the market will cause traders to either buy or sell. This will cause the price to change. The outcome of that action is represented in the price bar. By comparing the current price bar to the previous price bar, we can see that this new information has had either a positive effect or a negative effect on price.

Either way, you are looking at how the market is responding to new information such as a news event. In the ART approach to price bar meaning, it is important to realize that ART determines whether a price bar is bullish or bearish by *where prices close* in relation to where prices have traveled on the price bar itself. Notice I did not say where prices open.

Color Meaning for ART Price Bars

- Bullish price bar = green.
- Neutral price bar = black.
- Bearish price bar = red.

Note: These are the default colors. You can change the defaults by referring to your *ART Trading Software User's Manual* and following the "User Input" instructions.

OHLC: Open, High, Low, and Close

Technical analysis is based on charts, and very often price bars are used on bar charts to indicate the current price action in the market. The anatomy of a price bar includes four important items, which are the:

1. Open.
2. High.
3. Low.
4. Close.

In just one simple price bar you can read all of this information at once. An acronym to describe this price bar information is OHLC. Look at Figure B.12 to see an example of how this information looks on a price bar.

ART Defines Price Bars Differently, It's All about the Close

These price bar rules are all programmed into the software, so you will not need to implement them manually. But we want to show you how the ART

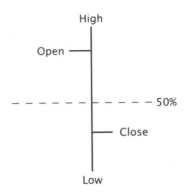

FIGURE B.12   OHLC Price Bar
This illustration of a typical price bar shows the open, high, low, and close of the
time interval of the price bar. The acronym to describe this is OHLC.

software is interpreting market data in a unique way so you will have a better
understanding of how ART is based on reality even on the price bar level.

- An **ART bullish price bar** is one *where prices close* on the upper half
  of the price bar.
- An **ART bearish price bar** is one *where prices close* on the lower half
  of the price bar.

Given that the definition of an ART price bar is different than other systems' price bar definitions, here are a few possibilities you should be aware of:

- It is possible to have a bearish price bar (by the ART definition) even
  though prices go higher than the previous price bar's close.
- It is possible to have a bearish price bar (by the ART definition) when
  the close is higher than the open on the same price bar.
- It is possible to have a bullish price bar (by the ART definition) even
  though prices go lower than the previous price bar's close.
- It is possible to have a bullish price bar (by the ART definition) when
  the close is lower than the open on the same price bar.

Remember: With ART a bullish or bearish price bar is determined
based on where the *close* is in relation to the price bar interval (the distance
between the price bar's high and low prices). If the open and close are both
exactly at the 50 percent mark on the price bar, then the bar is neutral with
little meaning except that the bulls and bears are in stalemate.

By evaluating the market's response to new information (by concentrating on the *close*) instead of evaluating the new information itself, you are tuned in to the reality of the marketplace. Don't look at the content of any news event—because the content is more information than you need.

ART Price Bar Definitions

How a price bar closes is an important truth we must be aware of. Here are seven examples of ART price bar definitions:

1. **Bullish—closing price at the very top of the price bar**. This means buyers are in control. (See Figure B.13.)

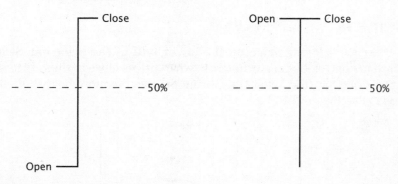

FIGURE B.13 Very Bullish Price Bars

2. **Bullish—closing price on the upper half of the price bar.** Buyers are in control, but not as much as when prices close at the very top of the price bar (the higher the closing price is the more bullish the bar is). (See Figure B.14.)

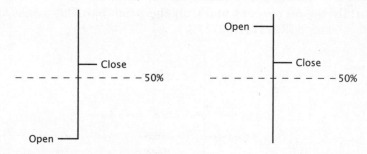

FIGURE B.14 Bullish Price Bars

3. **Bearish—closing price at the very low of the price bar.** This means sellers are in control. (See Figure B.15.)

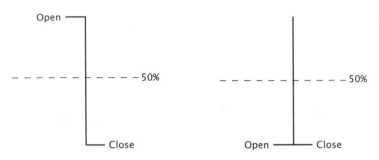

FIGURE B.15   Very Bearish Price Bars

4. **Bearish—closing price on the lower half of the price bar.** Sellers are in control, but not as much as when prices close at the very low of the price bar (the lower the closing price is the more bearish the bar is). (See Figure B.16.)

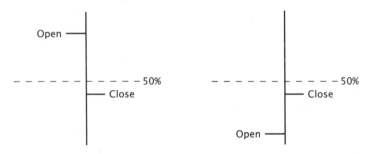

FIGURE B.16   Bearish Price Bars

5. **Bullish—closing price above the open of the price bar and at exactly the 50 percent mark on the price bar.** This means buyers are in control. (See Figure B.17.)

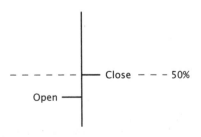

FIGURE B.17   Bullish Price Bar

6. **Bearish—closing price below the open of the price bar and at exactly the 50 percent mark on the price bar.** This means sellers are in control. (See Figure B.18.)

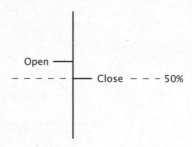

FIGURE B.18 Bearish Price Bar

7. **Neutral—closing price equal to the opening price and at exactly the 50 percent mark on the price bar.** This means buyers and sellers are in a stalemate. (See Figure B.19.)

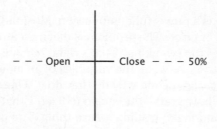

FIGURE B.19 Neutral Price Bar

Elongated Price Bars Represent High Emotion in the Market

A large price range, called an elongated price bar, has significant meaning (see Figure B.20). This type of price bar is *at least one-third longer* than the previous two to five price bars. These bars can signal the beginning or end of a trend. When you see an ART One-Bar Reversal that is elongated, it represents high emotions in the market between buyers and sellers and is one of the highest-probability ART One-Bar Reversal signals.

The Second Market Truth Is Volume

Volume is a market truth because it represents the number of trades (activity) in the current price bar. Like price, volume is not distorted; it is actual activity, a truth. Using volume along with price allows us to see what the

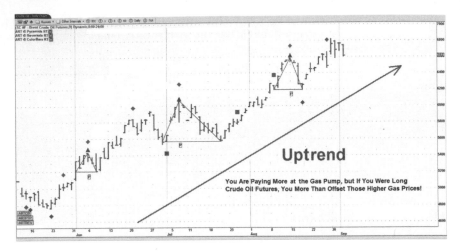

FIGURE B.20 Elongated Bullish ART One-Bar Reversal Forms on May 23, Signaling Beginning of Uptrend

Source: eSignal (www.eSignal.com).

market is saying. It is a powerful combination. Most indicators are derived from either volume or price. The problem is that indicators can be tweaked. And guess who does the tweaking? That's right, humans!

When a trader tries to tweak the variables of an indicator, the truth can be distorted. You may ask: Then why do they do it? One answer is that they are looking for the holy grail—the magic indicator that will solve all their trading problems and make trading a sure thing. The other reason is that the media have brainwashed traders into believing they must have these indicators to be successful.

One positive note about indicators is that once you realize that they are not the truth of the market and they can cause destructive opinions, they can be useful. Using indicators is an advanced technique, and if you would like to know more about how to use them in conjunction with the ART software, refer to the "Advanced Techniques" chapters in my book *The ART of Trading* (John Wiley & Sons, 2008). Remember, indicators are useful only if you are mentally tough enough to resist forming destructive opinions. Use indicators only as a confirmation and filtering tool. ART does not use indicators to forecast the market.

The Meaning of Volume

The meaning of volume is determined by its intensity. Here are two ways volume can have meaning.

First, when volume is higher than the previous price bar, more traders are trading. This may be either bullish or bearish, depending on how the price is moving. The more volume a price bar has, the more significant it is. The more volume present, the less likely it is to have price manipulation from locals on the floor or market makers. An increase in volume usually means trades are coming in from outside the community of locals and market makers. This means that new information has entered the market, causing traders to increase volume.

Second, when volume is higher than the previous 20 price bars, this has great significance and means many traders are trading. New information has come into the market, causing traders to trade with increased activity. Prices have reached an emotional point, and traders are either panicking out of the market or trying to get into the market. It can also be a combination of fear and greed; the two groups of buyers and sellers cause high volume. This type of activity usually occurs around market tops or market bottoms. It can also occur during breakouts when buyers want to buy the market.

ART REVERSAL BARS

Now we're going to work on combining price bar information with volume information. By combining these two market truths, we can benefit from significant trading signals called ART Reversal bars.

The ART One-Bar Reversal (1B) and the ART Two-Bar Reversal (2B) can help you:

- Scale out of trends.
- Scale into trends.
- Scalp.
- Countertrend trade.

The ART One-Bar Reversal occurs at market tops and bottoms. It is often seen as an elongated price bar at the end of a runaway market trend. This is a strong signal with relatively low risk. Within five bars after entering the position, you will know whether it will be successful.

The ART software identifies all ART Reversal bars (both one-bar and two-bar patterns) and is designed to be flexible enough to accommodate your personal style. This flexibility allows you to set the ART Reversals to occur aggressively or conservatively. (See the *ART Trading Software User's Manual* that you downloaded from the TradersCoach.com website to learn how to optimize this software to your needs).

On-Screen Icons for ART Reversals

♦ = **Green diamond** indicates a bullish ART One-Bar Reversal.

♦ = **Red diamond** indicates a bearish ART One-Bar Reversal.

♦ = **Gray diamond** indicates a voided bullish or bearish ART One-Bar Reversal.

■ = **Green square** indicates a bullish ART Two-Bar Reversal.

■ = **Red square** indicates a bearish ART Two-Bar Reversal.

■ = **Gray square** indicates a voided bullish or bearish ART Two-Bar Reversal.

Note: These are the default colors. You can change the defaults by referring to your *ART Trading Software User's Manual* and following the "User Input" instructions.

ART One-Bar Reversal Rules

Bullish ART 1B Rules

- The signal price bar is identified by a *green* icon on the chart.
- Go long on the next bar if prices go one tick above this ART One-Bar Reversal signal price bar.
- Set your initial stop-loss exit one tick below the low of the bullish ART One-Bar Reversal signal price bar.
- The signal is voided if prices on the next bars go below the ART One-Bar Reversal signal bar before going above it.

See Figure B.21.

Bearish ART 1B Rules

- The signal price bar is identified by a *red* icon on the chart.
- Go short on the next bar if prices go one tick below this ART One-Bar Reversal signal price bar.
- Set your initial stop-loss exit one tick above the high of the bearish ART One-Bar Reversal signal price bar.
- The signal is voided if prices on the next bars go above the ART One-Bar Reversal signal bar before going below it.

See Figure B.22.

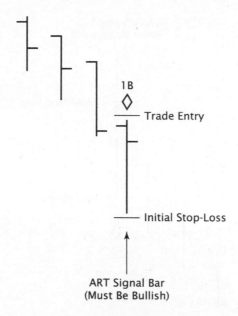

FIGURE B.21   Bullish ART One-Bar Reversal Diagram

Entry and exit rules: The bullish ART One-Bar Reversal signal price bar is identified by a green icon on the chart; go long on the next bar if prices go one tick above this ART One-Bar Reversal signal price bar; set your initial stop-loss exit one tick below the low of the bullish ART One-Bar Reversal signal price bar; the signal is voided if prices on the next bars go below the ART One-Bar Reversal signal bar before going above it.

Highest-Probability ART One-Bar Reversal

An elongated price bar and increasingly high volume combine for the highest-probability ART One-Bar Reversal.

An elongated price bar will be at least one-third longer than the previous three to five bars. Some reversals do occur on nonelongated price bars as long as the volume is high and the trend has been sharply in place. When you see an ART One-Bar Reversal that is elongated, it represents high emotions in the market between buyers and sellers. It is the highest-probability ART One-Bar Reversal signal, especially when combined with high volume.

If there is higher volume than the previous price bar's volume, that is a high-probability signal. Better yet, if there is higher volume than the previous two price bars, the signal is strengthened even more.

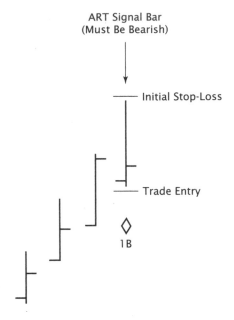

FIGURE B.22   Bearish ART One-Bar Reversal Diagram

Entry and exit rules: The bearish ART One-Bar Reversal signal price bar is identified by a red icon on the chart; go short on the next bar if prices go one tick below this ART One-Bar Reversal signal price bar; set your initial stop-loss exit one tick above the high of the bearish ART One-Bar Reversal signal price bar; the signal is voided if prices on the next bars go above the ART One-Bar Reversal signal bar before going below it.

Once you see an elongated price bar combined with increasingly high volume, you have a very high-probability ART One-Bar Reversal. Not all ART One-Bar Reversals are elongated, but when you see one that is, it is a high-probability trade signal.

The ART One-Bar Reversal signal becomes void if prices go one tick beyond the opposite side of the reversal bar before triggering the expected trade. If this happens, it indicates a possible trade in the other direction. Also, a new ART One-Bar Reversal cancels the previous ART Reversal price bar signal. As long as prices stay inside the highs and lows of the reversal bar, the signal(s) remain(s) valid.

What we will not know when trading this technique is whether the reversal will be a major change in trend or just a normal correction in the ongoing trend. You must accept this. Your personality will determine if and how you use this technique.

Three Methods of Monitoring an ART One-Bar Reversal Position

1. Trading as a possible beginning of a new trend in the opposite direction: Keep your stop in place until you have your first correction in the new trend. Once this new trend resumes and forms a new high, move your initial stop loss up one tick under the first pullback. Keep doing this until either you get stopped out or you see a sharp increase in the current trend. Then look for a reversal bar to get out, or get out and do a stop and reverse.

   Figure B.23 illustrates examples of ART One- and Two-Bar Reversal signals on increasing volume along with adjusted stops. ART One- and Two-Bar Reversals are shown with square and diamond icons.

2. Trading as if this is a correction in the current trend and not a change in trend direction: Once you initiate a trade against the trend, keep your initial stop loss in place. Then look for an ART Reversal indicating that the correction is possibly over. If you are trading this as a correction, the best you should expect from the trade is that the correction will retrace the trend by 50 percent. So the idea is to take a quick profit.

   Figure B.24 shows a bearish trend trade on an intraday chart with an exit at the end of the trading day. However, there is also a countertrend

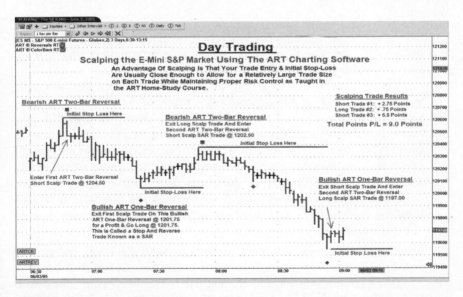

FIGURE B.23 Using ART One- and Two-Bar Reversal Signals on Increasing Volume to Take Advantage of a Possible Change in Trend Direction

Source: eSignal (www.esignal.com).

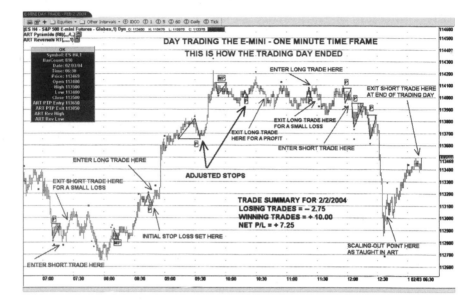

FIGURE B.24   Using ART Reversal Signals to Take Advantage of Countertrend Opportunities

Source: eSignal (www.esignal.com).

trade opportunity: the pullback in the downtrend as indicated by the bullish ART One-Bar Reversal occurring at approximately 12:30 P.M. on this one-minute E-mini S&P 500 chart.

This countertrend trade off that bullish ART One-Bar Reversal would have been at an approximate price of $1,130.50. As prices rebound, you would not know whether the downtrend would continue, but the bearish Primary Pyramid Trading Point indicates the trend is still down. However, this rebound or countertrend movement of prices provides an excellent opportunity to countertrend trade using the bullish ART One-Bar Reversal. You could exit this countertrend trade when prices retrace 50 percent of the downtrend or wait until the next bearish ART signal indicating a possible resumption of the downtrend.

3. Trading as if this is a new trend in the opposite direction, but getting out if it appears to be just a correction in the current trend:

Once you initiate a trade against the trend, keep your initial stop loss in place. When prices move 50 percent against the trend, use a trailing stop on half your positions. If your stop is triggered, you then are long half your original size. Keep the stop for your remaining position

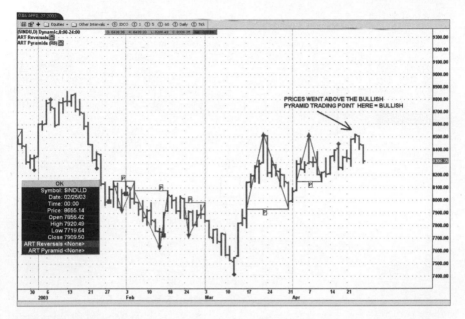

FIGURE B.25 Using the ART Trading Software to Take Advantage of a Change in Trend or a Correction

Source: eSignal (www.esignal.com).

at the original stop-loss location. Either you now will get stopped out or a new trend will emerge. Then you can revert to placing stops in accordance with the trend.

Figure B.25 illustrates a change in trend using the ART charting software. Note the elongated bullish ART Reversal bar at the bottom of the trend. A bullish One-Bar Reversal signals a new uptrend on March 12.

ART Two-Bar Reversal Rules

Bullish ART 2B Rules

- The signal price bar is identified by a *green* icon.
- Go long on the next price bar if prices go one tick above the signal bar.
- Set your initial stop-loss exit one tick under the low of the first price bar in the bullish ART Two-Bar Reversal pattern.
- The signal is voided if prices on the next price bars go below the signal bar before going above it.

See Figure B.26.

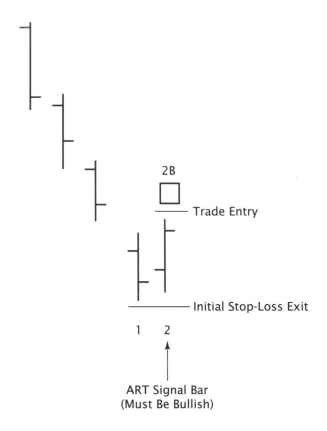

FIGURE B.26 Bullish ART Two-Bar Reversal Diagram
Entry and exit rules: The bullish ART Two-Bar Reversal signal bar is identified by
a green icon; go long on the next price bar if prices go one tick above the signal
bar; set your initial stop-loss exit one tick under the low of the first price bar in the
bullish ART Two-Bar Reversal pattern; the signal is voided if prices on the next price
bars go below the signal bar before going above it.

Bearish ART 2B Rules

- The signal price bar is identified by a *red* icon on the chart.
- Go short on the next price bar if prices go one tick below the signal bar.
- Set your initial stop-loss exit one tick above the high of the first price
  bar in the bearish ART Two-Bar Reversal pattern.
- The signal is voided if prices on the next price bars go above the signal
  bar before going below it.

See Figure B.27.

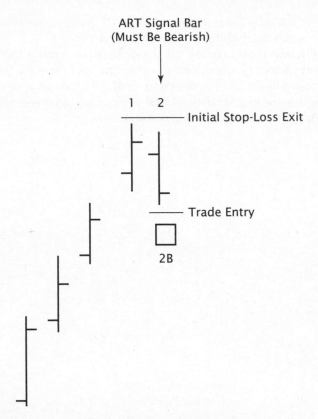

FIGURE B.27   Bearish ART Two-Bar Reversal Diagram

Entry and exit rules: The bearish ART Two-Bar Reversal signal bar is identified by a red icon; go short on the next price bar if prices go one tick below the signal bar; set your initial stop-loss one tick above the high of the first price bar in the bearish ART Two-Bar Reversal pattern; the signal is voided if prices on the next price bar go above the signal bar before going below it.

ART REVERSALS TELL YOU WHEN THE TREND ENDS

If trends don't end on an ART One-Bar Reversal bar, then they will usually end on an ART Two-Bar Reversal pattern. So, one way or another, we are going to have a high probability of spotting a potential change in trend from the ART Reversal signals. Because with the ART Two-Bar Reversal we are using two bars instead of one, volume may not be as high as the volume on other bars. This is why there is no volume minimum required on this setup. If high volume is present, the ART Two-Bar Reversal patterns will have a significantly higher probability of success.

When intraday trading below the five-minute time frame, the ART Two-Bar Reversal pattern is more common than the ART One-Bar Reversal. In fast time frames like a one-minute chart, traders' reaction to new information coming into the market may take two price bars to represent itself. The ART Two-Bar Reversal catches this phenomenon.

Resources: Front-End Platforms, Brokers, Data Providers, and More

This resources appendix has a wealth of information for both the newbie and the seasoned professional alike. With your finances, as in life, very often it is whom you know that can make or break the outcome of any situation. This is why we want to give you our personal "little black book" or "yellow pages" of terrific products and services that can speed you along on the path to greater profitability.

Keep in mind that we do not make any guarantees that you will be successful using the following resources. As in the markets, your success with these kinds of professional relationships depends entirely on you and how you select, manage and cultivate them. For most of the categories listed, you will see that we generally have a variety to choose from. This gives you a list to select from when it comes to brokers, a front-end platform, market data, and so forth.

It is essential that you interview each potential resource prior to signing up and be sure that it is a good fit for your personality, your trading and investing needs, and your budget. This means you are in the driver's seat and you will need to do your homework in order to obtain the best results.

Keep us posted and give us your feedback with regard to the following resources. And of course let us know if you find any outstanding firms or individuals that we can add to the list. Contact us via e-mail: Info@ TradersCoach.com.

Important Note: for the latest and most current resources information, we will be posting an updated version of this appendix online. You can access this up to the minute information by going to the following link:

www.traderscoach.com/survivalguide.php

FRONT-END PLATFORMS

The following list contains all the front-end charting platforms that the Applied Reality Trading (ART) software plugs into at the time of the printing of this book (which is September 2011). Keep in mind that these platforms are also exceptional for other software packages and tools in addition to the ART software. We encourage you to visit each platform's website to gather as much current information as possible. This will enable you to develop a custom plan perfectly suited to you.

TradeStation

- Website: www.TradeStation.com
- Phone: 1-800-292-3476
- Phone: 1-954-652-7441
- Markets Currently Available: All markets, including forex, equities, futures, and options. Contact this company to find out the latest information on products and services available.
- TradeStation is a premier and first-class front-end platform, broker, data provider, and ART platform. It provides a variety of services, products, and tools for virtually every trading and investing market. It is *not* compatible with other brokers or data vendors.

eSignal

- Website: www.eSignal.com
- E-mail: ray.fitzgerald@interactivedata.com
- Phone: 1-800-322-0940
- Phone: 1-510-723-1671
- Contact: Ray Fitzgerald
- Markets Currently Available: All markets including forex, equities, futures, and options. Contact this company to find out the latest information on products and services available.

- Free eSignal service and CME exchange fee waivers: Some eSignal brokers offer free eSignal service, including GAIN Capital, and MF Global. This offer is between the subscriber and the broker, and if a certain number of trades are completed each month by the subscriber, the broker reimburses the subscriber for their eSignal fees. Some brokers also offer CME exchange fee waivers. Contact this company to find out the latest information.
- eSignal is a premier and first-class data provider and ART platform. It is a front-end platform, and it is *not* a broker but is compatible with many brokers. Some of the brokers it is compatible with are: MB Trading, PFGBEST.com, Interactive Brokers, GAIN Capital, and optionsXpress.

NinjaTrader

- Website: www.NinjaTrader.com
- E-mail: support@ninjatrader.com
- Markets Currently Available: Equities, forex, futures, and options. Contact this company to find out the latest information on products and services available.
- NinjaTrader is a premier and first-class trading and investing ART platform. It is a front-end platform and is *not* a broker and *not* a data provider. Some of the brokers it is compatible with are: Interactive Brokers, MB Trading, AMP Futures, and Mirus Futures. Some of the data providers it is compatible with are: Kinetick, eSignal, Zen-Fire, and DTN.IQ.
- **Important Note:** This platform is compatible with the Zen-Fire trading engine and the Patsystems broker technology.

Trade Navigator (Genesis)

- Website: www.TradeNavigator.com
- E-mail: sales@tradenavigator.com
- Phone: 1-800-808-3282
- Phone: 1-719-884-0244
- Markets Currently Available: Equities, forex, futures, and options. Contact this company to find out the latest information on products and services available.
- Trade Navigator is a premier and first-class trading and investing ART platform. It is a front-end platform and is *not* a broker. Some of the brokers it is compatible with are: PFGBEST.com, Infinity Futures, TransAct Futures, and MF Global.

Market Analyst

- Website: www.Market-Analyst.com
- E-mail: sales@Market-Analyst.com
- Phone: 1-800-557-2702—United States
- Phone: 0-800-680-0428—United Kingdom
- Phone: 800-130-1604—Singapore
- Phone: 1-300-655-262—Australia
- Phone: +61-7-3118-9580—All countries
- Markets Currently Available: Equities, forex, futures, and options. Contact this company to find out the latest information on products and services available.
- Market Analyst is a premier and first-class trading and investing ART platform. It is a front-end platform and is *not* a broker. Two of the brokers it is compatible with are GFT and Interactive Brokers. Two of the data feeds it connects to are DTN IQFeed and eSignal.

Patsystems (Third-Party Broker Technology)

- ART Platform that Patsystems plugs into: NinjaTrader
- Website: www.PatSystems.com
- E-mail: sales@patsystems.com
- Phone: 1-312-922-7600
- Markets Currently Available: Futures, forex, and options. Call Ninja-Trader or Patsystems for the latest information on products and services available.
- If your broker uses the Patsystems technology (more than 100 brokers are using the Patsystems technology at this time) to route its trades to the exchanges, you will be able to have the ART trading software interface with your broker through Patsystems (sometimes called J-Trader). This means that you may be able to obtain free data (if your broker provides this) and direct order execution.
- This can currently be done by using the NinjaTrader platform of the ART software; see details in this appendix on this platform. There are four ways for you to see if your broker is using Patsystems: (1) call your broker to ask if it is on Patsystems; (2) call Patsystems to see if it supports the broker you are interested in using; (3) look in this appendix to see if your broker is currently set up on Patsystems; and (4) go to www.traderscoach.com/survivalguide.php for the latest availability and specifics on platform interface.
- Here is a brief list of brokerages that connect to NinjaTrader through Patsystems technology: MF Global, ND Global Trading, RCG, R.J. O'Brien, and Zaner.

BROKERS

The following list contains all the brokers that offer compatible order execution with the Applied Reality Trading (ART) system and software at the time of the printing of this book (which is September 2011). Keep in mind that these brokers are compatible with other software packages and tools in addition to the ART software. We encourage you to visit each broker's website to gather as much current information as possible. This will enable you to develop a custom plan perfectly suited to you.

TradeStation

- ART Platform Required: TradeStation
- Website: www.TradeStation.com
- Phone: 1-800-292-3476
- Phone: 1-954-652-7441
- Markets Currently Available: All markets, including equities, futures, options, and forex. Contact this company to find out the latest information on products and services available.

Mirus

- ART Platform Required: NinjaTrader or eSignal
- Website: www.MirusFutures.com
- Phone: 1-800-496-1683
- Phone: 1-312-423-2230
- Markets Currently Available: Futures. Contact this company to find out the latest information on products and services available.
- **Important Note:** This company offers Zen-Fire data.

Global Futures

- ART Platform Required: NinjaTrader or eSignal
- Website: www.globalfutures.com
- Email: globalfutures@globalfutures.com
- Phone: 1- 818-996-0404
- Markets Currently Available: Futures and forex. Contact this company to find out the latest information on products and services available.

- **Important Note:** Global Futures offers excellent international support for traders all over the world. They have brokers that speak virtually every language and are located in the same time zone as their customers. This broker is highly recommended for traders interested in speaking with their broker in their native language.

Optimus Futures

- ART Platform Required: Ninja Trader
- Website: www.optimusfutures.com
- Email: support@optimusfutures.com
- Phone: 1-561-367-8686
- Markets Currently Available: Futures. Contact this company to find out the latest information on products and services available.

Rogers Trading LLC Guaranteed by PFGBEST.com

- ART Platform Required: Trade Navigator, eSignal, or NinjaTrader
- Website: www.pfgbest.com
- E-mail: nrogers@pfgbest.com
- Phone: 1-800-546-9423
- Phone: 1-312-775-3543
- Markets Currently Available: Futures, options, stocks, and forex. Contact this company to find out the latest information on products and services available.

MF Global (Man Financial)

- ART Platform Required: (Patsystems compatible) NinjaTrader, eSignal, or Trade Navigator
- Website: www.mfglobal.com
- Phone: 1-800-421-5851
- Phone: 1-312-548-3243
- Markets Currently Available: Futures equities, forex, and options. Contact this company to find out the latest information on products and services available.

Interactive Brokers

- ART Platform Required: eSignal, Market Analyst or NinjaTrader
- Website: www.InteractiveBrokers.com
- Phone: 1-877-442-2757

- Phone: 1-312-542-6901
- Markets Currently Available: All markets, including equities, futures, options, and forex. Contact this company to find out the latest information on products and services available.

Vision Financial Markets

- ART Platform Required: eSignal or NinjaTrader
- Website: www.visionfinancialmarkets.com
- E-mail: inquiry@visionfinancialmarkets.com
- Phone: 1-203-388-2714
- Markets Currently Available: Futures, securities, and options. Contact this company to find out the latest information on products and services available.

TransAct Futures

- ART Platform Required: Trade Navigator or eSignal
- Website: www.transactfutures.com
- E-mail: info@TransActFutures.com
- Phone: 1-877-872-3303
- Phone: 1-312-341-9090
- Markets Currently Available: Equities, futures, options, and forex. Contact this company to find out the latest information on products and services available.

GAIN Capital (Forex.com)

- ART Platform Required: eSignal or NinjaTrader
- Website: www.GAINCapital.com
- E-mail: clientservices@gaincapital.com
- Phone: 1-877-424-6227
- Phone: 1-908-731-0700
- Market Currently Available: Forex. Contact this company to find out the latest information on products and services available.

GFT

- ART Platform Required: Market Analyst or NinjaTrader
- Website: www.gftforex.com
- E-mail: new.accounts@gftforex.com

- Phone: 1-800-465-4373
- Phone: 1-616-956-9273
- Markets Currently Available: Equities, futures, options, and forex. Contact this company to find out the latest information on products and services available.

MB Trading

- ART Platform Required: eSignal or NinjaTrader
- Website: www.MBTrading.com
- Phone: 1-866-628-3001
- Phone: 1-310-647-4281
- Markets Currently Available: Forex, options, futures, and equities. Contact this company to find out the latest information on products and services available.

AMP Futures & Forex

- ART Platform Required: NinjaTrader or eSignal
- Website: www.ampfutures.com
- Phone: 1-800-560-1640
- Phone: 1-312-893-6400
- Markets Currently Available: Equities, futures, options, and forex. Contact this company to find out the latest information on products and services available.
- **Important Note:** This company offers Zen-Fire data.

RCG (Rosenthal Collins Group)

- ART Platform Required: (Patsystems compatible) NinjaTrader
- Website: www.rcgdirect.com
- E-mail: info@rcgdirect.com
- Phone: 1-312-795-7770
- Market Currently Available: Futures. Contact this company to find out the latest information on products and services available.
- **Important Note:** This company offers Zen-Fire data.

Dorman Trading

- ART Platform Required: NinjaTrader or eSignal
- Website: www.dormantrading.com

- E-mail: support@dormantrading.com
- Phone: 1-800-552-7007
- Markets Currently Available: Futures, options, and forex. Contact this company to find out the latest information on products and services available.

optionsXpress

- ART Platform Required: eSignal
- Website: www.optionsxpress.com
- Phone: 1-888-280-6505
- Phone: 1-888-280-8020
- Markets Currently Available: Equities, futures, and options. Contact this company to find out latest information on products and services available.

FXCM

- ART Platform Required: eSignal or NinjaTrader
- Website: www.fxcm.com
- E-mail: info@fxcm.com
- Phone: 1-212-897-7660
- Market Currently Available: Forex. Contact this company to find out the latest information on products and services available.

R.J. O'Brien

- ART Platform Required: (Patsystems compatible) Ninja
- Website: www.rjofutures.com
- Phone: 1-800-441-1616
- Phone: 1-312-373-5478
- Market Currently Available: Futures. Contact this company to find out the latest information on products and services available.

Zaner

- ART Platform Required: (Patsystems compatible) eSignal or NinjaTrader
- Website: www.zaner.com
- E-mail: sales@zaner.com
- Phone: 1-800-621-1414
- Phone: 1-312-277-0050

- Markets Currently Available: Futures, options, and forex. Contact this company to find out the latest information on products and services available.
- **Important Note:** This company offers Zen-Fire data.

Infinity Futures

- ART Platform Required: eSignal, or Trade Navigator
- Website: www.infinitybrokerage.com
- Phone: 1-800-322-8559
- Phone: 1-312-373-6220
- Market Currently Available: Futures. Contact this company to find out the latest information on products and services available.

TradeKing

- ART Platform Required: NinjaTrader
- Website: www.TradeKing.com
- E-mail: service@tradeking.com
- Phone: 1-877-495-5464
- Markets Currently Available: Options. Contact this company to find out the latest information on products and services available.

ND Global

- ART Platform Required: (Patsystems compatible) NinjaTrader
- Website: www.ndglobaltrading.com
- E-mail: info@ndglobaltrading.com
- Phone: 1-888-513-6464
- Markets Currently Available: Equities, futures, options, and forex. Contact this company to find out the latest information on products and services available.
- **Important Note:** This company offers Zen-Fire data.

DATA PROVIDERS

Data feeds are your connection to the markets. You will receive price and volume data from the exchanges and it will be delivered through a data service. The firms listed here all provide quality data.

eSignal

- ART Platform Required: eSignal, Market Analyst, or NinjaTrader
- Website: www.eSignal.com
- E-mail: ray.fitzgerald@interactivedata.com
- Phone: 1-800-322-0940
- Phone: 1-510-723-1671
- Contact: Ray Fitzgerald
- Markets Currently Available: All Markets.

Kinetick

- ART Platform Required: NinjaTrader
- Website: www.kinetick.com
- E-mail: sales@kinetick.com
- Contact: Ryan Sindelar
- Markets Currently Available: Futures, stocks and forex. Contact this company to find out latest information on products and services available.

Zen-Fire (Data and Trading Engine)

- ART Platform Required: NinjaTrader or eSignal
- Website: www.zen-fire.com
- E-mail: support@zen-fire.com
- Markets Currently Available: Futures and options. Contact this company to find out latest information on products and services available.
- **Important Note:** Platforms with Zen-Fire data compatibility are NinjaTrader and eSignal. Brokers that provide Zen-Fire data are Mirus, Zaner, ND Global, AMP, and RCG.

TradeStation

- ART Platform Required: TradeStation
- Website: www.TradeStation.com
- Phone: 1-800-292-3476
- Phone: 1-954-652-7441
- Markets Currently Available: All markets.

DTN IQFeed (Telvent)

- ART Platform Required: NinjaTrader, TradeStation, or Market Analyst
- Website: www.dtniq.com
- Phone: 1-800-511-0096 ext. 8435

- Phone: 1-402-255-8435
- Contact: Trent Smalley
- Markets Currently Available: All markets.

BarchartMarketData.com

- ART Platform Required: NinjaTrader
- Website: www.barchartmarketdata.com
- Phone: 1-866-333-7587
- Phone: 1-312-566-9235
- Markets Currently Available: All markets.

TECHNOLOGY SUPPORT

Technology is a modern-day essential, especially if you are trading for a living. The following vendor and the tools it specializes in are basic necessities for every trader.

Custom Trading Computers, Inc. (COBRA)

- Website: www.customtradingcomputers.com
- E-mail: info@customtradingcomputers.com
- Phone: 1-801-447-0080
- Contact: Jordan Peterson

Suggested Reading and Education

This appendix has a wealth of information. Keep in mind that we do not make any guarantees that you will be successful using the following information. As in the markets, your success with educational resources depends entirely on you and how you select, manage, and apply them. For most of the categories listed you will see that we generally have a variety to choose from. This gives you a list to select from when it comes to education and so forth. You are in the driver's seat and you will need to do your homework in order to obtain the best results.

Keep us posted and give us your feedback with regard to the following list of books, websites, and inspiration. And of course let us know if you find any other outstanding education material that we can add to the list. Contact us via e-mail: Info@TradersCoach.com.

BOOKS

One of the best ways to keep up to date with current (and classic) trading and investing approaches is to read, read, and read some more. What I find is that when reading a variety of material, one new idea or approach may be all it takes to cultivate a more profitable approach. I may not agree or use every idea of each author, but if their observations and commentary open my eyes by presenting the material in a way not expressed before, it can be very valuable indeed.

Now, if you've been in this business very long at all, you know that books we as traders benefit the most from are generally not in your local public library. The reality is that active traders are a very small segment of the population, so your local library often will not utilize its limited resources to purchase and carry excellent trading books. That may be due in no small part to the fact that excellent trading books tend to be far more expensive than most mainstream literature.

And, unless a trading book has just been released, chances are you will not be able to find it in your local bricks-and-mortar bookstore. Again, for the same reasons that public libraries don't often carry trading books, bookstores will rarely carry books in this genre, since they are now more than ever trying to sell to the mainstream.

With this said, books are the most cost-effective way to educate yourself on a variety of topics utilizing a minimum of resources. If you were studying at a university, you no doubt would allocate a significant portion of your resources to textbooks. So, from my standpoint, your survival depends on keeping current and educating yourself constantly just as if you were going to a university. Reading trading books is the way to do that.

Out of the many hundreds of trading books in my own library, those listed here are ones that I have found to be the most useful. Some of them are expensive, but a few of the bookstores listed here allow you to rent some books for a quarter of what you would pay to buy them outright. Renting is of course an option; like video rentals from Blockbuster, this is a cost-effective way to sample these books before deciding to take the plunge and purchase them. Buying used books is another effective solution.

Another cost-saving tip is to consider what you are spending on shipping. We've listed a variety of Amazon.com locations just to assist you in finding the best price. Sometimes if you purchase the book you are interested in from a location that is closer to you, it will save you significant money in shipping.

And of course comparison shopping is worth the time it takes to do the search. A number of websites sort booksellers for a particular title from least expensive to most expensive. One such site is AllBookstores.com. It is a helpful tool to utilize.

One last note on books is that some titles are out of print or are difficult to locate. For these titles you may have more success in finding them by going to a bookseller that specializes in trading books, such as Trader's Library.

Booksellers

Trader's Library—United States

- Website: www.TradersLibrary.com
- Phone: 1-800-272-2855
- Phone: 1-410-964-0026

Amazon.com—United States

- Website: www.amazon.com
- E-mail: order@amazon.com
- Phone: 1-800-201-7575
- Phone: 1-206-694-2992
- Kindle versions of many trading and finance books are available for immediate download to your Kindle device.

Traders Press—United States

- Website: www.TradersPress.com
- E-mail: customerservice@traderspress.com
- Phone: 1-800-927-8222
- Phone: 1-864-298-0222

John Wiley & Sons—United States

- Website: www.wiley.com
- E-mail: support@wiley.com
- Phone: 1-877-762-2974
- E-books available on many John Wiley & Sons trading and finance books can be immediately sent to you in PDF form to your e-mail address.

AllBookstores.com—United States

- Website: www.allbookstores.com
- Website: www.allbookstores.com/book/compare
- This website compares the prices of many different Internet booksellers so you can see which one has the lowest price at the current time. The site does not compare prices to Traders Press and Traders Library (which often have very low prices), so you may want to check those sites out in addition to this one.
- Rental prices are also quoted and compared on this site, so for those readers who are interested in renting a trading book for a short time, that is an alternative solution.

TextbooksRus.com—United States

- Website: www.textbooksrus.com
- This site provides prices for rentals, and has an A+ Better Business Bureau rating at the time of this printing.

Books-A-Million—United States

- Website: www.booksamillion.com
- Phone: 1-800-201-3550

Barnes & Noble—United States
- Website: www.barnesandnoble.com
- Phone: 1-800-843-2665
- Phone: 1-201-559-3882
- Nook versions of many trading and finance books are available for immediate download to your Nook device.

Borders—United States
- Website: www.borders.com
- Phone: 1-800-770-7811
- Kobo versions of many trading and finance books are available for immediate download to your Kobo device.

Amazon.com—Canada
- Website: www.amazon.ca
- E-mail: info@amazon.ca

Amazon.com—United Kingdom
- Website: www.amazon.co.uk
- E-mail: order@amazon.co.uk

Amazon.com—Germany
- Website: www.amazon.de

Amazon.com—China
- Website: www.amazon.cn

Amazon.com—France
- Website: www.amazon.fr

Amazon.com—Italy
- Website: www.amazon.it

Technical Analysis Books

The ART of Trading
Bennett McDowell
John Wiley & Sons, 2008

Technical Analysis of the Financial Markets: A Comprehensive Guide to Trading Methods and Applications
John Murphy
New York Institute of Finance, 1999

Technical Analysis: The Complete Resource for Financial Market Technicians
Charles Kirkpatrick
FT Press, Second Edition 2010

The Encyclopedia of Technical Market Indicators
Robert Colby
McGraw-Hill, Second Edition 2002

Technical Analysis Explained: The Successful Investor's Guide to Spotting Investment Trends and Turning Points
Martin Pring
McGraw-Hill, 2002

Encyclopedia of Chart Patterns
Thomas Bulkowski
John Wiley & Sons, Second Edition 2005

Fundamental Analysis Books

The Secrets of Economic Indicators: Hidden Clues to Future Economic Trends and Investment Opportunities
Bernard Baumohl
Pearson Prentice Hall, Second Edition 2007

The Wall Street Journal Guide to the 50 Economic Indicators That Really Matter
Simon Constable
Harper Paperbacks, 2011

Common Stocks and Uncommon Profits and Other Writings
Philip Fisher
John Wiley & Sons, Second Edition 2003

The Intelligent Investor
Benjamin Graham
Collins Business, Revised Edition 2003

Elliott Wave Analysis

R. N. Elliott's Masterworks
Ralph Nelson Elliott
Edited by Robert Prechter Jr.
New Classics Library, 1994

Money Management Books

A Trader's Money Management System: How to Ensure Profit and Avoid the Risk of Ruin
Bennett McDowell
John Wiley & Sons, 2008

Money Management Strategies for Futures Traders
Nauzer Balsara
John Wiley & Sons, 1992

The Handbook of Portfolio Mathematics: Formulas for Optimal Allocation & Leverage
Ralph Vince
John Wiley & Sons, 2007

Beyond Technical Analysis: How to Develop and Implement a Winning Trading System
Tushar Chande
John Wiley & Sons, Second Edition 2001

Psychology Books

Trading in the Zone: Master the Market with Confidence, Discipline and a Winning Attitude
Mark Douglas
Prentice Hall Press, 2001

The Psychology of Trading: Tools and Techniques for Minding the Markets
Brett Steenbarger
John Wiley & Sons, 2002

Trading to Win: The Psychology of Mastering the Markets
Ari Kiev
John Wiley & Sons, 1998

The Disciplined Trader: Developing Winning Attitudes
Mark Douglas
John Wiley & Sons, 1990

The Art of War
Sun Tzu
Edited and translated by Thomas Cleary
Shambhala Publications, 1988

The Courage to Fail: Art Mortell's Secrets for Business Success
Art Mortell
McGraw-Hill, 1992

Candlesticks

Japanese Candlestick Charting Techniques
Steve Nison
Prentice Hall Press, Second Edition 2001

Stocks

How to Make Money in Stocks: A Winning System in Good Times and Bad
William O'Neil
McGraw-Hill, Fourth Edition 2009

Options

McMillan on Options
Lawrence McMillan
John Wiley & Sons, Second Edition 2004

Options as a Strategic Investment
Lawrence McMillan
Prentice Hall Press, Fourth Edition 2001

Futures

A Trader's First Book on Commodities: An Introduction to the World's Fastest Growing Market
Carley Garner
FT Press, 2010

Forex

Day Trading and Swing Trading the Currency Market: Technical and Fundamental Strategies to Profit from Market Moves
Kathy Lien
John Wiley & Sons, 2008

Trading History

Rogue Trader
Nick Leeson
Warner, 1997

Reminiscences of a Stock Operator
Edwin Lefevre
John Wiley & Sons, Revised Edition 2006

Market Wizards
Jack Schwager
Marketplace Books, Original Classic Edition 2006

The New Market Wizards: Conversations with America's Top Traders
Jack Schwager
Marketplace Books, Original Classic Edition 2008

Lessons from the Greatest Stock Traders of All Time: Jesse Livermore, Bernard Baruch, Nicolas Darvas, Gerald Loeb and William O'Neil
John Boik
McGraw-Hill, 2004

Inspirational and Motivational Books

Awaken the Giant Within: How to Take Immediate Control of Your Mental, Emotional, Physical and Financial Destiny!
Anthony Robbins
Free Press, 1992

The Secret
Rhonda Byrne
Atria Books, Beyond Words, 2006

What the Bleep Do We Know!?: Discovering the Endless Possibilities for Altering Your Everyday Reality
William Arntz, Betsy Chasse, and Mark Vicente
HCI, Mti edition 2007

You Can Heal Your Life
Louise Hay
Hay House, Gift edition 1999

Health and All Around Fitness

Fit for Life
Harvey and Marilyn Diamond
Wellness Central, Reprint edition 2010

MOVIES

These movies for a variety of reasons not only are entertaining but also are educational to traders and investors. Look for my comment at the end of each movie description to see how the movie can assist you in attaining greater insight into taking your trading up to the next level.

Rogue Trader

Miramax, 2000

Running Time: 97 minutes

Starring: Ewan McGregor

Director: James Dearden

This is a true story of Nick Leeson, who is famous for causing the collapse of the Barings Bank in 1995. Barings was the oldest bank in the world (operating for 232 years before the collapse), and Leeson was a trader for the bank. The film does an amazing job of showing how an ordinary young man can allow small losses to spiral into huge $1 billion losses because of his own fear, greed, denial, and lack of risk control. It also shows how an established, reputable bank could be so oblivious as to let it happen. This is a remarkable story that illustrates how emotions and psychology can get the better of anyone in the trading environment if one is not careful.

What the Bleep Do We Know!?

20th Century Fox, 2004

Running Time: 108 minutes

Starring: Marlee Matlin

Directors: William Arntz, Betsy Chasse, and Mark Vicente

Here's a great film that is part Hollywood and part independent film documentary. It stars Marlee Matlin playing a divorced photographer who tumbles down a metaphysical rabbit hole. Her mind-bending voyage through the worlds of science and metaphysical spirituality is mixed with actual interviews with some of the world's leading scientists, doctors, and metaphysical philosophers, including Ramtha (JZ Knight). The film (there is also a companion book) will certainly help you think outside the box and possibly see how your thoughts and addictions may very intensely create your reality. It includes lots of scientific data on the brain and how it works, quantum physics, and how these both affect our consciousness and our reality.

The Right Stuff

Warner Bros., 1983

Running Time: 193 minutes

Starring: Sam Shepard, Dennis Quaid, Barbara Hershey, and Ed Harris

Director: Philip Kaufman

This movie is based on the history of modern aviation, and the screenplay is adapted from the book by Tom Wolfe. The film begins out in the desert with the most famous test pilot of all time, Chuck Yeager. You get to see Yeager as the first man on earth to break the sound barrier by going Mach 1. The government demanded secrecy for this groundbreaking development because this was top secret stuff, but any pilot in the United States knew that Yeager was the fastest man on the planet. From Yeager to John Glenn, the examples in this film exhibit how determination and the passion for pushing the envelope enable us to achieve greatness. The courage to go above and beyond and to risk failure made these men heroes, and much can be learned from them about exploration, fear, failure, and success. These lessons all directly apply to trading and investing in the financial markets.

Wall Street

20th Century Fox, 1987

Running Time: 126 minutes

Starring: Michael Douglas, Charlie Sheen, and Daryl Hannah

Director: Oliver Stone

Pure Hollywood, this film is about an ambitious young broker (Charlie Sheen) who is lured into the illegal, lucrative world of corporate espionage when he is seduced by the power, status, and financial wizardry of Wall Street legend Gordon Gekko (Michael Douglas). He soon discovers that the pursuit of overnight riches comes at a price that's too high to pay. Gordon Gekko's famous line in the movie is "Greed is good!" Very entertaining Wall Street fiction, this movie is fun to watch.

Boiler Room

New Line Films, 2000

Running Time: 120 minutes

Starring: Giovanni Ribisi and Ben Affleck

Director: Ben Younger

This is a fictional story of Seth Davis (Giovanni Ribisi), who runs a small-time gambling casino operation out of his apartment. He gets recruited by the city's newest and hottest stock brokerage firm, an aggressive, renegade firm far from the traditions of Wall Street. The firm has a huge team of high-pressure telemarketing stockbrokers who relentlessly call until they sell whatever the stock du jour for the firm is. The movie is an interesting and disturbing look at what can happen when unethical individuals gain the trust of unsuspecting investors.

Apollo 13

NBC Universal, 2005

Running Time: 141 minutes

Starring: Tom Hanks, Bill Paxton, Kevin Bacon, Gary Sinise, and Ed Harris

Director: Ron Howard

An amazing true story of how a routine space flight becomes a desperate battle for survival. This is a triumphant adventure of courage and faith that shows how the NASA team works together to bring the crew of Apollo 13 safely home. James Lovell was the commander of this now-famous mission into outer space that he referred to as the most successful failure in history. The story is an example of how even when looking into the face of disaster, the NASA team, led by Gene Krantz, was able to use their determined and creative mind-set to bring home the space ship and crew when many feared the worst. This is a truly inspiring story.

PERIODICALS

Periodicals are quickly changing, given the new technology of our times. The old-fashioned magazines and newspapers are soon to be extinct. They will be replaced by periodicals that will be instantly delivered to our mobile devices and will be more current and instantaneous than ever.

Regardless of the method of delivery, it is crucial to be up to date on the latest news and information that you can get from periodicals, whether they are monthly, weekly, or daily. The following are some periodicals that offer industry-specific information useful to traders and investors.

Technical Analysis of Stocks & Commodities

Website: www.Traders.com

Phone: 1-800-832-4642

Phone: 1-206-938-0570

Publishes 13 issues per year.

Traders World

Website: www.tradersworld.com

Phone: 1-800-288-4266

Phone: 1-417-882-9697

Publishes four issues per year.

Futures

Website: www.futuresmag.com

Phone: 1-800-458-1734

Phone: 1-847-763-9252

Publishes 11 issues per year.

Active Trader

Website: www.activetradermag.com

Phone: 1-800-341-9384

Phone: 1-312-775-5421

Publishes 12 issues per year.

SFO (Stocks, Futures, and Options)

Website: www.sfomag.com

Phone: 1-800-590-0919

Phone: 1-319-268-0441

Publishes 12 issues per year.

Traders'

Website: www.traders-mag.com

Publishes four issues per year in both English and German.

IBD (Investor's Business Daily)

Website: www.investors.com

Phone: 1-800-831-2525

Phone: 1-310-448-6600

Publishes 250 issues per year.

Wall Street Journal

Website: www.wsj.com

Phone: 1-800-568-7625

Publishes 312 issues per year.

Barron's

Website: www.barronsmag.com

Phone: 1-800-568-7625

Publishes 45 issues per year.

WEBSITES

Today more than ever, you can get an infinite amount of information on the Internet—and often at little or no cost. The key with researching on the web is to verify that the information you are obtaining is valid and reliable.

This is why you need to select reputable sources, which will assist you in achieving your business goals. With that in mind, we are providing you with the following list of websites that we have found to be useful. Remember that we do not make any guarantees that you will be successful in using the following websites. As in everything, your success with these resources depends entirely on you. It is also important to verify your findings to determine the validity of the information you uncover.

Let us know if you find any other outstanding websites that we can add to the list. Contact us via e-mail: Info@TradersCoach.com.

www.TradersCoach.com

- E-mail: info@traderscoach.com
- Phone: 1-800-695-6188
- Phone: 1-858-695-0592
- Description: Provides many products and services for traders and investors in all markets. Extensive software library available to assist in: entries, exits, filtering, scanning, and money management. Featuring education on a variety of subjects including technical analysis, money

management, psychology, Elliott Wave, options, stocks, forex, futures, business management for traders, and much more.

www.ToniTurner.com

- E-mail: info@toniturner.com
- Phone: 1-949-509-6588
- Description: This website provides a variety of products and services for all traders and investors. Featuring Toni Turner, an exceptional educator, the student has access to her Market Club, books, DVD videos, and much more.

www.CandleCharts.com

- E-mail: paul@candlecharts.com
- Phone: 1-732-561-2152
- Description: Premier Candlestick education center featuring methods and software developed by Steve Nison. These techniques were first introduced to the western world by Nison himself and he is the authority on the proper use of candlesticks in trading and investing.

www.OptionStrategist.com

- E-mail: info@optionstrategist.com
- Phone: 1-800-724-1817
- Description: This is the leading options education website and it features the expertise of Lawrence McMillan, author of McMillan on Options. Provides a variety of market education and newsletters all focused on options trading.

www.TradingLiveOnline.com

- E-mail: leslie@tradingliveonline.com
- Description: Educational website providing one on one mentoring for traders based on the book *Trade What You See, How to Profit from Pattern Recognition.*

www.GeometricTrading.com

- E-mail: ross@geometrictrading.com
- Description: This website explains Gartley patterns and their use in optimal trading performance. Software tools related to this topic are also offered.

www.TradingPub.com

- E-mail: support@tradingpub.com
- Description: The Pub is the place to receive quality trading education on stocks, futures, options, and forex, all while interacting with traders and investors who are just like you—so pull up a stool and join us!

www.BKforexadvisors.com

- Description: This site specializes in forex trading and features both Kathy Lien and Boris Schlossberg as the primary educators.

www.MoneyMentor.com

- E-mail: sunny@moneymentor.com
- Phone: 1-760-908-3070
- Description: Site owner is Sunny Harris and it offers a variety of fundamental and technical support for traders. Sunny is experienced in developing strategies for the TradeStation platform.

www.RDStrader.com

- E-mail: support@rdstrader.com
- Phone: 213-784-0887
- Description: Professional traders and CME Group Members, Mike and Stephanie Radkay teach forex and futures trading to their students through this site.

www.TraderInterviews.com

- Phone: 1-949-829-3409
- Description: Tim Bourquin interviews top traders and provides the recordings to his subscribers so that they can learn from the lessons of these professional traders.

www.GabrielWisdom.com

- E-mail: gwisdom@amminvest.com
- Phone: 1-888-999-1395
- Phone: 1-858-755-0909
- Description: Gabriel Wisdom is an extraordinary financial radio talk show host and money manager. His website offers extensive content on topics related to finance.

www.StockCharts.com

- E-mail: support@stockcharts.com
- Phone: 1-425-881-2606
- Description: Winner for nine years in a row for best technical analysis website by the Technical Analysis of Stocks & Commodities Reader's Choice Award, this site offers fantastic charts.

www.Worden.com

- E-mail: support@worden.com
- Phone: 1-800-776-4940
- Phone: 1-919-294-1111
- Description: Offers effective scanning products and services.

www.MoneyShow.com and www.TradersExpo.com

- Phone: 1-800-970-4355
- Description: Content-rich website with videos, courses, and commentary from hundreds of trading and investing experts. Live tradeshows with speakers presenting educational workshops are also presented around the world.

www.TradingTutor.com

- E-mail: larry@tradingtutor.com
- Description: Fibonacci and Astrological Cycles expert, Larry Pesavento teaches his students pattern recognition skills and much more through this site.

www.Investopedia.com

- Description: Informative site so that you can find answers to trading and investing questions quickly and easily.

www.Wikpedia.com

- Description: Similar to Investopedia.com but with more in-depth content and the ability to translate to any language. Their tagline is "The Free Encyclopedia" and that is an accurate summation. Good for doing research on new topics to get an overview.

www.AAII.com

- Phone: 1-800-428-2244
- Phone: 1-312-280-0170
- Description: AAII is an acronym for American Association of Individual Investors. Excellent resource for a multitude of material from portfolio models to financial planning to investing strategies.

www.Finance.Yahoo.com

- Description: Must see site with free data feeds from the exchange, videos, news, education, and more.

www.DJAverages.com

- E-mail: DJIndexSupport@djindexes.com
- Phone: 1-609-520-7249
- Description: Informative and fun site to visit. Lots of history on the DJIA and complete data from the last 100 years.

www.NeedToKnowNews.com

- Phone: 1-312-663-7176
- Description: News feed services both audio and written.

www.GreenCompany.com

- E-mail: info@greencompany.com
- Phone: 1-888-558-5257
- Phone: 1-646-224-6923
- Description: CPA firm offering virtual tax and investment management services for traders. Robert Green, CPA and CEO, consults, lectures, and authors books and articles on traders' tax topics.

Market Exchanges

This appendix has a listing of many of the worldwide financial exchanges that investors and traders work with. Some of the exchanges listed now operate as subsidiaries of other exchanges, and this list is current at the time of this book's printing. For the latest list of exchanges, you can go to the following link:

www.traderscoach.com/survivalguide.php

ASE (or ATHEX)

Exchange Name: Athens Stock Exchange

Website: www.athex.gr/

Location of Exchange: Athens, Greece

ASX

Exchange Name: Australian Securities Exchange

Website: www.asx.com.au/

Location of Exchange: Sydney, NSW, Australia

BATS

Exchange Name: Better Alternative Trading System

Website: www.batstrading.com/

Location of Exchange: Kansas City, MO, United States

BCBA

Exchange Name: Buenos Aires Stock Exchange, Bolsa de Comerciao de Buenos Aires

Website: www.bcba.sba.com.ar/

Location of Exchange: Buenos Aires, Argentina

BM&F BOVESPA

Exchange Name: Bolsa de Valores, Mercadorias & Futuros de Sao Paulo

Website: www.bmfbovespa.com.br/

Location of Exchange: Sao Paulo, Brazil

BME

Exchange Name: Madrid Stock Exchange

Website: www.bolsamadrid.es/

Location of Exchange: Madrid, Spain

BMV

Exchange Name: Mexican Stock Exchange, Bolsa Mexicana de Valores

Website: www.bmv.com.mx/

Location of Exchange: Mexico City, Mexico

BORSA

Exchange Name: Borsa Italiana

Website: www.borsaitaliana.it/

Location of Exchange: Milan, Italy

BOX

Exchange Name: Boston Options Exchange

Website: www.bostonoptions.com/

Location of Exchange: Boston, MA, United States

BSE

Exchange Name: Budapest Stock Exchange

Website: www.bse.hu/

Location of Exchange: Budapest, Hungary

BSX

Exchange Name: Bermuda Stock Exchange

Website: www.bsx.com/

Location of Exchange: Hamilton, Bermuda

BVC

Exchange Name: Caracas Stock Exchange, Bolsa de Valores de Caracas

Website: www.caracasstock.com/esp/

Location of Exchange: Caracas, Venezuela

BVL

Exchange Name: Lima Stock Exchange, Bolsa de Valores de Lima

Website: www.bvl.com.pe/

Location of Exchange: Lima, Peru

BVRJ

Exchange Name: Rio de Janeiro Stock Exchange

Website: www.bvrj.com.br/

Location of Exchange: Rio de Janeiro, Brazil

CBOE

Exchange Name: Chicago Board Options Exchange

Website: www.cboe.com/

Location of Exchange: Chicago, IL, United States

CHX

Exchange Name: Chicago Stock Exchange

Website: www.chx.com/

Location of Exchange: Chicago, IL, United States

CME GROUP

Exchange Name: Chicago Mercantile Exchange

Website: www.cmegroup.com/

Location of Exchange: Chicago, IL, United States

CME GROUP, CBOT

Exchange Name: Chicago Board of Trade

Website: www.cmegroup.com/company/cbot.html

Location of Exchange: Chicago, IL, United States

CME GROUP, COMEX

Exchange Name: Commodity Exchange, Inc.

Website: www.cmegroup.com/company/comex.html

Location of Exchange: New York, NY, United States

CME GROUP, NYMEX

Exchange Name: New York Mercantile Exchange

Website: www.cmegroup.com/company/nymex.html

Location of Exchange: New York, NY, United States

DEUTSCHE BORSE

Exchange Name: Deutsche Borse

Website: http://deutsche-boerse.com/

Location of Exchange: Frankfurt, Germany

DME

Exchange Name: Dubai Mercantile Exchange

Website: www.dubaimerc.com/

Location of Exchange: Dubai, United Arab Emirates

EUREX

Exchange Name: Eurex

Website: www.eurexchange.com/

Location of Exchange: Zurich, Switzerland

EURONEXT, AMSTERDAM

Exchange Name: Amsterdam Stock Exchange

Website: www.euronext.com/landing/indexMarket-18812-NL.html

Location of Exchange: Amsterdam, Netherlands

EURONEXT, BRUSSELS

Exchange Name: Brussels Stock Exchange

Website: www.euronext.com/

Location of Exchange: Brussels, Belgium

EURONEXT, LISBON

Exchange Name: Euronext Lisbon
Website: www.euronext.com/landing/indexMarket-18812-EN.html
Location of Exchange: Lisbon, Portugal

EURONEXT, PARIS

Exchange Name: Euronext Paris
Website: www.euronext.com/landing/indexMarket-18812-FR.html
Location of Exchange: Paris, France

HKEX

Exchange Name: Hone Kong Stock Exchange
Website: www.hkex.com.hk/eng/
Location of Exchange: Hong Kong

ICE

Exchange Name: IntercontinentalExchange
Website: https://www.theice.com/
Location of Exchange: Atlanta, GA, United States

ICE FUTURES, CANADA

Exchange Name: Winnipeg Commodity Exchange (former name)
Website: https://www.theice.com/clear_canada.jhtml
Location of Exchange: Winnipeg, Canada

ICE FUTURES, NYBOT

Exchange Name: New York Board of Trade
Website: https://www.theice.com/
Location of Exchange: New York, NY, United States

ISE

Exchange Name: Irish Stock Exchange
Website: www.ise.ie/
Location of Exchange: Dublin, Ireland

JSE

Exchange Name: Johannesburg Stock Exchange
Website: www.jse.co.za/
Location of Exchange: Johannesburg, Africa

KCBT

Exchange Name: Kansas City Board of Trade

Website: www.kcbt.com/

Location of Exchange: Kansas City, MO, United States

KRX

Exchange Name: Korea Stock Exchange

Website: www.krx.co.kr/

Location of Exchange: Busan, South Korea

LME

Exchange Name: London Metal Exchange

Website: www.lme.com/

Location of Exchange: London, United Kingdom

LSE

Exchange Name: London Stock Exchange

Website: www.londonstockexchange.com/

Location of Exchange: London, United Kingdom

MEFF

Exchange Name: Spanish Futures & Options Exchange

Website: www.meff.es/

Location of Exchange: Barcelona, Spain

MGEX

Exchange Name: Minneapolis Grain Exchange

Website: www.mgex.com/

Location of Exchange: Minneapolis, MN, United States

MX

Exchange Name: Montreal Exchange

Website: www.m-x.ca/accueil_fr.php

Location of Exchange: Montreal, Canada

MYX

Exchange Name: Bursa Malaysia Stock Exchange

Website: www.bursamalaysia.com/

Location of Exchange: Kuala Lumpur, Malaysia

NASDAQ GROUP

Exchange Name: National Association of Securities Dealers Automated Quotations, NASDAQ Stock Market

Website: www.nasdaq.com/

Location of Exchange: New York, NY, United States

NASDAQ OMX GROUP, BX

Exchange Name: Boston Stock Exchange

Website: www.nasdaqtrader.com/Trader.aspx?id=Boston_Stock_Exchange

Location of Exchange: Boston, MA, United States

NASDAQ OMX GROUP, CSE, COPENHAGEN

Exchange Name: Copenhagen Stock Exchange

Website: www.nasdaqomxnordic.com/nordic/Nordic.aspx

Location of Exchange: Copenhagen, Denmark

NASDAQ OMX GROUP, STOCKHOLM

Exchange Name: Stockholm Stock Exchange

Website: www.nasdaqomxnordic.com/nordic/Nordic.aspx

Location of Exchange: Stockholm, Sweden

NASDAQ OMX PBOT

Exchange Name: Philadelphia Board of Trade

Website: www.nasdaqomx.com/whatwedo/trading/usmarkets/futures/?languageId=1

Location of Exchange: Philadelphia, PA, United States

NASDAQ OMX PHLX

Exchange Name: Philadelphia Stock Exchange

Website: www.nasdaqtrader.com/Micro.aspx?id=phlx

Location of Exchange: Philadelphia, PA, United States

NSE

Exchange Name: National Stock Exchange of India

Website: www.nse-india.com/

Location of Exchange: Mumbai, India

NSX

Exchange Name: National Stock Exchange
Website: www.nsx.com/
Location of Exchange: Chicago, IL, United States

NYSE EURONEXT

Exchange Name: New York Stock Exchange
Website: www.nyse.com/
Location of Exchange: New York, NY, United States

NYSE EURONEXT, NYX, AMEX

Exchange Name: American Stock Exchange
Website: www.nyse.com/attachment/amex_landing.htm
Location of Exchange: New York, NY, United States

NZX

Exchange Name: New Zealand Exchange
Website: www.nzx.com/
Location of Exchange: Wellington, New Zealand

ONECHICAGO

Exchange Name: One Chicago
Website: www.onechicago.com/
Location of Exchange: Chicago, IL, United States

OSE

Exchange Name: Osaka Securities Exchange
Website: www.ose.or.jp/
Location of Exchange: Osaka, Japan

OSLO

Exchange Name: Oslo Stock Exchange
Website: http://oslobors.no/
Location of Exchange: Oslo, Norway

SAFEX

Exchange Name: South African Futures Exchange
Website: www.safex.co.za/
Location of Exchange: South Africa

SET

Exchange Name: Stock Exchange of Thailand
Website: www.set.or.th/
Location of Exchange: Bangkok, Thailand

SFE

Exchange Name: Sydney Futures Exchange
Website: www.asx.com.au
Location of Exchange: Sydney, Australia

SGX

Exchange Name: Singapore Exchange
Website: www.sgx.com/
Location of Exchange: Singapore

SIX SWISS

Exchange Name: Six Swiss Exchange
Website: www.six-swiss-exchange.com/
Location of Exchange: Zurich, Switzerland

SSE

Exchange Name: Santiago Stock Exchange, Bolsa de Comercio de Santiago
Website: www.bolsadesantiago.com/
Location of Exchange: Santiago, Chile

TASE

Exchange Name: Tel Aviv Stock Exchange
Website: www.tase.co.il/TASEEng/
Location of Exchange: Tel Aviv, Israel

TFX

Exchange Name: Tokyo Financial Exchange
Website: www.tfx.co.jp/en/
Location of Exchange: Tokyo, Japan

TGE

Exchange Name: Tokyo Grain Exchange
Website: www.tge.or.jp/english/
Location of Exchange: Tokyo, Japan

TSE

Exchange Name: Tokyo Stock Exchange

Website: www.tse.or.jp/english/

Location of Exchange: Tokyo, Japan

TSX

Exchange Name: Toronto Stock Exchange

Website: www.tmx.com/

Location of Exchange: Toronto, Canada

TWSE

Exchange Name: Taiwan Stock Exchange

Website: www.twse.com.tw/en/

Location of Exchange: Taiwan, Republic of China

WIENER BORSE

Exchange Name: Vienna Stock Exchange

Website: www.vienna-stock-exchange.com/

Location of Exchange: Vienna, Austria

WSE

Exchange Name: Warsaw Stock Exchange

Website: www.gpw.pl/

Location of Exchange: Warsaw, Poland

Glossary

accumulation/distribution (A/D) A momentum indicator that attempts to gauge supply and demand by determining whether traders or investors are accumulating (buying) or distributing (selling) a certain financial instrument by identifying divergences between price and volume flow.

American Stock Exchange (AMEX) The third-largest stock exchange in the United States, renamed NYSE Amex Equities. Generally, the listing rules are more lenient than those of the NYSE, and therefore it has a larger representation of stocks and bonds issued by smaller companies. It is located in New York City.

annual percentage rate (APR) The periodic rate times the number of periods in a year. Example: A 5 percent quarterly return has an APR of 20 percent.

Applied Reality Trading® (ART®) A technical analysis system developed by Bennett A. McDowell that focuses on trading the realities of the financial markets. The ART software works on any time frame and in any market for both investors and day traders. The software generates charts that illustrate clear entry and exit signals and sound money management rules.

APR See *annual percentage rate*.

ART bear price bar When prices close on the *lower* half of the bar, it is an ART bear price bar. The bar is defined by the relationship between the *close* and the price bar interval. The bears are in control at the close of the price bar. (ART determines bear and bull differently than other systems.)

ART bull price bar When prices close on the *upper* half of the bar, it is an ART bull price bar. The bar is defined by the relationship between the *close* and the price bar interval. The bulls are in control at the close of the price bar. (ART determines bear and bull differently than other systems.)

ART elongated price bar A price bar that is at least one-third longer than the previous three to five price bars.

ART inside price bar A compressed price bar forming directly after the signal bar in an ART Reversal. It can be used to aggressively enter an ART Reversal trade.

ART neutral price bar   On this price bar, the open and the close are at the 50 percent point on the bar when it closes. Bulls and bears are in a stalemate at the close of the price bar.

ART One-Bar Reversal (1B)   This scalp signal identifies exact entries and exits, and can also be used for scaling in and scaling out of trends. This reversal signal requires only one price bar that is the signal bar, which determines both the entry and also the stop-loss exit. It can be used on all markets and all time frames.

ART signal price bar   The price bar used for a trade entry when making an ART Reversal trade. The ART trading software designates the ART signal bar with a 1B or 2B directly above or below the price bar.

ART Two-Bar Reversal (2B)   This scalp signal identifies exact entries and exits, and can also be used for scaling in and scaling out of trends. This reversal signal requires two price bars; the first price bar is used for the stop-loss exit, and the second price bar or signal bar is used for the entry. It can be used on all markets and all time frames.

ask price   The price a seller is willing to accept. It is also known as the offer. The difference between the bid and ask is known as the bid-ask spread.

asset   Any possession that has value in an exchange.

asset allocation   The process of deciding what types of assets you want to own, and the percentage of each. As conditions change, the percentage allotted to each asset class changes.

at-the-money   An option is at-the-money if the strike price of the option is equal to the market price of the underlying asset.

average true range (ATR)   An indicator that helps determine a market's volatility over a given period. It is calculated by taking an average of the true ranges over a set number of previous periods. It is the (moving) average of the true range for a given period.

back-testing   The use of historical data to test technical or fundamental theories or systems to determine the historical performance of a given set of rules. Back-testing can give information on what the performance would have been but does not guarantee future results. eSignal has a playback feature that enables you to test your trading skills using historical data and playing it forward to determine what your performance would have been. The value of the playback is that you do not see the right side of the chart, so you are testing your own ability to make decisions without knowing what the next price bar will bring.

balance sheet   A listing of all assets and liabilities for an individual or a business. The surplus of assets over liabilities is the net worth, or what is owned free of debt.

basis   The cost of the asset. If you pay $10 per share for a stock plus $1 per share for commission, your basis is $11 per share.

bear   Someone who believes prices will decline and is generally pessimistic about future market returns.

bear market   A market characterized by prolonged broadly declining prices. Some negative information has entered the market to create this condition. Generally the downturn in prices is in excess of 20 percent. It is not to be confused with a correction.

bid-ask spread   The difference between the bid and the ask. The spread narrows or widens according to the supply of and demand for the security being traded.

bid price   The price a buyer is willing to pay.

black box system   A 100 percent mechanical system that requires absolutely *no* discretion. The concern with these systems is that they are unable to adapt to ever-changing market cycles. The reality is that over time, all systems require some form of discretionary decision making to be consistently profitable. ART is not a black box system.

Black Monday   Refers to October 19, 1987, when the Dow Jones Industrial Average fell 508 points after sharp drops the previous week.

blue-chip company   A large, nationally recognized, financially sound firm with a long track record, usually selling high-quality and widely accepted goods and services. Examples: General Electric and IBM.

bond   A debt investment. Investors lend money to an institution by buying bonds and receive fixed interest payments in return. When the bond matures, the investor receives the principal back.

bond market   The bond market, also known as the debt, credit, or fixed income market, is a financial market where participants buy and sell debt securities.

bracketed market   This is also known as a consolidating, range-bound, sideways, nontrending, choppy, channeling, sleepy, or drunk market. When a market is bracketed, it is stuck in a price range between identifiable resistance and support levels. On a chart, a bracket will be seen as a sideways horizontal line. Some of the most powerful and profitable trends come out of markets that have been bracketed for more than 20 price bars.

breakout   A sharp change in price movement after the market has traded sideways for at least 20 price bars. This is beyond a previous high (or low) or outside the boundaries of a preceding price bracket.

broker   An individual or online firm that is paid a commission for executing customer orders; an agent specializing in stocks, bonds, commodities, or options. The broker must be registered with the exchange where the securities are traded.

bull   Someone who believes that prices will rise and is generally optimistic about future market returns.

bull market   A market characterized by prolonged broadly rising prices. Positive information has entered the market to create this condition. Over 70 percent of historic periods have been bull markets.

buy   To purchase an asset.

buyer's market   A market in which the supply exceeds the demand, creating lower prices.

call option   An options contract with the right to buy a specific number of shares of a stock at a specified price (the strike price) on or before a specific expiration date, regardless of the underlying stock's current market price. A call option writer sells the right to a buyer.

candlestick chart   A type of bar chart developed by the Japanese, in which the price range between the open and the close is either a white rectangle (if the close is higher) or a black rectangle (if the close is lower).

capital   The money you need to trade or invest. This should be risk capital, meaning that you can afford to lose this money.

cash per share   The amount of cash divided by the total number of common stock shares outstanding for a given stock. A corporation with high cash per share ratio is said to be cash rich and may be considered low-risk or undervalued.

central bank   The institution in each country responsible for setting monetary policy, printing money, managing reserves, and controlling inflation. In the United States, the central bank is the Federal Reserve System, also known as the Fed.

channeling market   This is also known as a bracketed, consolidating, range-bound, sideways, or nontrending market. See *bracketed market.*

chart   A graph that depicts the price movement of a given market. The most common type of chart is the bar chart, which denotes each interval's open, high, low, and close for a given market with a single price bar.

chart analysis   The study of price charts in an effort to find patterns that in the past preceded price advances or declines. The basic concept is that the development of similar patterns in a current market can signal a probable market move in the same direction. Practitioners of chart analysis are often referred to as *technical analysis* traders or investors.

Chicago Board of Trade (CBOT)   Established in 1848, the CBOT is a leading exchange for futures and options on futures. More than 3,600 CBOT members trade 50 different futures and options products at the exchange through open auction and/or electronically. CME Group is a combined entity formed by the 2007 merger of the Chicago Mercantile Exchange (CME) and the Chicago Board of Trade (CBOT).

Chicago Board Options Exchange (CBOE)   Founded in 1973, the CBOE is an exchange that focuses on options contracts for individual equities, indexes, and interest rates. The CBOE is the world's largest options market. It captures a majority of the options traded. It is also a market leader in developing new financial products and technological innovation, particularly with electronic trading.

Chicago Mercantile Exchange (CME)   Founded in 1898 as the Chicago Butter and Egg Board, this is an American financial exchange based in Chicago. Originally the exchange was a not-for-profit organization. The exchange demutualized in November 2000, went public in December 2002, and merged with the Chicago Board of Trade in July 2007. CME trades several types of financial instruments: interest rates, equities, currencies, and commodities. CME has the largest options and futures contracts open interest (number of contracts outstanding) of any futures exchange in the world. Trading is conducted in two methods: an open outcry format and the CME Globex® electronic trading platform. Approximately 70 percent of total volume at the exchange occurs on CME Globex.

choppy market   See *bracketed market.*

churning   When a broker excessively trades an account for the purpose of increasing his or her commission revenue. This practice is entirely unethical and does not serve the customer's investment or trading goals.

close   The period at the end of the trading session; sometimes refers to the closing price.

CME Group   The world's largest and most diverse exchange. Formed by the 2007 merger of the Chicago Mercantile Exchange (CME) and the Chicago Board of Trade (CBOT), CME Group serves the risk management needs of customers around the globe. As an international marketplace, CME Group brings buyers and sellers together on the CME Globex electronic trading platform and on its trading floors.

commission   Fee paid to a brokerage house to execute a transaction.

commission ratio   Total dollars of commission paid divided by total dollars of profit earned equals the commission ratio. This formula is not applicable to traders who are not generating a profit or who have a payoff ratio of less than 1 to 1.

commodities   Physical goods that are traded at a futures exchange, such as grains, foods, meats, metals, and so on.

consolidating market   This is also known as a bracketed, range-bound, sideways, nontrending, choppy, or channeling market. See *bracketed market.*

consumer price index (CPI)   Issued by the U.S. Bureau of Labor Statistics, this figure is a popularly used measure of inflation. It measures the relative change in prices of a basket of consumer products and services.

contract   A single unit of a commodity or future. This is similar to shares in stocks.

contrarian   One who trades or invests on contrary opinion using the theory that one can profit by doing the opposite of the majority of traders or investors in the market.

correction   A short, sharp reverse in prices during a longer market trend.

corrective Elliott wave   Refers to an Elliott wave structure made up of impulsive wave counts and corrective wave counts. Usually refers to a correction wave sequence in an impulsive trend wave sequence.

countertrend trade   A trading strategy where an investor or trader attempts to make small gains through a series of trades against the current trend.

cover   To liquidate an existing position (such as sell if one is long; buy if one is short).

covered call   To sell a call option at the same time you own the same number of shares represented by the option in the underlying stock.

covered put   To sell a put option at the same time you are holding a short position in the underlying stock.

data   Live streaming market data is provided to the trader or investor by data providers and brokerage houses. This data is used to conduct technical analysis and provide price and volume information. Real-time data is sent by the minute during the trading day. Generally data providers charge more for real-time data because it is more labor-intensive to provide. Real-time data is used by day traders. End-of-day data is provided at the end of the day and gives you final price and volume information for the market you are analyzing. Data providers charge less for end-of-day data, and this type of data is used more by investors and position traders.

day trade   A trade that is liquidated on the same day it is initiated.

day trader   Refers to the practice of buying and selling financial instruments within the same trading day such that all positions will usually (not necessarily always) be closed before the market close. Traders who participate in day trading are day traders.

debt-to-equity ratio   Ratio demonstrating an institution's debt relative to its equity. It is just one component used by corporations in assessing optimal capital structures.

decimal   Increment of movement in the stock market.

deflation   A drop in average product and services price levels, usually caused by excessive tightening of the money supply. Deflation can lead to reduced economic demand and higher unemployment. It is not to be confused with disinflation.

discretionary trader   A trader who makes decisions based on his or her own analysis of the market, rather than in response to signals generated by a computerized black box system. The best discretionary traders are those who develop a systematic approach and then use discretion in their entries, exits, and position sizing to improve performance.

disinflation   The slowing growth of average product and services price levels. This can be thought of as the slowing of inflation, and is not to be confused with deflation.

divergence The failure of a market or an indicator to follow suit when a related market or indicator sets a new high or low. Some analysts look for divergences as signals of impending market tops and bottoms.

diversification Trading or investing in a variety of markets and sectors to reduce risk. Don't put all your eggs in one basket!

dividend A payment made to stockholders, usually quarterly, out of a firm's current or retained earnings.

DJIA See *Dow Jones Industrial Average*.

dollar cost averaging Averaging the cost per share of a particular security by investing a fixed sum regularly.

double witching A term used for the day when both options and futures expire.

doubling down Adding onto a losing position.

Dow Jones Industrial Average (DJIA) A price-weighted index of 30 blue-chip U.S. stocks. This index is also known as the Dow.

downtrend A general tendency for declining prices in a given market.

drawdown A decrease in the value of an account because of losing trades or because of paper losses, which may occur simply because of a decline in the value of open positions. No or low drawdown is a desirable performance feature of a trader or investor.

earnings per share (EPS) A firm's total after-tax net earnings divided by the number of common shares outstanding.

earnings-to-price (E/P) ratio Ratio of a company's earnings per share to its share price. This is the reverse of the price-to-earnings ratio.

edge The advantage you and your system give you over the market by dollars earned. See *payoff ratio*.

efficient market The theory that the financial markets quickly and efficiently compensate and price in all widely known information.

Elliott wave analysis A method of market analysis based on the theories of Ralph Nelson Elliott. Although relatively complex, the method is based on the concept that markets move in waves, forming a general pattern of five waves (or market legs) in the direction of the main trend

e-mini Used in the futures market to represent a smaller trading market of its parent market.

entry The point at which you place or open your trade or investment. This is the opposite of your exit. When placing your entry, you should already know what your initial exit will be—see *stop-loss exit*. The distance between your entry and your exit will determine what your trade size will be.

equities markets   Stock markets.

equity   The total dollar value of an account.

equity curve   The value of your account over time, illustrated in a graph.

exchange-traded fund (ETF)   A security that tracks a specific index, equity category, or other basket of assets but is traded on an exchange like a single stock.

exercise   To buy or sell a call or put option by the expiration date on the option contract.

exit   The point at which you close your trade or investment. This is the opposite of your entry. It can also be known as your *stop-loss exit*. It is a crucial part of your money management risk control plan. The distance between your entry and your exit will determine what your trade size will be.

expiration date   The last day on which an option may be exercised. For stock options, this date is the third Friday of the expiration month.

false breakout   A short-lived price move that penetrates a prior high or low before succumbing to a pronounced price move in the opposite direction. For example, if the price of a stock that has been trading between $18 and $20 rises to $21 and then quickly falls below $18, the move to $21 can be termed a false breakout.

Federal Open Market Committee (FOMC)   A 12-member committee responsible for setting credit and interest rate policy for the Federal Reserve System. The members set the discount rate directly and control the federal funds rate by buying and selling government securities impacting the rate. They meet eight times a year under the direction of a chairman.

Federal Reserve Board of Governors   The governing arm of the Federal Reserve System, which seeks to regulate the economy through the implementation of monetary policy. The seven members of the Board of Governors are appointed by U.S. presidents to serve 14-year terms.

Federal Reserve System (Fed)   The central banking system of the United States, responsible for regulating the flow of money and credit. It serves as a bank for other banks and the U.S. government.

Fibonacci retracement   The concept that retracements of prior trends will often approximate 38.2 percent and 61.8 percent—numbers derived from the Fibonacci sequence.

Fibonacci sequence   A sequence of numbers that begins with 1, 1, and progresses to infinity, with each number in the sequence equal to the sum of the preceding two numbers. Thus, the initial numbers in the sequence would be 1, 1, 2, 3, 5, 8, 13, 21, 34, 55, 89, and so on. The ratio of consecutive numbers in the sequence converges to 0.618 as the numbers get larger. The ratio of alternate numbers in the sequence (for example, 21 and 55) converges to 0.382 as the numbers get larger. These two ratios—0.618 and 0.382—are commonly used to project retracements of prior price swings.

fill The price at which an order is executed. For example, if a trade was placed at $32.00 and executed at $32.25, the fill price would be $32.25.

filter An indicator that selects only data that meet specific criteria. Too many filters can lead to overoptimization.

financial instrument A term used to denote any form of funding medium. Financial instruments can be categorized by whether they are cash instruments or derivative instruments. Cash instruments are financial instruments whose value is determined directly by markets. They can be divided into securities, which are readily transferable, and other cash instruments such as loans and deposits, where both borrower and lender have to agree on a transfer. Derivative instruments are financial instruments that derive their value from some other financial instrument or variable. They can be divided into exchange-traded derivatives and over-the-counter (OTC) derivatives. If it is debt, it can be further categorized into short-term (less than one year) or long-term debt. Foreign exchange instruments and transactions are neither debt nor equity based and belong in their own category.

flat When you are not in the market with a live position or when you close out all your positions before the end of the trading day, you are considered flat.

floor trader A member of the exchange who trades on the floor for personal profit.

forecasts Individuals who attempt to predict future market behavior are said to be forecasting the market. They tend to use indicators such as moving average convergence/divergence (MACD), stochastics, and Elliott waves to determine their forecasts. Forecasting the markets is often like forecasting the weather; it is difficult to do with any consistent accuracy.

forex market The foreign exchange (forex) market exists wherever one currency is traded for another. It is by far the largest financial market in the world, and includes trading between large banks, central banks, currency speculators, multinational corporations, governments, and other financial markets and institutions.

fundamental analysis The use of economic data and news data to analyze financial markets. For example, fundamental analysis of a currency might focus on such items as relative inflation rates, interest rates, economic growth rates, and political factors. In evaluating a stock, a fundamental analyst would look at financials, value, earnings, debt, management, operations, competition, and other relative data. Fundamental analysis is often contrasted with technical analysis, and some investors and traders use a combination of the two.

futures When commodity exchanges added stock index contracts and currency contracts, the term *futures* was developed to be more inclusive.

futures market   An auction market in which participants buy and sell commodity/futures contracts for delivery on a specified future date. Trading is carried on through open outcry and hand signals in a trading pit.

Gann analysis   Market analysis based on a variety of technical concepts developed by William Gann, a famous stock and commodity trader during the first half of the twentieth century.

gap   A price zone at which no trades occur. For example, if a market that has previously traded at a high of $20 per share opens at $22 on the following day, the price zone between $20 and $22 is referred to as a gap up. If the price zone were to go from $22 to $20, it would be a gap down. Sometimes Fed announcements or corporate earnings announcements can create an immediate gap even in the middle of a trading day.

Globex®   Today the CME Globex trading system operates at the heart of CME. Proposed in 1987, it was introduced in 1992 as the first global electronic trading platform for futures contracts. This fully electronic trading system allows market participants to trade from booths at the exchange or while sitting in a home or an office thousands of miles away.

good till canceled (GTC) order   By choosing GTC, you ensure that your order will remain open until it is executed or canceled, regardless of the number of trading days.

gross domestic product (GDP)   The monetary value of all products and services produced in a country over a certain time period. In the United States, GDP growth is a popularly used indicator of overall economic health.

grounded assessments   Trading and investing rules that are based on reality versus forecasts or predictions. For example, trade and investment entries based on price and volume would be considered grounded assessments. The ART signals are all grounded assessments.

hedge   To reduce risk in an investment or trade by offsetting it with another investment or trade.

hedge fund   A managed portfolio of investments that is generally unregulated (unlike a mutual fund) and may invest in any highly speculative markets, including options.

hedger   A market participant who implements a position to reduce price risk. The hedger's risk position is exactly opposite that of the speculator, who accepts risk in implementing positions to profit from anticipated price moves.

higher time frame filter   A filter technique used to look at the market you are trading or investing in on a higher time frame to see if it confirms your primary time frame.

high probability   Refers to trades or investments that statistically are more likely to succeed.

hyperbolic move   A sharp and significant move to the upside or downside of your position. You might decide to scale out of a position to lock in profit if this type of move occurs. See *scaling out*.

immediate or cancel (IOC) order   By choosing IOC, you ensure that your order will have immediate execution of all or part of the quantity of stock you specified. Any portion of the order that is not executed immediately is automatically canceled.

index fund   A mutual fund that tracks a stated market index.

individual retirement account (IRA)   A retirement account that any employed person (or spouse of an employed person) can open and contribute to. Assets in the account grow tax deferred, and contributions may be tax deductible. Distributions taken before age 59 are subject to penalty.

inflation   Rate of increase in average product and service price levels. Different indexes use different baskets of products and services to compute the average prices. A popular index is the consumer price index.

initial public offering (IPO)   The first sale of equities (stocks) to the public by a private firm. In making an IPO, a private firm has gone public.

insider trading   Trading by officers, directors, major stockholders, or others who hold private inside information allowing them to benefit from buying or selling stock. It is a misuse of inside information to profit more quickly than the average shareholder would.

institutional investor   A bank, mutual fund, pension fund, or other corporate entity that trades financial instruments in large volumes.

in-the-money   When an option's current market price is above the strike price of a call or below the strike price of a put. An in-the-money option would produce a profit if exercised.

intraday time frame   A shorter time frame (from the one-minute to the 60-minute) that day traders use in making their entry and exit decisions.

investing   A term with several closely related meanings in business management, finance, and economics, related to saving or deferring consumption. An asset is usually purchased, or equivalently a deposit is made in a bank, in hopes of getting a future return or interest from it. Think of it as using financial instruments to invest savings for future gain; it usually is not considered a short-term endeavor.

investor   Generally, one who favors a buy-and-hold approach using weekly and monthly charts to evaluate the market. An investor can be a trader when timing long-term investments. Investors are more likely to incorporate fundamental analysis into their approach than a day trader would.

Kelly formula   See *optimal f formula*.

large cap   Refers to the size of a firm's market capitalization. Generally, any firm with a market cap above $10 billion is referred to as large cap.

left brain   The human brain is divided into two hemispheres, the left and the right, each of which is responsible for specific functions in human behavior and existence. The left brain is responsible primarily for speech, logic, planning, and analysis abilities. It tends to think in words as opposed to pictures and looks at the details as opposed to the big picture. Those who are analytical and scientific in nature are generally referred to as left-brain thinkers.

leverage   The ability to control a dollar amount of a commodity or financial instrument greater than the amount of personal capital employed. This ability is obtained by using borrowed money, such as a margin account. The greater the leverage of the position, the greater the potential profit or loss.

limit order   An order in which you set the maximum price you will pay for your purchase, or a minimum price you will accept as a seller.

limit position   For many futures contracts, government regulations specify a maximum position size (such as number of contracts) that a speculator may hold.

limit price move   For many futures contracts, the exchanges specify a maximum amount by which the price can change on a single day. A market that increases in price by this specified maximum is said to be limit-up, while a market that declines by the maximum is said to be limit-down.

liquidity   The degree to which a given market is liquid. When volume is high, there is usually a lot of liquidity. Low liquidity in markets can result in poor fills.

liquidity risk   The risk when you enter a trade that you may not have sufficient liquidity to exit at your desired exit point.

liquid market   A market in which there are a large number of trades daily so that most buy and sell orders can be executed without dramatically moving prices. In other words, a liquid market allows you the ease of entry and exit.

long   A position established with a buy order, which profits in a rising price market. The term is also used to refer to the person or entity holding such a position.

long call   To buy a call option.

long put   To buy a put option.

lot   The quantity of shares in which stocks are bought or sold. In futures markets, a lot is called a *contract*.

MACD   See *moving average convergence/divergence*.

margin   To borrow money from a financial provider (broker or bank) to purchase certain financial instruments.

margin call   A Federal Reserve Board and financial service provider requirement that you deposit additional funds or sell some of your holdings to increase the equity in your margin account if it has fallen below the minimum.

margin debit The amount of money borrowed from a financial service provider.

margin risk The risk that you can lose more than the dollar amount in your margined trading account.

market index The weighted average of companies comprising an index. The index represents a category or market (such as the S&P 500 or the NASDAQ).

market maker A broker, bank, or firm such as Goldman Sachs or Merrill Lynch, which buys or sells a security, currency, or futures contract.

market order An order to execute a purchase or sale at the best price available at the time the order is received.

market risk Uncontrolled risk possibilities that are always present in open trade and investment positions. Economic and world events can cause market risk where the market could move so quickly that you may not be able to exit at your stop-loss exit point.

Minneapolis Grain Exchange (MGEX) This exchange was founded as a not-for-profit membership organization and maintains that structure today with a membership base of 390 outstanding seats or memberships. In 1883, MGEX launched its first futures contract, hard red spring wheat, which is the exchange's most heavily traded product today.

Minor Pyramid Trading Point® (MP) An MP indicates a correction in the dominant trend.

momentum investing and trading Momentum represents the change in price now from some fixed time period in the past. This strategy attempts to capture short-term price movements based on the belief that price patterns are indicative of future results.

money flow index (MFI) A volume-weighted momentum indicator that measures the strength of money flowing in and out of a financial instrument. It compares *positive* money flow to *negative* money flow to create an indicator that can be compared to price in order to identify the strength or weakness of a trend. The MFI is measured on a 0 to 100 scale and is often calculated using a 14-day period.

money management The use of various methods of risk control in trading and investing. These methods include: (1) using proper trade size, (2) not risking more than 2 percent of your risk account on any one trade, and (3) diversifying your trading or investing account over a number of markets and sectors. This is also known as risk management.

moving average (MA) An average of data for a certain number of time periods. It moves because for each calculation we use data from latest number of time periods. By definition, a moving average lags the market. An exponentially smoothed moving average (EMA) gives greater weight to the more recent data in an attempt to reduce the lag time.

moving average convergence/divergence (MACD)   This indicator, developed by Gerald Appel, is calculated by subtracting the 26-period exponential moving average of a given financial instrument from its 12-period exponential moving average. By comparing moving averages, MACD displays trend-following characteristics, and by plotting the difference between the moving averages as an oscillator, MACD displays momentum characteristics. The MACD histogram is the visual representation of the difference between the MACD line and the MACD signal line.

mutual fund   An investment company investing in a variety of securities as dictated by the specific fund's prospectus. Investors do not own the underlying investments; they buy shares of the fund itself.

naked option   A short option position by a trader who does not own the underlying commodity or financial instrument.

naked put   A put option in which the seller does not own the short position. Loss potential is total except for the premium.

narrowing the spread   Reducing the difference between the bid and ask prices of a security.

NASDAQ   See *National Association of Securities Dealers Automated Quotations System.*

NASDAQ-100 index   A modified capitalization-weighted index designed to track the performance of the 100 largest and most actively traded nonfinancial domestic and international securities listed on the NASDAQ.

National Association of Securities Dealers Automated Quotations System (NAS-DAQ)   An American stock market founded in 1971 by the National Association of Securities Dealers (NASD), which divested it in a series of sales in 2000 and 2001. It is owned and operated by the NASDAQ Stock Market, Inc., the stock of which was listed on its own stock exchange in 2002. NASDAQ is the largest electronic screen-based equity securities market in the United States. With approximately 3,200 companies, it lists more companies and on average trades more shares per day than any other U.S. market.

National Association of Securities Dealers, Inc. (NASD)   This self-regulatory organization of the securities industry is responsible for the regulation of the NASDAQ stock market and the over-the-counter markets.

nearest month   The expiration date of an option or future that is closest to the present.

net asset value (NAV)   An increment of movement in the mutual fund market.

net worth   Total assets minus total liabilities.

New York Cotton Exchange (NYCE)   Founded in 1870 by a group of 100 cotton brokers and merchants in New York City, the NYCE is the oldest commodities exchange in the city. Well into the twentieth century, cotton was a leading American commodity for both export and domestic consumption.

New York Futures Exchange (NYFE)   An exchange on which trading occurs for Treasury bond futures and some currency futures.

New York Mercantile Exchange (NYMEX)   The world's largest physical commodity futures exchange, located in New York City. Its two principal divisions are the NYMEX and the New York Commodities Exchange (COMEX), which were once independent companies but are now merged.

New York Stock Exchange (NYSE)   Known as the Big Board, this is a New York City–based stock exchange. The NYSE provides an efficient method for buyers and sellers to trade shares of stock in companies registered for public trading. The exchange provides efficient price discovery via an auction environment designed to produce the fairest price for both parties. As of January 24, 2007, NYSE stocks can be traded via its electronic hybrid market (except for a small group of very high-priced stocks). Customers can now send orders for immediate electronic execution or route orders to the floor for trade in the auction market. In excess of 50 percent of all order flow is now delivered to the floor electronically.

nontrending market   This is also known as a bracketed, consolidating, range-bound, sideways, choppy, or channeling market. See *bracketed market*.

NYSE Composite index   A capitalization-weighted index designed to track the performance of all common stocks listed on the New York Stock Exchange.

OBV   See *on balance volume*.

on balance volume (OBV)   A method is used in technical analysis to detect momentum, the calculation of which relates volume to price change. OBV provides a running total of volume and shows whether this volume is flowing into or out of a given financial instrument. It attempts to detect when a stock, bond, or other instrument is being accumulated by a large number of buyers or sold by many sellers. Joe Granville developed this indicator.

opening price guaranteed (OPG) order   By choosing OPG at the opening, you ensure that your order will be executed at the opening price. If it is not executed at the opening, it will be canceled automatically.

open interest   In futures markets, the total number of long and short positions is always equal. This total is called the open interest. By definition, when a contract month first begins trading, the open interest is zero. The open interest builds to a peak and then declines as positions are liquidated as the contract approaches its expiration date.

open order   An order to buy or sell a security that remains in effect until it is either canceled by the customer or executed.

optimal *f* formula   A formula that calculates for you the optimum fraction of capital, or percent of capital, to risk on any one trade based on your win ratio and payoff ratio. It gives you a more aggressive calculation than the risk of ruin tables do. It is sometimes referred to as the Kelly formula.

optimization   Refers to optimizing software and the process of discovering what impact is the result of varying a particular parameter across different values, and then using that information to make an informed decision about which specific parameter values to use in actual trading or investing.

option   The right to buy or sell an underlying asset at a fixed price up to some specified date in the future. The right to buy is a *call option*, and the right to sell is a *put option*.

options market   An open market to trade options.

oscillator   A technical analysis tool that is a trend indicator for discovering short-term overbought and oversold conditions. Most oscillators go from 0 to 100. Analysts believe that when the indicator is near zero the price is oversold and when it is near 100 it is overbought.

out-of-the-money   When an option's current market price is below the strike price of a call or above the strike price of a put.

overbought/oversold indicator   An indicator that attempts to define when prices have risen (or fallen) too far, too fast, and hence are vulnerable to a reaction in the opposite direction.

overtrading   You are overtrading when your commission fees are eating into your profit or when you feel out of control. Stop and reverse (SAR) traders can overtrade because of the speed of their entries and exits.

Pacific Exchange (PCX)   Originally a regional stock exchange located in San Francisco, California. Its history began with the founding of the San Francisco Stock and Bond Exchange in 1882. Seven years later, the Los Angeles Oil Exchange was founded. In 1957, the two exchanges merged to form the Pacific Coast Stock Exchange, though trading floors were kept in both original cities. A name change to the Pacific Stock Exchange took place in 1973. Options trading began three years later. In 1997, *Stock* was dropped from the exchange's name. In 1999, the Pacific Exchange was the first U.S. stock exchange to demutualize. In 2001, the Los Angeles trading floor was closed, and the next year the San Francisco trading floor was closed as well. Pacific Exchange equities trading now takes place exclusively through NYSE Arca (formerly known as ArcaEx), an electronic communication network. In 2003, the Pacific Exchange launched PCX plus, an electronic options trading platform.

paper gain   Unrealized capital gain on securities held based on a comparison of the current market price to the original cost.

paper loss   Unrealized capital loss on securities held based on a comparison of the current market price to the original cost.

pattern recognition   A price-forecasting method that uses historical chart patterns to draw analogies to current situations.

payoff ratio   Average winning trade divided by average losing trade equals the payoff ratio. For example, a 2 to 1 payoff ratio means that you are winning two dollars for every dollar you lose.

P/E ratio   See *price-to-earnings (P/E) ratio.*

percentage in point (PIP)   The increment of movement in the forex market.

percentage price oscillator (PPO) histogram   An indicator based on the difference between two moving averages; it is expressed either as a percentage or in absolute terms. The plot is presented as a histogram so that the centerline crossovers and divergences are easily identifiable. The same principles apply to the MACD histogram.

pit   The area where a futures contract is traded on the exchange floor.

playback feature   See *back-testing.*

position   A trader's or investor's financial stake in a given financial instrument or market.

position trader   A trader who uses daily and weekly charts on which to base decisions and holds positions for days, weeks, or months.

price   In trading and investing, *price* refers to the last trade price.

price bar   The price bar represents the high and low price behavior in a measured time interval, such as a one-minute, five-minute, 60-minute, daily, or weekly time frame.

price gap   See *gap.*

price-to-earnings (P/E) ratio   The current price of a stock divided by the company's annual earnings. One of the most commonly used stock valuation ratios.

Primary Pyramid Trading Point® (P)   This ART signal indicates entries into and exits out of a primary trend trade or investment.

profit margin   An indicator of profitability, determined by dividing net income by revenue for the same 12-month period. Also known as net profit margin.

put-call ratio   The ratio of the volume of put options traded to the volume of call options traded, which is used as an indicator of investor sentiment (bullish or bearish).

psychology   Mastering the psychology of trading and investing is a crucial part of becoming successful. The *trader's mind-set* is our definition of what you will attain when you have mastered your financial psychology. Some of the challenges in developing strong psychology are overcoming fear, greed, ego, and anger when trading and investing.

PTP apex   The PTP apex is the point of the pyramid (triangle) and always points in the direction of the trend. It tells you where to enter based on current market dynamics.

PTP base leg   The base leg is the flat base of the pyramid (triangle) and tells you where to set your stop-loss exit based on current market dynamics.

PTP confirmed   When the market moves beyond the PTP apex in the direction of the trend, it will be confirmed. At that moment, the triangle will turn either *green* or *red*, depending on whether it is a bull or a bear trend.

PTP MinScore   This adjustable setting on the ART software determines the number of pyramids you will see on your chart.

PTP potential   When the pyramid is potential, it will be *yellow* in color. Once the market moves beyond the apex of the pyramid, it will then be confirmed and will turn either *green* or *red*, depending on whether it is a bull or a bear trend. If the market does not confirm the pyramid by exceeding the apex, the yellow pyramid (triangle) will disappear.

PTP voided   If a potential *yellow* pyramid is not confirmed, it will be voided and will disappear.

put option   An options contract with the right to sell a security at a specified exercise price (the strike price) on or before a specific expiration date. A put option writer sells the right to a buyer. If the option exercises, the buyer puts the stock to the writer, and the writer must buy it.

Pyramid Trading Point® (PTP)   This ART trend trading signal was developed by Bennett A. McDowell and identifies exact entries and exits. It enables you to trade and invest utilizing the realities of the markets. It can be used on all markets and in all time frames.

rally (recovery)   An upward movement of prices.

range-bound market   See *bracketed market*.

reality-based trading   Living in reality is to be seeing and reacting to the environment as events are occurring, without attempting to predict future events. When traders are living in reality, they are dealing with what is actually occurring to them at any given moment. When trading and investing in reality, they are focusing on the current moment. They are free of opinions and other past or future distractions or thoughts. Reality-based trading and investing involve looking at what is real in the market, such as *price* and *volume*.

recession   A contraction in the business cycle, usually manifesting in slow or negative GDP growth.

relative strength index (RSI) An indicator developed by J. Welles Wilder Jr. that is used to ascertain overbought and oversold conditions. It works on a scale of 99 to 1, with 99 being the strongest and 1 being the weakest. In the stock market, it is a measure of a given stock's price strength relative to a broad index of stocks. The term can also be used in a more general sense to refer to an overbought/oversold type of indicator.

resistance level In technical analysis, a price area at which a rising market is expected to encounter increased selling pressure sufficient to stall or reverse the advance.

retracement A price movement in the opposite direction of the previous trend. A retracement is usually a price correction. For example, in a rising market, a 55 percent retracement would indicate a price decline equal to 55 percent of the prior advance.

return on investment (ROI) Book income as a proportion of net book value.

reward-to-risk ratio The average winning trade divided by the size of the average losing trade. This formula will enable you to determine the estimated potential loss or gain of future transactions. Provided that you have more winners than losers, a ratio of 3:1 is excellent.

right brain The human brain is divided into two hemispheres, the left and the right, each of which is responsible for specific functions in human behavior and existence. The right brain is considered to be primarily responsible for feelings, emotions, and creativity. The right brain tends to think in pictures as opposed to words and is able to look at the big picture as opposed to minute detail. Those who are more creative tend to be considered right-brain thinkers.

right side of the chart When trading the live market, the right side of the chart is the unknown. Hindsight is 20/20, and when in the live market there is always uncertainty as to where the market actually will go. It is the not knowing that is on the right side of the chart.

risk The price of being wrong about an investment or trade.

risk control See *money management*.

ROI See *return on investment*.

RSI See *relative strength index*.

Russell 2000 index A capitalization-weighted index designed to track the performance of the 2,000 smallest U.S. stocks included in the Russell 3000 index.

Russell 3000 index A capitalization-weighted index designed to track the performance of the 3,000 largest and most liquid U.S. stocks.

S&P See *Standard & Poor's Corporation*.

S&P 500 composite stock price index A capitalization-weighted index designed to track the performance of 500 stocks that are included in the index based on their liquidity, market capitalization, and sector. While not necessarily the 500 largest U.S. companies, these are generally the 500 most widely held.

S&P 500 E-mini Designated by the commodity ticker symbol ES and often abbreviated as E-mini, this is a stock market index futures contract traded on the Chicago Mercantile Exchange's Globex electronic trading platform.

SAR See *stop and reverse.*

scaling in Refers to adding onto your current trade position to increase your *trade size.* Scale in only if the trade or investment is already profitable.

scaling out Exiting 30 percent of your position when your trading rules tell you to. This is a technique that is effective in reducing stress and locking in profit.

scalper A trader who seeks to profit from very small price fluctuations. Scalpers buy and sell quickly to make a quick profit. They often use *stop and reverse* (SAR) techniques. They can trade larger trade sizes than trend traders and still maintain proper risk control.

seasonal trading Trading based on consistent, predictable changes in price during the year due to production cycles or demand cycles.

SEC See *Securities and Exchange Commission.*

sector Used to characterize a group of securities that are similar with respect to maturity, type, rating, and/or industry.

securities Also known as *stocks.* There are a number of categories of securities such as debt securities, equity securities, common stock and derivative contracts, and options and swaps.

Securities and Exchange Commission (SEC) The federal agency that is designed to promote full public disclosure and protect the investing public against fraudulent practices in the securities markets.

seller's market A market in which demand exceeds supply. As a result, the seller can dictate the price and terms of a sale.

sell-off The sale of securities under pressure.

setup When your trading rules identify certain criteria that must be present prior to entering the market.

share A unit of measure for financial instruments, including stocks, mutual funds, limited partnerships, and real estate investment trusts (REITs).

shareholder A person or entity that owns shares or equity in a corporation.

short When you sell before you have bought the item, you are *shorting* the market. This position is implemented with a sale that profits from a declining price market. The term also refers to the trader or entity holding such a position.

short call   Refers to selling a *call option* that you don't already own.

short put   Refers to selling a *put option* that you don't already own.

sideways market   Also known as a bracketed, consolidating, range-bound, non-trending, choppy, or channeling market. See *bracketed market*.

slippage   The difference in price between what you expect to pay when you enter the market and what you actually pay. For example, if you attempt to buy at 20 and you end up buying at 20.5, you have a half point of slippage.

small cap   Refers to the relative size of a firm's market capitalization. Traditionally, any firm with a market cap under $10 billion is referred to as small cap.

speculator   A person who willingly accepts risk by buying and selling financial instruments or commodities in hopes of profiting from anticipated price movements.

split   The division of outstanding shares of a corporation into a larger or smaller number of shares. For example: in a three-for-one split, each holder of 100 shares before would now have 300 shares.

spread   The difference between the bid price and the ask price.

Standard & Poor's Corporation (S&P)   A company well known for its ratings of stocks and bonds according to investment risk (the Standard & Poor's rating) and for compiling the Standard & Poor's 500 index.

stochastic   An overbought/oversold indicator, made popular by George Lane, which is based on the observation that prices tend to close near the high of the day in an uptrend, and in a downtrend they tend to close near the low of the day.

stock   A financial instrument that signifies an ownership position in a corporation. Stock is the capital raised by a corporation through the issuance of shares. A person who holds at least a partial share of stock is called a *shareholder*.

stock market   A market for the trading and investing in company stock that is listed on a stock exchange.

stop and reverse (SAR) order   An order that is used to close the current trade and open a new trade in the opposite direction.

stop limit order   An order that is triggered when the stop price is reached but can only be executed at the limit price.

stop-loss exit   Also referred to as a stop, stop loss, initial stop, or trailing stop. It is your designated price level where you have determined you must exit your trade if it goes against you. It is used to help control your *trade risk*. This is the worst-case scenario if the trade or investment does go against you. It is important to determine the exit point *before* entering the trade or investment.

stop order   A buy order placed above the market (or sell order placed below the market) that becomes a market order when the specified price is reached.

stopped out   A purchase or sale executed under a stop order at the stop price specified by the customer.

straddle   The purchase or sale of an equal number of puts and calls with the same terms at the same time.

strike price   The fixed price of an option.

supply = demand   When supply equals demand, both the seller and buyer agree on price but disagree on value. This is the relationship between the availability of a good or service and the need or desire for it among consumers.

support level   In technical analysis, a price area at which a falling market is expected to encounter increased buying pressure sufficient to stall or reverse the decline.

swing trading   A short-term trading approach designed to capture quick moves in the market.

technical analysis   Price forecasting methods based on a study of price itself (and volume) as opposed to the underlying fundamental (such as economic) market factors. Technical analysis traders and investors use charts to detect price patterns in the market. Technical analysis is often contrasted with fundamental analysis, and some investors and traders use a combination of the two.

tick   The increment of movement and price fluctuation up or down in a market is called a tick. The value of a tick movement will vary from market to market.

ticker symbol   Standard abbreviation used to refer to a stock when placing orders or conducting research.

time frame   The length of time represented by a price bar interval, such as a two-minute chart, 60-minute chart, or daily chart.

trade   When a buyer and seller agree on price but disagree on value, a trade occurs. More simply stated, the trade occurs at the point where the value of selling and the value of receiving are equal.

trade risk   The risk that traders attempt to control through money management and risk control.

The Trader's Assistant™   A complete trade posting and trade record-keeping system created by Bennett A. McDowell to streamline trading and keep a trader organized by recording all trade information on trade posting cards and in trade ledgers.

trader's mind-set   See *psychology*.

trade size   Also known as position size, this is the size of your trade or investment represented in the number of units (shares, contracts, etc.) of the market you are trading or investing in. Selecting optimal trade size is important in maintaining solid risk control.

Trade Size Calculator™ Risk control software created by Bennett A. McDowell to determine a trader's maximum *trade size* based on certain variables such as percent risk and equity account size.

trading Opening a position in a financial market, either long or short, with the plan of closing it out at a substantial profit. If the trade goes against you, the plan is to cut losses quickly by using effective risk control.

trailing stop A stop-loss exit that moves in the direction of a trend trade, locking in profit in either a long or a short trend.

transaction The delivery of a security by a seller and its acceptance by the buyer.

trend The tendency of prices to move in a given general direction (up or down).

trend channel A trend line or series of trend lines used to identify upward-sloping or downward-sloping trends by placing the trend lines on the highs and lows of the channel.

trend exhaustion When a trend ends, it has reached trend exhaustion. With the ART system, trend exhaustion generally occurs after four to five consecutive *Primary Pyramid Trading Points* in the same direction.

trending day A day that continued primarily in one trend direction, either up or down, from open to close.

trend trader A trader who trades or invests in the direction of the overall trend.

true range The greatest difference, either between the current high and the current low, between the current high and the previous close, or between the current low and the previous close.

ungrounded assessments Trading and investing rules that try to forecast or predict the market. For example, MACD, stochastics, and Elliott wave analysis are ungrounded assessments.

unrealized gain The appreciation in value of an asset that has not been sold—paper gain.

unrealized loss The depreciation in value of an asset that has not been sold—paper loss.

uptrend A general tendency for rising prices in a given market.

volatility Refers to the range of prices in a given time period. A highly volatile market has a large range in daily prices, whereas a low-volatility market has a small range of daily prices. This is a measure of price variability in a market. A volatile market is a market that is subject to wide price fluctuations.

volume The total number of shares or contracts traded during a given period.

whipsaw A price pattern characterized by repeated, abrupt reversals in trend. The term is often used to describe losses resulting from a choppy or trendless market.

win ratio The number of winning trades divided by the total number of trades equals the win ratio. For example, if you have six winning trades out of a total of 10 trades, the result is a win ratio of 60 percent, meaning you have 60 percent winning trades.

About the Author

Bennett A. McDowell, founder of TradersCoach.com, began his financial career on Wall Street in 1984, and later became a registered securities broker and financial adviser for Prudential Securities and Morgan Stanley.

As a financial adviser, Bennett's niche was active trading and investing for a community of high-net-worth clients using his own proprietary trading system. This system later became known as the Applied Reality Trading® (ART®) system.

Bennett brought the ART software to the public in the year 2003. This was in answer to his clients' many requests for him to share with them his successful trading and investing techniques. Today the ART system is used in over 50 countries around the world by sophisticated hedge fund managers, individual investors, and active traders alike.

Considered an expert in technical analysis and complex trading platforms, Bennett lectures nationally and writes articles for many leading trading publications, including *Technical Analysis of Stocks & Commodities* magazine. Internationally recognized as a leader in trading education, Bennett teaches trading to students worldwide through his company, Traders Coach.com.

He is honored to be included as a member of the eSignal "Trading with the Masters" team. In addition, TradersCoach.com, Applied Reality Trading, and The Traders Assistant® record-keeping system have received numerous *Technical Analysis of Stocks & Commodities* Readers' Choice awards.

He has also written two best-selling books published by John Wiley & Sons, *The ART of Trading* and *A Trader's Money Management System*, both released in 2008.

Bennett resides in San Diego, California, with his wife and two children. He can be reached by e-mail via Info@TradersCoach.com.

Index